1 PETER

ABINGDON NEW TESTAMENT COMMENTARIES

1 PETER

M. EUGENE BORING

Abingdon Press
Nashville

7-14-00

ABINGDON NEW TESTAMENT COMMENTARIES:
1 PETER

Copyright © 1999 by Abingdon Press

All rights reserved.

This book is printed on recycled, acid-free, elemental-chlorine–free paper.

Library of Congress Cataloging-in-Publication Data

Boring, M. Eugene.
    1 Peter / M. Eugene Boring.
        p.   cm. — (Abingdon New Testament commentaries)
    Includes bibliographical references.
    ISBN 0-687-05854-6 (alk. paper)
    1. Bible. N.T. Peter, 1st—Commentaries. I. Title. II. Title:
First Peter. III. Series.
    BS2795.3.B65   1999
    227'.92077—dc21   99-11067
                                                                                          CIP

Scripture quotations, unless otherwise indicated, are from the New Revised Standard Version Bible, copyright © 1989, by the Division of Christian Education of the National Council of the Churches of Christ in the United States of America.

Scripture quotations noted AT are the author's translation.

Scripture quotations noted KJV are from the King James Version of the Bible.

Scripture quotations noted NAB are from the Revised New Testament—New American Bible. © 1986 Confraternity of Christian Doctrine, Washington, D.C.

Scripture quotations noted NIV are taken from the *Holy Bible: New International Version.* Copyright © 1973, 1978, 1984 by the International Bible Society. Used by permission of Zondervan Bible Publishers.

Scripture quotations noted REB are from *The Revised English Bible.* Copyright © 1989 by The Delegates of the Oxford University Press and The Syndics of the Cambridge University Press. Reprinted by permission.

99 00 01 02 03 04 05 06 07 08—10 9 8 7 6 5 4 3 2 1

MANUFACTURED IN THE UNITED STATES OF AMERICA

*To the Faculty, Staff, and Students
of Brite Divinity School,
especially the students
in my seminars
on 1 Peter in 1996 and 1997*

CONTENTS

FOREWORD

The *Abingdon New Testament Commentaries* series provides
compact, critical commentaries on the writings of the New
Testament. These commentaries are written with special
attention to the needs and interests of theological students, but they
will also be useful for students in upper-level college or university
settings, as well as for pastors and other church leaders. In addition
to providing basic information about the New Testament texts and
insights into their meanings, these commentaries are intended to
exemplify the tasks and procedures of careful, critical biblical
exegesis.

The authors who have contributed to this series come from a
wide range of ecclesiastical affiliations and confessional stances. All
are seasoned, respected scholars and experienced classroom teachers. They take full account of the most important current scholarship and secondary literature, but do not attempt to summarize that
literature or engage in technical academic debate. Their fundamental concern is to analyze the literary, socio-historical, theological,
and ethical dimensions of the biblical texts themselves. Although
all of the commentaries in this series have been written on the basis
of the Greek texts, the authors do not presuppose any knowledge
of the biblical languages on the part of the reader. When some
awareness of the grammatical, syntactical, or philological issue is
necessary for an adequate understanding of a particular text, they
explain the matter clearly and concisely.

The introduction of each volume ordinarily includes subdivisions dealing with the *key issues* addressed and/or raised by the
New Testament writing under consideration; its *literary genre,
structure, and character;* its *occasion and situational context,* in-

cluding its wider social, historical, and religious contexts; and its *theological and ethical significance* within these several contexts.

In each volume, the *commentary* is organized according to literary units rather than verse by verse. Generally, each of these units is the subject of three types of analysis. First, the *literary analysis* attends to the unit's genre, most important stylistic features, and overall structure. Second, the *exegetical analysis* considers the aim and leading ideas of the unit, deals with any especially important textual variants, and discusses the meanings of important words, phrases, and images. It also takes note of the particular historical and social situations of the writer and original readers, and of the wider cultural and religious contexts of the book as a whole. Finally, the *theological and ethical analysis* discusses the theological and ethical matters with which the unit deals or to which it points, focusing on the theological and ethical significance of the text within its original setting.

Each volume also includes a *select bibliography,* thereby providing guidance to other major commentaries and important scholarly works, and a brief *subject index.* The New Revised Standard Version of the Bible is the principal translation of reference for the series, but the authors draw on all of the major modern English versions, and when necessary provide their own original translations of difficult terms or phrases.

The fundamental aim of this series will have been attained if readers are assisted, not only to understand more about the origins, character, and meaning of the New Testament writings, but also to enter into their own informed and critical engagement with the texts themselves.

Victor Paul Furnish
General Editor

PREFACE

I remember a conversation with Fred Craddock of several years ago in which we both expressed our deep interest in 1 Peter as one of the meatier documents of the New Testament, though it was somewhat neglected in the scholarship of that time. We each indicated that we hoped the occasion would arise in the future to do an in-depth study of 1 Peter.

The years that have passed since that time have seen much change. First Peter is no longer an "exegetical stepchild" of academic and theological study, thanks in considerable degree to one of the editors of this series, John H. Elliott. Fred Craddock has published a commentary on 1 Peter (see bibliography). I have occasionally lectured to church groups on 1 Peter, have written an article or two, and from time to time have offered a seminary course or seminar on the Petrine tradition in the New Testament. It was an unanticipated pleasure when Victor Paul Furnish invited me to write the commentary on 1 Peter for this series, and I was glad to accept.

To me the most significant results of my engagement with 1 Peter that resulted in this commentary are

1. the realization that the letter functions to bring about change in the readers' lives primarily by projecting indirectly a narrative world the author assumes to be the real world, a challenge to the world of the readers' assumptions;

2. the effort to take seriously the "social code" of 1 Peter 2:11–3:12 that is so troublesome to many modern readers because of its assumption of imperial Roman rule, the patriarchal household, and the institution of slavery;

3. the attempt by the reader both to make what sense can be made of the mythological section 3:18-22 portraying Christ's "descent into hell" (as it has often been traditionally known) and to recognize the limitations necessarily involved in our apprehension of the author's original meaning;

4. the inseparable connection between Christology and ecclesiology in the author's presentation.

I am grateful for the incisive counsel during the writing and final editing of this manuscript offered by John H. Elliott of the Editorial Board of the Abingdon New Testament Commentary series, to Victor Paul Furnish, the General Editor of the series, to Edward J. McMahon for helpful observations, and to Kate Hawthorne for secretarial assistance. I also express my gratitude to the community of Brite Divinity School that provided both resources and a stimulating context for academic work in the service of the church. In particular, I would like to offer my thanks to Brenda J. Wilson and Randall W. Foster, graduate students in my seminar who read the manuscript with judicious eyes and annotated it with insight.

M. Eugene Boring

LIST OF ABBREVIATIONS

1 [2] Clem.	*First [Second] Clement*
1 Enoch	Ethiopic *Book of Enoch*
1QH	*Thanksgiving Hymns* (Qumran Cave 1)
1QpHab	Habbakuk Commentary (Qumran Cave 1)
1QS	*Rule of the Community* (Qumran Cave 1)
2 Apoc. Bar.	*Syriac Apocalypse of Baruch*
4QFlor	*Florilegium* [or *Eschatological Midrashim*] (Qumran Cave 4)
4Q'Amram	*Visions of Amram* (Qumran Cave 4)
4QpPs37	*Pesher on Psalm 37* (Qumran Cave 4)
AB	Anchor Bible
ABD	D. N. Freedman (ed.), *Anchor Bible Dictionary*
Abr.	Philo, *On Abraham*
Adv. Haer.	Irenaeus, *Against Heresises*
AnBib	Analecta biblica
Ann.	Tacitus, *Annals*
ANRW	*Aufstieg und Niedergang der römischen Welt*
Ant.	Josephus, *The Antiquities of the Jews*
ANTC	Abingdon New Testament Commentaries
ASNU	Acta seminarii neotestamentici upsaliensis
BAGD	W. Bauer, W. F. Arndt, F. W. Gingrich, and F. W. Danker, *Greek-English Lexicon of the NT*
Barn.	Barnabas
CBQ	Catholic Biblical Quarterly
CD	Cairo text of the *Damascus Document*
CEV	*The Bible for Today's Family* (Contemporary English Version)
Dial. Trypho	Justin Martyr, *Dialogue with Trypho*

Did.	*Didache*
EKKNT	Evangelisch-katholischer Kommentar zum Neuen Testament
Epic.	*Epictetus*
Gen. Rab.	*Genesis Rabbah*
Gos. Pet.	*Gospel of Peter*
Herm. Man.	*Hermas, Mandate(s)*
Herm. Vis.	*Hermas, Vision(s)*
Hist. Eccl.	Eusebius, *The History of the Church*
HNT	Handbuch zum Neuen Testament
HTKNT	Herders theologischer Kommentar zum Neuen Testament
IBC	Interpretation: A Bible Commentary for Teaching and Preaching
ICC	International Critical Commentary
IDB	G. A. Buttrick (ed.), *Interpreter's Dictionary of the Bible*
IDBSup	Supplementary volume to *IDB*
Ign. *Eph.*	Ignatius, *Letter to the Ephesians*
Ign. *Mag.*	Ignatius, *Letter to the Magnesians*
Ign. *Phld.*	Ignatius, *Letter to the Philadelphians*
Ign. *Rom.*	Ignatius, *Letter to the Romans*
Ign. *Smyrn.*	Ignatius, *Letter to the Smyrnaeans*
JB	*The Jerusalem Bible*
JBL	*Journal of Biblical Literature*
Jos. As.	*Joseph and Aseneth*
JSNT	*Journal for the Study of the New Testament*
JSNTSUP	Journal for the Study of the New Testament— Supplement Series
Jub.	*Jubilees*
KJV	King James Version
LXX	Septuagint
Mart. Pol.	*Martyrdom of Polycarp*
MeyerK	H. A. W. Meyer, Kritisch-exegetischer Kommentar über das Neue Testament
Midr. Ps.	*Midras Psalms*
MNTC	Moffatt NT Commentary

Mor.	Plutarch, *Moralia*
MT	Massoretic Text
NAB	*The New American Bible*
NABPR	National Association of Baptist Professors of Religion
NCB	New Century Bible
NEB	*The New English Bible*
NICNT	New International Commentary on the New Testament
NIV	*The Holy Bible, New International Version*
NRSV	New Revised Standard Version
NTD	Das Neue Testament Deutsch
NTS	*New Testament Studies*
Pol. *Phil.*	Polycarp, *Letter to the Philippians*
Prot. James	*Protevangelium of James*
PSTJ	*Perkins (School of Theology) Journal*
RB	*Revue biblique*
REB	*The Revised English Bible*
RSV	Revised Standard Version
SBLDS	SBL Dissertation Series
SBLMS	SBL Monograph Series
Sobr.	Philo, *On Sobriety*
Spec. Leg.	Philo, *On the Special Laws*
Syb. Or.	*Sibylline Oracles*
T. Ash.	*Testament of Asher*
T. Benj.	*Testament of Benjamin*
T. Levi	*Testament of Levi*
TDNT	G. Kittel and G. Friedrich (eds.), *Theological Dictionary of the New Testament*
TEV	*The Bible in Today's English Version* (Good News Bible)
TRu	*Theologische Rundschau*
WBC	Word Biblical Commentary
ZNW	*Zeitschrift für die neutestamentliche Wissenschaft*

INTRODUCTION

How may Christians live faithfully in a non-Christian society that misunderstands and abuses them? First Peter addresses this theme with more single-mindedness than any other New Testament document, and from this point of view may be the most significant book in the New Testament (Frankemölle 1990, 26). Since "Christian life in a non-Christian society" describes the current situation of the church in every country in the world, 1 Peter needs to be rediscovered not only by scholars but by the contemporary church, to which it has something to say.

But it does not say it directly. First Peter was not written to us. The first principle of authentic biblical interpretation is to acknowledge that nothing in the Bible was written directly to us, and that we are bound seriously to misunderstand it if we read our own situation and ideologies into it. We are neither residents of Cappadocia (1:1), nor subject to the emperor (2:13), nor does our social situation include slavery and the patriarchal family (2:18-20; 3:1-7), nor do we anticipate the soon coming of the Lord (4:7). In order to hear what 1 Peter might say to us, we need to hear it within its own context. This is not only common sense, but a matter of theological authenticity, for the Incarnation affirms the appearance of the absolute God in the concreteness of one particular history. Likewise, the documents that bear authentic witness to that event are not abstract generalities, but always express the meaning of the gospel in the time-bound categories of a particular time and place. To understand such a text (rather than simply use it for our own purposes), it is necessary to come within hearing distance of its own historical setting.

THE MAN: THE HISTORICAL SIMON PETER

The first word of 1 Peter is the name of a man, a real, historical person. Simon Peter was not only a character in a story, but, like Jesus of Nazareth, a figure who was born, lived, and was killed in the first-century Mediterranean world. Since the significance of Simon's life was preserved and communicated by elaborating and reinterpreting stories about him in a variety of later situations, Simon's story, like that of other New Testament figures, cannot be read directly from the pages of the Bible, but must be reconstructed (cf. Cullmann 1953; Brown, Donfried, and Reumann 1973; Brown 1976; Thiede 1987; Donfried 1992; Perkins 1994).

Simon Before Jesus

Simon's father's name was Jonah (Matt 16:17) or John (John 1:42; 21:15)—two different names are represented in Aramaic and Greek, as in English. His mother's name is unknown. As a contemporary of Jesus, Simon was presumably born sometime in the period between 10 BCE–10 CE, perhaps in the bilingual and multicultural Bethsaida (cf. John 1:44; 12:21). Simeon (Hebrew)/Simon (Greek) apparently received this double name at birth. His brother Andrew is known to us only by his Greek name, for which there is no Hebrew counterpart. It is likely that, like many people in Galilee, he could handle Greek as well as his native Aramaic, but the extent to which he may have been competent in Greek is not known. It is not necessary to portray him as a crude fisherman uninfluenced by the sophisticated hellenistic forces present in some streams of Galilean culture, just as we have no reason to picture him as an erudite scholar at home in the subtleties of Greek literature (*contra* Grudem 1988, 27-30).

Simon was married (Mark 1:30-31) and was accompanied by his wife on later mission trips (1 Cor 9:5). We know the name neither of his wife nor his mother-in-law. He, along with his brother Andrew, was in the fishing business. This means that Simon belonged neither to the upper class of *telōnēs* who received fishing rights from the government and farmed them out to other fishermen (Matthew/Levi belonged to this social class [Mark 2:14; Matt 9:9]), nor to the lower class of day-laborers who did most of the actual work—and who were largely illiterate—but to the "middle class" of small businessmen and craftsmen such as Paul the tentmaker (Wuellner 1962, 50-58, who cites evidence that occasionally a professional fisherman was also a scribe).

We know nothing of Simon's religious orientation before he became a disciple of Jesus. The tradition preserved in John 1:35-42 suggests that both Andrew and Simon may have been disciples of John the Baptist prior to the call to follow Jesus, that is, they already were oriented to the apocalyptic stream of Judaism. Similarly, it needs to be emphasized that we know little if anything about Simon's "personality." Though often pictured in sermons and popular legend as "volatile and impulsive" (e.g., even the sober historian Filson 1962, 751), this romanticized image of popular piety is based on the ways the literary character of Simon is portrayed in New Testament narratives, which were written for theological purposes. Biblical narrative did not share the modern interest in "personality." Traits usually attributed to "personality" pertain to the literary figures in the various stories, not to the historical Simon.

Simon with Jesus

Sometime during his ministry, Jesus of Nazareth called Simon to be his disciple, and Simon responded. The three versions of this encounter in the New Testament (Mark 1:16-20 = Matt 4:18-22; Luke 5:1-11; John 1:35-42) vary not only in details, but in major elements of chronology and their understanding of the significance of the event (e.g., was Simon called first, as in Mark and Matthew, or not, as pointedly in John?). Further, the similarities between Luke 5:1-11 and John 21:1-19 show that the post-Easter perspective of the church influenced the retelling of all the stories. None are simply biographical, but exhibit the later theological reflection of the church and the evangelists. In their present form and contexts, the stories of Simon's call communicate early Christian understandings of the call to discipleship, how one "becomes a Christian."

Jesus called and Simon responded. In becoming a disciple of Jesus, his life was completely reoriented. He left home, family, and business, and became a participant in the "Jesus movement" and its mission. Not only did he become a disciple, it is clear that he became a leading member of the group of disciples. He is pictured as belonging to the inner circle (e.g., Mark 9:2; 13:3; 14:33), as being the spokesperson for the other disciples (e.g., Mark 8:29; 9:5—it is such texts that give rise to the picture of Peter as "impulsive"), as being the disciples' representative to whom Jesus speaks and with whom he deals (e.g., Mark 8:33), and as the representative member of the group whom others approach (e.g., Matt 17:24). While later interpretations are at work in these stories, it is also clear that already during Jesus' ministry Simon was the leader of the twelve, and is always named first in the various lists (Matt 10:2; Mark 3:16; Luke 6:14; Acts 1:13).

It is also historically true that Simon not only failed to understand Jesus during his earthly ministry, but misunderstood and finally denied him (e.g., Mark 8:29-33; 14:66-72). During Jesus' ministry Peter may have made some sort of confession of Jesus as uniquely sent from God ("Messiah," Mark 8:29; "the Messiah of God," Luke 9:20; "Messiah, the Son of the living God," Matt 16:16; "Holy One of God," John 6:69). These accounts, however, are colored by later Christian faith; the historical reality is that insight into the true meaning of Jesus' life, death, and identity awaited the Resurrection.

Peter in the Early Church

The risen Jesus appeared to Simon and (re-)constituted him to be the "Rock" on which the new Christian community is established. That Jesus appeared first to Cephas/Peter is declared in what may be the oldest piece of early Christian tradition preserved in the New Testament, the creedal statement of 1 Cor 15:3-5. In this early Christian creed, "appeared to Cephas" functions as the validating element for "raised on the third day" just as "buried" functions as the validating element for "died." The primary role of Peter in the resurrection appearances is also documented in Luke 24:34 and suggested in Mark 16:7. The later narratives in which Jesus appears first to the women (Matt 28:8-10) or to Mary Magdalene (John 20:11-18) have their own theological validity, but cannot be understood merely as correctives to the earliest testimony with regard to Peter's role in the resurrection appearances and the reconstitution of the community of disciples (cf. Luke 22:31-32; for a different interpretation cf. Setzer 1997). Despite his misunderstanding and failure during Jesus' earthly ministry, the encounter with the risen Lord enabled Peter to become the principal leader in regathering the disciples and in the formation of what was to become the church.

Jesus gave Simon a new name that embodied this role in the establishment of the church: "Rock" (Aramaic: "Cephas"; Gk. "Peter"; Matt 16:16-19; John 1:42). Since "Peter" has become a common name in Western culture influenced by Christianity, it is important to remember that "Cephas/Peter" was not a name at all in first-century Judaism, but was a metaphorical title, "Rock." Neither *kēphas* nor *petros* occurs as a name prior to Simon Peter. (The one possible exception in each case is extremely doubtful. See Hort 1898, 152; Bauer 1979, 654.) Jesus' designation of Simon as "Rock" was not merely a nickname, but corresponds to the biblical tradition in which a new name signals a new reality: Jacob becomes Israel (Gen 32:22-32), Abram becomes Abraham (Gen 17:1-8), Sarai becomes Sarah (Gen 17:15-16).

By the time of Paul's first letter to the Corinthians, Peter is already a well-known figure in Gentile Christianity far beyond Palestine (9:5). Regardless of whether or not Peter had personally visited Corinth, a group appealing strictly to Petrine authority existed within the Corinthian congregation (1:12). Paul may have already found it necessary to polemicize subtly against what he considers a misunderstanding of Peter's role as the "Rock" on which the church is founded (3:11; cf. Matt 16:18). In writing to the Galatians, even while emphasizing the minimal contacts he had had with the original apostles, Paul nevertheless indicates that he went up to Jerusalem "to visit Cephas" (1:18), and that fourteen years later Peter (along with James and John) was still one of the three "pillars" of the Jerusalem church (2:7-8).

Peter was clearly the principal leader of the earliest Christian community in Jerusalem, which was composed of both "Hebrews" and "Hellenists," that is, Christians of Aramaic-speaking Palestinian culture and Christians of Greek-speaking hellenistic culture. Acts 2–6 pictures Peter as a bridge between the two groups, not just as the leader of one. Early in the church's development, Peter's influence extended into Gentile Christianity. The later picture of Acts 2–12, 15, though written from Luke's perspective, is still essentially correct in its broad outline: Peter was from the beginning both a principal leader and agent of unity in what was already becoming a church containing internal tensions.

Peter's role in the early church in the years 30 to 50 CE is complex and should not be oversimplified, either in its reality or in the ease with which we claim to reconstruct it. It is clear, however, that Peter was no rigid advocate of the Torah; Paul never makes the Law an issue between Peter and himself. Peter's conduct at Antioch (Gal 2:11-14) to which Paul objected can in fact be seen as the application of Paul's own principle articulated in 1 Cor 8–10: while one may be inwardly free, in particular situations one should give up one's freedom for the sake of those who have scruples. The incident would also illustrate how difficult the principle is to put into practice (Paul himself received similar criticism on this point; cf. 1 Cor 9:19-23). Peter's leadership of the Jerusalem church receded in favor of the more strict James, brother of Jesus, but this need not be attributed to theological conflict. Even if so, it indicates that Peter advocated a more moderate position closer to Paul than to James. We should, indeed, not speak simplistically of "Jewish" and "Gentile" Christianity as though these were the two mutually exclusive compartments of early Christianity, but of a spectrum of at least four types of Jewish/Gentile Christianity (Brown and Meier 1983, 2-8).

In Paul's letters, Peter appears at first as the leading figure in the Jerusalem church (Gal 1:18), then several years later as one of the three "pillars" (Gal 2:9), then as an influential leader in the Antioch church (Gal 2:11-14). We lose sight of Peter after the Antioch incident (c. 50 CE), though he apparently continued various missionary journeys (1 Cor 9:5), that, however, did not include the provinces to which 1 Peter is addressed (1 Pet 1:12; cf. Brox 1979, 70). In Acts, Peter disappears abruptly from the narrative at 12:17 (mid-40s CE) and departs Jerusalem for "another place," to reappear only once at the Jerusalem Conference (c. 49 CE). Although in some older interpretations the "other place" was Rome, it appears that Peter did not arrive in Rome until after Paul had written Romans (c. 56 CE), and that (if Philemon and Philippians were written from Rome, which I consider unlikely) Peter was not yet in Rome by the late 50s, since he is not mentioned in any of these letters.

Peter did, however, come to Rome, where he continued his apostolic ministry, which he finally sealed with a martyr's death (*1 Clem.* 5–6; Ign. *Rom.* 4:3; cf. John 21:18-19). While falling short of absolute proof, convincing evidence indicates that Peter died as a martyr in Rome under Nero in the mid-60s (Cullmann 1953, 70-154; Brown and Meier 1983, 124; Perkins 1994, 131-50). As was the case with Paul, who likewise suffered martyrdom in Rome about the same time, Peter's ministry and message continued to be effective in the tradition initiated by him that continued after his death.

THE TRADITION: PETER'S HERITAGE

During the several generations after his death an enormous amount of literature associated with the name of Peter was produced, much of it claiming his authorship. In addition to the canonical Petrine texts and noncanonical texts associated with the apostles as a group, in which Peter plays a leading role, the following documents testify to the continuing importance of the figure of Peter (for texts and introductory material, see especially Hennecke and Schneemelcher 1964; Schneemelcher 1991; and individual articles in *ABD*):

The Gospel of Peter; The Letter of Peter to James; The Kerygma Petrou; The Kerygmata Petrou; The Acts of Peter; The Pseudo-Clementines; The Apocalypse of Peter; The Passion of Peter and Paul; The Acts of Peter and the Twelve Apostles; The Act of Peter; The Martyrdom of Peter; The Passion of Peter.

Much of this material is generations or even centuries later than the historical Simon Peter, with whom it has only a nominal connection. After the church became a worldwide institution within which Peter was an accepted authority figure, material was associated with him or even attributed to him that had no connection with the life and ministry of Simon Peter. Nonetheless, there is solid canonical and patristic evidence that the ministry of the apostle Peter continued among disciples influenced by him and in a stream of tradition emanating from him, somewhat analogously to the Pauline school that continued to reinterpret Paul's message after his death (cf. Brown, Donfried, Reumann 1973; Soards 1988).

Struggle for the Apostolic Tradition

In the second and third Christian generations, the issue of who represented the authentic tradition, who could legitimately present themselves as representatives of the Christian faith, meant that several streams of Christian tradition vied with one another for recognition. The primary means of legitimization was the claim to represent apostolic tradition, hence the tendency both to connect anonymous works such as the Gospel of Mark with apostolic names and to present new works under the name of an accepted apostolic authority.

It is not the case that all the churches looked back to all the apostles as authorities. There was a tendency to think in terms of one apostle who represented the one Jesus Christ who represented the one God. The Pastorals, for instance, represent Paul as apostle, and never hint that there are others. There was Jacobite Christianity, Johannine Christianity, and so on, each with its single apostolic hero and symbol of the link between them and Christ, the sole symbol of authentic Christianity. Marcion with his one apostle (Paul) was only an exaggerated instance of a widespread approach. This is conceptually neater and more attractive than the concept that finally won out and is represented in the New Testament canon, namely that of a limited plurality. The canonical scheme was (and is) that while not just any way of representing the faith is acceptable, more than one way is acceptable. This affirmation of unity-within-[limited]-variety was also already congealing within the New Testament period, in Acts, the Synoptics, Ephesians, 2 Peter, and Revelation, and the final redaction of the Gospel of John. It was the genius of later catholic and canonizing Christianity that standardized the view of a limited plurality, but this perspective was already present in Paul, who not only affirmed other and different apostles besides himself (1 Cor 3:21-23; 15:11), but also combated those he considered false apostles (2 Cor 10–13).

Although 1 Peter itself does not directly participate in this struggle, it cannot be understood apart from this background that played such a formative role in the development of the Petrine tradition. The major item on 1 Peter's agenda is to equip the church for its life in a hostile non-Christian world—but this equipment includes living out of a theologically true view of the world. First Peter simply assumes that the faith it represents is shared by and is normative for the addressees in Asia Minor, so that the establishment or preservation of orthodoxy is not part of its agenda. This does not mean that the author is oblivious to issues of orthodoxy and heresy as though he were above the fray, but that he simply assumes that the traditions represented in his letter are normative for the church so that he speaks nonpolemically from within this context. Where did this tradition come from?

Roman Consolidation of Pauline and Petrine Traditions

In the late 50s and early 60s both Paul and Peter came to Rome. Paul came as a Roman citizen in protective custody awaiting trial (Acts 21:27–28:31). We do not know how Peter came. Paul's associates and fellow missionaries accompanied him, and after his death continued to propagate the Pauline understanding of the faith, in Rome and elsewhere (particularly Ephesus). Although we have no details, presumably the same was true of Peter. After both Paul and Peter had sealed their testimony with their own deaths, the Roman church became heir to the traditions of both the great apostles.

While the traditions represented by Paul and Peter were different, they were not mutually exclusive alternatives, and were not seen as such by the Roman church, which in the latter part of the first century began to see itself as supporter of and teacher to other struggling churches outside Rome. The Pseudo-Clementines represent a Petrine tradition that took Peter's side against Paul. Marcion was a Roman Christian leader who took Paul's side against Peter. But the mainstream Roman church held Peter and Paul together (cf. Brown and Meier 1983, 209). *First Clement* is the clearest testimony that the Roman church adopted both Paul and Peter as patron saints and saw itself as the world leader of both Jewish and Gentile Christianity in one church. That this development need not be seen in a sinister perspective as a power grab is apparent from Ignatius, who already in 110, from his Antiochene perspective considers "Paul and Peter" simply as THE apostles (Ign. *Rom.* 3:1). Twenty years later *Herm. Vis.* 2.4.3 refers to the Roman church as having previously sent writings to other churches. Thus by the end of the first century there had been an amalgamation of Pauline and Petrine traditions in Rome, which is acknowledged in the next generation by 2 Peter's claiming Paul as a brother apostle whose teaching, however, must be understood within the perspective of the Petrine tradition (2 Pet 3:14-16). The consolidation of Pauline and Petrine traditions into one whole is represented in another way by the author of Luke–Acts, who in about 90 CE (also in Rome?) retold the story of the early church in such a way that Peter and Paul are dual representatives of the one apostolic tradition. Acts is clear documentation that in some circles of early Christianity at the close of the first century there was deep interest in presenting the Christian message on the twin pillars of Petrine and Pauline tradition.

How and where does 1 Peter fit into this trajectory of developing Petrine tradition?

THE CANONICAL BOOK:
1 PETER AS THE ADDRESS OF PETRINE TRADITION
TO A PARTICULAR SITUATION

The question of the authorship and setting of 1 Peter has too often been reduced to an oversimplified and unhelpful either/or: either Simon Peter wrote the letter himself from Rome in the early 60s, or a later writer wrote pseudonymously in Peter's name.

However, there is actually a spectrum of possibilities, that may be delineated as follows:

1. Peter wrote the letter personally, from Rome, in the 60s. His thorough Greek education and experience made him fully capable of doing this without help from Silvanus or anyone else (Grudem 1988, 21-32).

2. Peter supplied the ideas but the vocabulary, syntax, and style belong to Silvanus, who did the actual writing at Peter's behest. Peter then approved and authorized it. This view usually dates 1 Peter in the 60s as above (Bigg 1901, 5), but J. Ramsey Michaels has recently revived the older view of A. M. Ramsey that Peter lived into the 80s when the letter was written by Peter with secretarial help from Silvanus (Michaels 1988, lxii).

3. Silvanus wrote representing Peter, who commissioned the letter. Peter is the authority that stands behind the letter, but Silvanus is its actual composer who made his "own contribution to the substance no less than to the language" of the letter (Selwyn 1947, 11; Davids 1990, 30).

4. Silvanus wrote in Peter's name after his death, using Petrine tradition. Silvanus is the actual author of the letter (Goppelt 1993, 50, considers this view sympathetically but finally rejects it; Kelly 1969, 33, with reservations; Brown 1983, 130, seems sympathetic to this view; much less so Brown 1997, 718-23).

5. An anonymous member of the "Petrine circle" in Rome wrote in Peter's name after his death. "Peter" is fictive, but "Silvanus," "Mark," and the "elect sister" are real people who are members of the Petrine group (Elliott 1981, 270-80).

6. An anonymous Roman Christian wrote on the basis of Petrine tradition (Goppelt 1993, 51-52, though also having sympathies for #4 above; Achtemeier 1996, 199).

7. A Paulinist wrote in Peter's name, primarily on the basis of Pauline tradition (Beare 1958, 24-30).

The exegetical work of the following commentary led to the conclusion that 1 Peter is best understood as a pseudonymous document written about 90 CE by an anonymous member of the

Roman church, that is, nearest to #6 above. First Peter represents the Roman amalgamation of Petrine and Pauline tradition focused in a particular letter to churches in Asia Minor to encourage and instruct them to live as Christians in response to their hostile social situation. The persuasive power of arguments for the position adopted comes only by testing the hypothesis in the detailed work on the text itself.

Authorship and Date:
1 Peter Is a Pseudonymous Document
of the Second Generation

The authorship question for 1 Peter is a different kind of question than, for example, the authorship of the Pastorals, where we have several undisputed letters of Paul and do not have to speculate as to what Paul would have actually written. But 1 Peter is the only possibility that we have of something in the New Testament written by Peter himself, or by any of the original disciples of Jesus. Thus while in the nature of the case all such historical judgments are less than absolutely certain, the following reasons are convincing to most contemporary scholars that 1 Peter was not written by Peter himself but by an anonymous disciple in Peter's name. ("Pseudonymous" does not, of course, mean "forgery," but represents a widespread practice of the hellenistic world in which a later disciple wrote in the name of a respected teacher or founder of a school tradition. Cf. below pp. 36-37.)

Language and Thought World: First Peter is written with a high level of literary and rhetorical competence by someone thoroughly at home in the Greek language, culture, and the LXX, the Greek translation of the Old Testament. First Peter exhibits a better level of Greek than does Paul, a hellenistic Jew who grew up in Tarsus, and better than 2 Peter, which could not have been written by the same person (details and lists in Achtemeier 1996, 3-9; Soards 1988, 3833 [with further bib.]; Selwyn 1947, 489-501). This argument does not presuppose that the historical Peter was an illiterate fisherman who knew no Greek, for this was probably not the case (see above). The difficulty is rather in believing that a

Palestinian Jew would be able to write the sophisticated and elegant Greek of 1 Peter, with its numerous allusions to classical and hellenistic culture, and that a Palestinian Jew would not only cite the LXX—this is credible enough in a missionary situation—but betray no knowledge of the original Hebrew texts and allude almost unconsciously to LXX phraseology, indicating that his own world of thought is represented by Greek literature and the LXX. First Peter sometimes *improves* the rough grammar and syntax when he cites the LXX (as in 3:10-12; cf. Beare 1958, 135).

Relation to Pauline and Deutero-Pauline Literature: While most scholarship has moved past the point where 1 Peter can be seen as merely another version of second-generation Paulinism (as still argued, e.g., by Koester 1982, 292-97), the letter does reflect knowledge and appropriation of the Pauline tradition in a way difficult to imagine for Paul's contemporary, the historical Peter. The extent and manner of 1 Peter's dependence on Pauline tradition will be discussed below and in the commentary. Here the point is that the letter form, as such, is an influence of Pauline tradition. Since our New Testament is composed chiefly of letters, it seems natural enough to us that 1 Peter should be in letter form. Yet it was not self-evident in the first generation of Christianity that the letter form should be chosen as the chief means of propagating the faith. It is not the case that the letter form as a means of Christian communication and instruction existed independently in early Christianity, which Paul and the author of 1 Peter coincidentally chose as their own medium of teaching. *It was Paul who made it so.* The author of 1 Peter does not, independently of Paul, choose the letter form from among a number of possibilities (e.g., essays, apocalypses, collections of sayings, hymns, creeds, church orders, narratives), but rather, the letter reflects a time and place when the Pauline letter form had become the accepted form of Christian communication from church leaders to congregations.

Not only the letter genre as such, but particular features of Paul's distinctive formal epistolary traits are found in 1 Peter, for example, "grace to you and peace" (AT) as the salutation, found only in Paul's writings and in literature dependent on him (1:2; cf. all the undisputed Pauline letters); "in Christ," apparently coined by Paul, found in the New Testament only in the Pauline tradition and in 1 Peter (3:16; 5:10, 14); Paul's distinctive and innovative word for spiritual "gift" *(charisma)* found only in the Pauline tradition and in 1 Pet 4:10; Paul's peculiar word for "fleshly" sinful desires *(sarkikos)* not found in the LXX or elsewhere in the New Testament except the Pauline letters (5x) and 1 Pet 2:11; the terminology of "angels, authorities, and powers," found outside the Pauline corpus only in 1 Pet 3:22. Such data do not necessarily indicate a direct literary connection between 1 Peter and the Pauline letters in the sense that the author of 1 Peter had the Pauline corpus open before him as he wrote, but do at least show that 1 Peter derives from a situation in which the Pauline letters and distinctive Pauline expressions circulated and could be adopted without comment as standard Christian vocabulary.

So also Paul's associates Mark and Silvanus (Silas) are incorporated into the fictive literary world projected by the document (5:12-13), which makes no reference to Paul himself. This represents a secondary amalgamation of Pauline and Petrine traditions (see below), not a strategy of the historical Simon Peter. It is hardly conceivable that the historical Peter in Rome would, in a letter to the Pauline mission territory of Asia and Galatia, allude to Mark and Silas, but not to Paul himself (contrast 2 Pet 3:14-16, where even the pseudepigraphical 2 Peter is constrained to do this).

These two features, the sophisticated language and style and the reflections of Pauline epistolary form and content, have caused practically all scholars who affirm Petrine authorship to attribute the actual composition of the letter to Silvanus, not directly to Simon Peter. But the secretary hypothesis cannot salvage Petrine authorship. On this hypothesis, Silvanus should at least have been included in 1:1, as in 1 Thessalonians (cf. Krodel 1977, 55). The message of 1 Peter is inextricably related to its language and rhetoric. We may take the first two literary units as examples, the salutation of 1:1-2 and the thanksgiving of 1:3-12. Each is a single sentence, a carefully composed unit in which form, syntax, and vocabulary are carefully chosen (see commentary). To explain the composition of such literary units in terms of "Peter gave Silvanus the basic idea, and Silvanus put it in sophisticated language," or "Peter composed the rough draft and Silvanus polished the language" is a last-ditch apologetic effort to salvage the letter, an attempt that fails to understand the relationship of thought and language. Even if the hypothesis is granted on the basis of questionable exegesis of 5:12 (see commentary ad loc.), the result is still that the letter is composed not by Peter himself but by a faithful disciple, and that the authority of Peter stands somehow behind it—which is precisely what the theory of pseudonymous authorship claims!

Date: When previous generations of scholars supposed that 1 Peter reflected a period of official Roman persecution of the church, it was thought that the letter must therefore be dated during the mid-60s (Nero's persecution of the church in Rome), the mid-90s (Domitian's persecution of Christians in Asia Minor reflected in Revelation), or the second decade of the second century (Trajan's persecution of Christians in Asia Minor reflected in Pliny's letter; cf. below pp. 44-45). More recent study has convinced most scholars that 1 Peter reflects a time of distress and social harassment, but not an official persecution initiated by the government, and that in any case there was no empirewide Roman persecution until the time of Decian in the third century (see on 3:13-17). Persecution "for the name" does not specifically indicate the period when 1 Peter was written (see commentary on 4:14, 16). Thus attempting to date 1 Peter on the basis of a specific persecution has not been helpful. Other data, however, point to the late 80s or early 90s as the period of the letter's composition:

• During the final days of both Nero and Domitian, some members of the church, in some locations, did sometimes face life-or-death decisions in their relation to the government. But for about twenty years in between, 72–92 CE the church in both Rome and the provinces lived in a precarious situation of marginalization and social harassment, but without the threat of martyrdom. This corresponds to the situation reflected in 1 Peter. Pliny's letter to Trajan (c. 112) refers to a period in Pontus twenty years previously during which Christians were harassed to the point that some had repudiated their new religion. This points to 90–92, and fits the situation of 1 Peter before the pressures intensified in the latter part of Domitian's reign. Likewise, the neutral description of the state and Christians' attitude toward it (2:13-17) are less positive than Paul's instructions in the mid-50s (Rom 13:1-7), but much less negative than Revelation's portrayal of Rome as apocalyptic beast (Rev 12–13 *et passim*), again pointing to the period after Nero but before Domitian's last days.

- Rome is represented as "Babylon" (see on 5:12), which did not happen until after the destruction of Jerusalem by the Romans in 70 CE.
- Cappadocia is mentioned as a separate province (1:1), which it did not become until 73 CE.
- If the author was indeed aware of the distinction between governors sent by the senate and governors sent by the emperor (cf. 2:14), his incidental description fits the late–first century better than earlier (cf. Beare 1958, 116).
- The numerous similarities in vocabulary and thought world shared by 1 Peter and *1 Clement* (written from Rome c. 95), while they do not point to literary dependence in either direction, do indicate that both derive from the same situation, making use of a common tradition.
- Elders as church leaders (5:1) are unknown to the undisputed letters of Paul, but are the standard form of congregational church leadership in the Pauline/Petrine tradition documented in Acts about 90 CE (Acts 11:30; 14:23; 15:2, 4, 6, 22; 16:4; 20:17, 18).
- The relation of the church to Judaism, and the church's direct appropriation of the Jewish Scriptures as its own, are simply not issues for the author (see commentary). A situation in which this could be assumed with no awareness of debate must reflect a period some time after Paul (cf. Rom 9–11) and even after Ephesians (cf. Eph 2).

Christology and Relation to Jesus Tradition: Perhaps the most compelling reason to attribute 1 Peter to a second-generation disciple rather than to Simon Peter himself is the absolute lack of the kind of material one would anticipate from a personal companion of Jesus and an eyewitness of his ministry. Except for the name in 1:1, the letter makes no claim to be from an eyewitness. Though writing to represent apostolic authority, the author presents himself not as an apostle but as a "fellow elder" (5:1 AT). The supposed contrast between the author as eyewitness and the addressees who are not is exegetically unsound (cf. commentary on 1:8). Nor does the author claim to be an eyewitness to Jesus' Passion (cf. commentary on 5:1). Even if these texts are understood differently, they would only represent the fictive literary world projected by the pseudonymous document, and would no more constitute evidence of actual authorship than the claims made, for example, by the *Gospel of Peter,* which does specifically claim eyewitness authorship.

The teaching of Jesus is reflected only minimally. A perusal of the margins of the Nestlé-Aland Greek text, which indicates all recognizable allusions, reveals that while the text is peppered with allusions to the Old Testament and to the parenetic tradition found in other New Testament epistles, the traditions from and about Jesus now found in the Gospels are quite meager. While there is some reflection of Jesus' sayings, these are not cited directly, but are incorporated into parenetic church tradition (see commentary on 3:8-12, 14; 4:7-11, 14). Traditional sayings of Jesus appropriate to points made in various texts of 1 Peter circulated in early Christianity (e.g., Mark 12:17 at 1 Pet 2:13-17). While these occur immediately to anyone who has read the Gospels, they are absent from 1 Peter, and instead we find the kind of Christian parenetic instruction utilized in Rom 13:1-7. Repeatedly, instead of citing the saying of Jesus one would anticipate from an eyewitness disciple, the Petrine point is made by citing the Old Testament (e.g., 3:14; 4:8, 14). Even the suffering of Jesus, paradigmatic for the Christian's own life, is described not in terms of the memory of an eyewitness, but by citing Scripture passages from Christian tradition (cf. commentary on 2:21-25). Although the connection between the Gospel of Mark and Simon Peter was made by the early second century (Papias in Eusebius, *Hist. Eccl.* 3.39.14-17), it is exegetically dangerous to rely on Mark as the supposed "preaching of Peter" as the key to interpreting 1 Peter, which shows no connections to the Gospel of Mark. For example, Jesus' words at the Last Supper in Mark 14:22-25 may not be used to explain the allusion to (covenantal) blood in 1 Pet 1:2 (*contra,* e.g., Selwyn 1947, 121). The lack of connection between 1 Peter and the Gospel of Mark is evidence against Simon Peter's having written 1 Peter, directly or indirectly.

Even more important, the Christology of 1 Peter is not expressed or illustrated by stories from the life of the historical Jesus, but by incorporating the life of Jesus within a cosmic framework in which the weakness of the earthly Jesus becomes part of the saving act of God (cf. Boring 1984, 49-72). In contrast to the epiphany Christology found in the Gospels in which Jesus is portrayed as being filled with the divine power (e.g., Mark 5), God's victory over the demonic powers that threaten human life is not thought of in terms of the exorcisms of the earthly Jesus as in the Gospel of Mark (also associated with Peter in early Christian tradition). Rather, the saving act of God in the Christ-event is portrayed as the cosmic victory accomplished by the Resurrection/Ascension, as in the Pauline *kenosis* Christology that portrays the earthly Jesus in the weakness of a truly human life (e.g., 2 Cor 13:4; Phil 2:5-11). This is a fundamental difference between the Gospel manner of conceptualizing the saving act of God in Jesus, and the Christology represented in all the Epistles. First Peter reflects the cosmic/*kenosis* Christology of the Epistles, not the epiphany Christology of the Gospels that functioned by reciting stories and sayings from the pre-Easter life of Jesus. One would anticipate that a letter from an eyewitness to the life of Jesus would at least make contact with the kind of Christology found in the Gospels, but it functions altogether within the framework of the epistolary christological tradition oriented to Paul. This consideration alone is decisive against authorship by a representative of the eyewitness tradition of a first-generation Palestinian disciple of Jesus.

The overtones of our terminology are important. It is unfortunate that in New Testament scholarship the designations that have become standard technical terms such as "authentic" and "pseudonymous" also in the popular mind have positive connotations in the former case and negative ones in the latter. These overtones should not be rhetorically exploited in responsible academic discussion. In the past, even those scholars who did not believe that Simon Peter wrote the letter personally but still claimed it as Petrine on the grounds that Silvanus composed it at Peter's behest, had sometimes spoken of the theory of pseudonymous authorship in terms of "deliberate falsification," "concoction," and "unscrupulous . . . forgery" (Bigg 1901, 79).

Something important was at stake in attributing 1 Peter to "Peter, apostle of Jesus Christ," but it was the claim to represent the authentic apostolic faith of the church, not the modern interest in truth understood as historical "fact." No one should make a decision with regard to the authorship and authority of 1 Peter (as well as the Deutero-Paulines and the other Catholic epistles) without having studied the phenomenon of pseudepigraphy in antiquity and its theological relevance. Brevard Childs has recently provided a good discussion of the canonical meaning of the phenomenon of pseudepigraphy, with summaries of recent research and additional bibliography (Childs 1984, 376-86).

Genre: 1 Peter Is a Real Letter

In the late–nineteenth century and first half of the twentieth century, many scholars argued that the bulk of 1 Peter was not originally composed as a letter. Already in 1887 Adolf Harnack confidently declared that 1 Peter was "a sermon not a letter," that a baptismal homily found in 1:3–5:11 had later been inserted into a letter framework. In 1911 E. R. Perdelwitz refined the theory to argue that 1:3–4:11 was a baptismal sermon to new converts, later incorporated into a letter that added exhortations to a new situation of persecution, a view of the document's composition that was widely adopted (e.g., Beare 1958, 6-9). Further research has shown the unity of the letter (e.g., Dalton 1965, 62-87), of which practically all scholars are now convinced (Krodel 1977 is an exception). Several commentaries and studies give the history of the rise and fall of such hypotheses, which need not be repeated here (e.g., Achtemeier 1996, 58-64; Soards 1988, 3834). First Peter was written all at once as a real letter, but does include a large proportion of traditional parenetic materials, including baptismal imagery and allusions, that have provided the occasion for other hypotheses.

The letter form is not part of the fictive literary world projected by the pseudonymous document; 1 Peter is a real letter to real churches. First Peter is not a letter to individual churches, but a circular letter to all the Christians in a wide area. Unlike the authentic Pauline letters, it does not reflect any awareness of particular events in the life of specific congregations. The Petrine author knows of the addressees' situation only what he knows theologically of Christians as such (cf. 2 Tim 3:12). Like the Pauline letters, it was intended for reading in the worship services of the congregations, not for private study. It thus contains preaching and teaching material appropriate to congregational instruction and edification. It is not essentially a catechetical letter concerned with Christian doctrine, but a parenetical letter designed to encourage a certain kind of conduct in a situation of testing and adversity (5:12).

Provenance: 1 Peter Was Written from Rome

The letter claims to have been written from "Babylon" (5:13). This cannot be meant literally. There is no evidence that Peter was ever in Babylon or that Petrine tradition was located there. The once-great city that had included a significant Jewish population was by the middle of the first century an insignificant small town that the Jewish community had left, and was practically uninhabited by the time 1 Peter was written (Diodorus Sic. 2.9.9; Strabo *Geog.* 16.1.5). Thus "Babylon" must be understood as a cryptogram for Rome. After 70 CE this became fairly common in Jewish apocalyptic documents (2 *Apoc. Bar.* 11:1-2; 67:7; 2 Esdr 3:1-2, 28; *Syb. Or.* 5.143, 155-161, 434, 440), and is clearly adopted by the Christian author of Revelation in the 90s (Rev 14:8; 16:19; 17:5; 18:2, 10, 21). Our choices are thus that 1 Peter was actually written from Rome, or that Rome = Babylon is part of the fictive literary world projected by the pseudonymous style. While the latter is not impossible, the close connections to the Roman *1 Clement* and Hebrews make an actual Roman provenance much more likely.

Sources: 1 Peter Represents the Roman Amalgamation of Petrine and Pauline Tradition Under the Heading of Peter

The common kerygmatic, parenetical, and liturgical elements in several New Testament documents that otherwise have no contact with one another show to what an extent the early church lived by its tradition. The claim that 1 Peter is a real letter does not mean that it was composed ad hoc; rather, it incorporates an extensive range of early Christian tradition that it focuses and applies to a particular situation. First Peter drew from a deep well of traditional materials comprised of Jewish Scripture and Christian tradition.

Jewish Scripture: The author uses the Old Testament as a Christian book in which what was once said to and about Israel passes seamlessly and unpolemically into address to the church. Since the Spirit of Christ spoke through the prophets (1:11) and in Christian preaching (1:12), the Old and New Testaments are a unity. When the relative size of the documents is considered, 1 Peter makes more extensive use of the Old Testament than any other New Testament author except Revelation (Best 1971, 29). His thought world is the LXX, from which the only direct quotations from any source are taken, and which is also the source of all his allusions. The montage of biblical imagery in 2:1-10 is one of the densest in the New Testament, though only 2:6 is a direct quotation. While the author knows the Old Testament thoroughly himself, the choice and combination of citations is not made independently, but itself reflects church tradition. He quotes some of the same obscure texts as other New Testament authors (e.g., Prov 3:34 in 5:5; cf. James 4:6) and the same combinations of texts (e.g., Isa 28:16 and 8:14 in 2:6-8; cf. Rom 9:33), which must be more than coincidence but need not be direct literary dependence. A tradition of textual selection and interpretation had developed that was shared by Paul, James, 1 Peter, and others. The Roman provenance of this hermeneutical tradition is suggested by the common use of Ps 34 (LXX Ps 33) in Hebrews, 1 Peter, and *1 Clement* (cf. Davids 1990, 128). If David Daube is correct in his argument that the large number of imperative participles in 1 Peter reflects rabbinic Hebrew usage but not ordinary hellenistic grammar, this may be a further indication of the influence of Palestinian tradition on 1 Peter (Daube in Selwyn 1947, 467-88), a probability enhanced by the general Jewish character of first- and second-generation Roman Christianity (Brown and Meier 1983, 92-158). The contacts between 1 Peter and James may suggest their dependence on common tradition with roots in Jerusalem Christianity (Brown 1997, 721).

Christian Tradition: The primary source from which 1 Peter draws its materials, concepts, and language is a stream of Christian tradition that has Palestinian roots, is reinterpreted and augmented by intense engagement with the world of hellenistic religions, and has received a stable form in the Roman church during the generation 60–90 CE.

This tradition has deep Jewish roots. There is no indication that the author had imbibed the kind of Jewish traditions cultivated in the rabbinic academies that later received written deposit in the Mishnah, Midrashim, and the Talmud. While there is no direct literary contact between 1 Peter and the Dead Sea Scrolls, the combination of thematic similarities such as election, purification by a water ritual, the community as eschatological house of God, eschatological interpretation of Scripture, the identification of the community itself as the people of God, and the call to holiness may well point to the earliest stage of the tradition now found in 1 Peter as having originated in the same thought world as that of Qumran, namely on the margins of Palestinian Judaism, in tension with the dominant religious authorities.

Included as part of the deposit of early Palestinian Christian tradition is the early *kerygma* of the saving event of Jesus' death and resurrection, and some reflection of the sayings of Jesus. While the difference between Peter and Paul on this point should not be exaggerated (1 Cor 15:11), there are no direct quotations from Jesus' teaching in 1 Peter. The extent of allusions to sayings of Jesus is disputed, but attempts to detect large numbers of them have not been convincing to most scholars (cf. Gundry 1967, 336-50, and the response by Best 1970, 95-113). However many such allusions there may be—I find relatively few myself—they bear the features not of personal memory but of church parenetic tradition.

First Peter is not a direct delivery of Palestinian tradition. In its present form, it has become thoroughly hellenized, and has incorporated many hellenistic elements, both from the hellenistic church and from hellenistic culture in general. While rabbinic points of contact are lacking, parallels to hellenistic religion and ethics abound (cf. Boring, Berger, and Colpe 1995, 528-36 and index). However, the extreme view of some scholars that the author was at home in the thought world of the mystery cults, or even that he had been an initiate in them prior to becoming a Christian (e.g., Perdelwitz 1911) has now been almost universally abandoned, but it cannot be denied that the conceptuality of hellenistic religion (such as "rebirth," 1:3, 23) has influenced the traditions from which 1 Peter draws.

Petrine Tradition: First Peter is a document of early Christian tradition. What was once seen by some scholars as a literary patchwork drawn from other early Christian writings (especially those of Paul and the Deutero-Paulines) is now widely (but not universally) acknowledged as a distinctively Petrine formulation of a stream of Christian tradition that was widely influential in early Christianity. This stream of tradition included hymnic, creedal, liturgical, and catechetical materials (see commentary on e.g., 1:18-20; 2:13–3:7; 2:21-25; 3:18-19). The existence and contents of this stream of tradition have been persuasively documented by the detailed charts cataloging identical and similar content, form, wording, and patterns representing the results of comparative analyses of 1 Peter and other New Testament documents (Selwyn 1947, 365-466). Comparing 1 Peter 5:5-9 to Jas 4:6-10 represents a sample of the more than one hundred pages of analysis provided by Selwyn, a sample in which even the casual reader can detect an underlying common tradition. While such analyses prove neither direct literary dependence nor that there was a rigidly fixed "early Christian catechism" known throughout early Christianity, the analyses of Selwyn and others have made the dependence of 1 Peter on earlier tradition impossible to deny.

This tradition should not be thought of as tradition-in-general. There was no such thing. There were only particular streams. Thus 1 Peter, for example, shows no contacts with the Johannine tradition. The degree of contact with Synoptic tradition is disputed, but seems to me to be minimal. First Peter is connected to 2 Peter, James, Hebrews, and *1 Clement,* but not to Johannine materials, including Revelation. First Peter represents a particular stream of tradition that can legitimately be called Petrine. John H. Elliott has made a convincing case that this tradition was cultivated in Rome after the death of Peter, though he has perhaps gone too far in proposing that Mark, Silvanus, and the "elect sister" were actual members of this "Petrine circle" (Elliott 1981, 267-95).

Pauline Tradition (Paul and Deuteropaul [Ephesians!]): The tradition found in 1 Peter also contains distinctively Pauline elements. A sample of Pauline characteristics has been given above (pp. 31-32), but extensive lists of linguistic, stylistic, formal, and theological features distinctive of Paul and found in 1 Peter (sometimes only in Paul's writings and 1 Peter) have been compiled (Beare 1958 *passim;* Achtemeier 1996, 15-19, with further bib.). This data was previously often explained as though 1 Peter was merely a "Paulinist" giving a rehash of the Pauline letters, even to the point of claiming that originally the letter was written in Paul's name, the abbreviation PS for "*Paulos*" being mistakenly expanded by later scribes into "*Petros*" (so Karl-Martin Fischer; cf. the designation "pseudo-Pauline" by Marxsen 1970, 236). This view was properly rejected by the next phase of scholarship, which tended to overreact and claim there was no contact between the author of 1 Peter and the letters of Paul. The pendulum is now swinging back to a more central position: 1 Peter represents an old and independent tradition and is not directly dependent on the Pauline letters in any scissors-and-paste manner, but the author has read them and been influenced by them (so e.g., Schelke 1988, 7).

The view represented in this commentary is that 1 Peter is written from a context that has combined the Petrine and Pauline traditions, which means that the Pauline letters, including the Deutero-Pauline Ephesians, were familiar and authoritative documents in the author's church. The Roman church represented semi-officially by *1 Clement* in about 95 CE regards Peter and Paul as the two pillars of the Church, including Paul in the category Paul had himself earlier spoken of with mild disdain (Gal 2:6-9), but placing Peter first. So also 2 Peter later incorporates the Pauline letters under the aegis of Petrine interpretation. First Peter represents the Roman affirmation of Pauline and Petrine tradition as its two foundational pillars, but with Peter as primary: much Pauline tradition is now set forth under the name of Peter, supported by the names of Paul's fellow missionaries Mark and Silvanus, and in the Pauline letter form. Peter again symbolically serves as peacemaker and symbol of unity as he had tried to be at Antioch.

Occasion: 1 Peter Was Written to Distressed Churches in Asia Minor Facing a Difficult Social Situation

First Peter is addressed to Christians in a broad geographical area: the five Roman provinces comprising most of present-day Turkey (see commentary on 1:1). This region represents a combination of Pauline mission territory (Galatia and Asia) and areas that by 90 CE were associated with Petrine preaching (cf. Acts 2:9 and Brown 1984, 76)—though 1 Pet 1:12 indicates no connection between the author, real or fictive, and the readers. These churches were suffering distress, and the church at Rome, site of the martyrdom of Paul and Peter, appears to have regarded itself as having ongoing responsibility for encouraging and instructing the churches of the Pauline and Petrine missions (*1 Clement;* Ign. *Rom.* 3:1).

While there were likely some Jewish Christians among the addressees, the letter indicates that the readers were primarily Gentiles who had formerly not known the true God and who had lived the sinful, idolatrous life of pagans (1:14, 18, 21; 2:1, 9-11, 25; 4:3), indeed that the principal reason for their social marginalization and distress was due to their having withdrawn from participation in aspects of their former life they now considered to be sinful (4:4).

Acts 28:22, written about the same time as 1 Peter, pictures the view of the church circulating in Rome as "the sect everywhere spoken against." This fits the perspective of 1 Peter: society at large considers the Christian community to be an unwelcome, even dangerous, sectarian movement, and subjects it to abuse. The situation is not merely local but worldwide (5:9). While Christians are called to suffer "for the name" (see 4:15-16), the abuse is mostly verbal (2:22-23; 3:9-12, 16). There is as yet no government persecution, except for occasional arbitrary acts by subordinate officials. First Peter's positive attitude toward the state (2:13-17) makes it clear that there was no government policy of persecution of Christians as such. This is not to minimize the seriousness of the situation of the Christian community that found itself pushed to the edges of society by a populace that regarded them as a superstitious and unpatriotic sect. The community tended to respond by intensifying its own sectarian and survival instincts, just as it was tempted to accept the outsider status imputed to it and to live irresponsibly in a world that had rejected it (cf. Elliott 1981, 101-64). First Peter attempts to offer realistic encouragement and instruction to Christians attempting to live faithfully in such a situation.

Pliny to Trajan: When Pliny arrived from Rome as the new governor of Pontus in about 111 CE he found some charges against Christians already on the court docket over which he had to preside and render judgments. A few citations from Pliny's letter to the emperor Trajan, written about twenty years after 1 Peter and from the same geographical area to which 1 Peter is directed, illuminates the way Christians were perceived by the government and their neighbors, and illustrates the precarious situation of a religious minority at the mercy of suspicious neighbors and arbitrary state power.

> I have handled those who have been denounced to me as Christians as follows: I asked them whether they were Christians. Those who responded affirmatively I have asked a second and third time, under threat of the death penalty. If they persisted in their confession, I had them executed. For whatever it is that they are actually advocating, it seems to me that obstinacy and stubbornness must be punished in any case. Others who labor under the same delusion, but who were Roman citizens, I have designated to be sent to Rome.
>
> In the course of the investigations, as it usually happens, charges are brought against wider circles of people, and the following special cases have emerged:

An unsigned placard was posted, accusing a large number of people by name. Those who denied being Christians now or in the past, I thought necessary to release, since they invoked our gods according to the formula I gave them and since they offered sacrifices of wine and incense before your image which I had brought in for this purpose along with the statues of our gods. I also had them curse Christ. It is said that real Christians cannot be forced to do any of these things.

Others charged by this accusation at first admitted that they had once been Christians, but had already renounced it; they had in fact been Christians, but had given it up, some of them three years ago, some even earlier, some as long as twenty-five years ago [note that this would be in the time of 1 Peter] (Pliny the Younger, *Letters*, X:96-97 translation by M. Eugene Boring).

Theology: 1 Peter Is Not a Theological Treatise, but Presupposes and Communicates a Profound Theology

Unlike, for example, Galatians, Romans, and Hebrews, 1 Peter does not directly address theological dangers within the church and cannot be considered in this sense a theological treatise. This does not mean that 1 Peter should be considered "practical advice" rather than "theological speculation." As is the case with all valid pastoral care, the instruction in 1 Peter presupposes profound theological commitments and understanding, but it is communicated mostly indirectly and incidentally. A key instance is the famous passage of 3:18-22 in which Christ, after his death, preaches to the spirits in prison, which is by no means a bit of speculative theology the author wants to explain, but is an aspect of his practical instruction on how Christians are called to live out their faith in the concrete social situation addressed in the letter. The underlying theology is projected indirectly to the reader through the narrative world that is presupposed, as the reader is called to accept as real the theocentric historical world of the creation-to-eschaton "mighty acts of God" defined by the Christ-event (cf. Appendix 1: The Narrative World of 1 Peter). Although it is possible to construct helpful systematic statements of "the theology of 1 Peter" in which the Christology, ecclesiology, eschatology, and so forth of the letter are delineated (cf., e.g., R. Martin

1994 and the relevant sections of standard New Testament theologies), it is more in tune with the author's own method to discuss theology as it emerges in the exegesis of individual texts.

Text and Canon: 1 Peter Was Faithfully Transmitted by the Church and Became a Part of the Church's Scripture

The first evidence for the existence of 1 Peter is in Polycarp's *Letter to the Philippians* early in the second century, perhaps as early as 110, no later than 135. The letter explicitly quotes 1 Peter several times, but not by name (this first occurs in *Adv. Haer.* 4.9.2, c. 185). It is significant that 1 Peter emerges in the correspondence of Polycarp as an apostolic letter that he had "read, learned, and inwardly digested," a letter by which he lived and died a martyr's death as an old man in 155 CE. The first echo of 1 Peter in history is a mighty one; Polycarp "suffered as a Christian" and "glorified God by that name" (1 Pet 4:16). First Peter was attested early and strongly, unlike the other Catholic epistles, and was never among the disputed documents on the edge of the canon (though its absence from the [incompletely preserved] Roman Muratorian Canon of the late–second century is puzzling). While much early Christian literature was written in Peter's name (cf. above), most of which finally failed to find acceptance in the church, 1 Peter was accepted as authentic testimony to the apostolic faith from the earliest times.

Likewise the text has been transmitted with great accuracy in the manuscript tradition, so that there are only minor variations to consider in the exegesis. Our earliest manuscript of 1 Peter is papyrus P^{72} from the late–third or early–fourth century, preserved in the Bodmer Library (Cologny/Geneva) as Bodmer Papyrus VII, VIII.

Structure: 1 Peter Is Effectively Structured to Achieve Its Purpose

The question of whether or not the author composed 1 Peter according to an intentionally thought through outline continues to be disputed, even after the work of some scholars who claim to have solved the problem when all others have failed (e.g., T. Martin

1992, 269, 275). Opinions range from Norbert Brox, who argues the author had no outline at all in mind and accordingly structures his commentary as a list of topics without major headings or subheadings (Brox 1979, 35-38) to Lauri Thurén, who sees in 1 Peter a thorough and subtle rhetorical structure (Thurén 1995, 88-185 *et passim*). The incorporation of a large amount of traditional material has obscured the author's own framework for his composition, but his parenesis is not the random stringing together of exhortations. The following outline seems to reflect the major turning points of the argument, and, with minor variations, is widely represented in current studies of 1 Peter.

1:1-2 Salutation
1:3-12 Thanksgiving
1:13–5:11 Body of the Letter
    1:13–2:10 The New Identity As the Elect and Holy People of
        God
    2:11–3:12 Christian Existence and Conduct in the Given
        Structures of Society
    3:13–5:11 Responsible Suffering in the Face of Hostility
5:12-14 Conclusion of the Letter

COMMENTARY

SALUTATION (1:1-2)

The author himself, of course, gave his letter no title, which was added to the document in various forms during the process of circulation and canonization. All the forms of the title designate it as the "first" epistle of Peter, indicating an acknowledgment of 2 Peter. Practically all manuscripts include "Catholic" in the title, understood either in the sense of "general, universal" (as opposed to letters to a particular congregation) or as "canonical, orthodox," or both.

It is not obvious that 1 Peter should be in the form of a letter. Neither the Old Testament nor the sacred writings of other religions contain series of letters. The author, even if he had a message to communicate directly to the churches of Asia Minor, could readily have expressed what he had to say in an essay, a collection of wisdom sayings, a sermon, a church order, or some other literary genre used by early Christians, and had it delivered and read in the churches by a messenger just as we presume Silvanus was (see on 5:12 below).

The epistolary form of 1 Peter is important theologically in that the letter genre corresponds to the nature of the Christian faith in its concreteness and particularity. The Christian gospel affirms that God has acted definitively in history in the particular person Jesus of Nazareth, rather than generally and abstractly. Like the Incarnation, letters are particular and concrete, not general and abstract, just as they correspond to the historical lives of their recipients—for we all live concrete, individual lives in a particular historical time and place. None of us lives "in general." Although 1 Peter is classified among the General Epistles in the sense that it is addressed to more than one congregation, it is the nature of a letter to be specific. This historical dimension of 1 Peter, like that of all letters and of the New Testament as such, both makes it relevant for historical beings and constitutes the hermeneutical problem of interpreting its message for people who live in a different historical situation.

First Peter's adoption of the letter form is a direct influence of Paul, who made letters a primary form of early Christian communication and theologizing. This is one of several indications that the author is indebted to major elements of the Pauline tradition (see Introduction, p. 42). First Peter's debt to Pauline tradition is seen immediately in the salutation, which is an adoption and adaptation of the Pauline form, including its distinctive elements.

The typical hellenistic letter began with the simple salutation "A to B, greetings." The stereotyped formula expressed by the word "greetings" is the infinitive of the word for "rejoice" *(chairein)*, but it had become a conventional formality. It was the customary form of greeting language, with no more content than "hi" as a colloquial English greeting or "Dear . . ." in business letters. Examples of this form are preserved in the New Testament (Acts 23:26; slightly modified Christian versions are found in Acts 15:23 and Jas 1:1).

Paul had elaborated on this form by making the author's name and title into a claim of apostolic authority, developing the reference to the addressees into a phrase or clause that characterized their existence as members of the Christian community, and by transforming the bland "greetings" into a distinctive "signature" in which *chairein* became the Christian theological term "grace" *(charis* for *chairein)*, which was combined with the Jewish letter salutation "peace" *(eirēnē = shalom)*. This combination was unique; although *charis* occurs 161 times in the LXX and *eirēnē* 275 times, they never appear together in a single verse. Since "grace and peace" has become something of a cliché in modern Christian circles accustomed to hearing it in the liturgy and reading it in the Bible, it may be difficult for modern readers to appreciate the fact that this was not the case for the first readers of the New Testament. It was Paul who combined "grace" and "peace" into this distinctive salutation form that appears in all his letters (Rom 1:7; 1 Cor 1:3; 2 Cor 1:2; Gal 1:3; Phil 1:2; 1 Thess 1:1; Phlm 1:3). This unique formulation was adopted by the Pauline school and appears in the

Deutero-Pauline letters, sometimes with slight modifications (Eph 1:2; Col 1:2; 2 Thess 1:2; 1 Tim 1:2; 2 Tim 1:2; Titus 1:4), and became the standard letter salutation in later Christian literature. *It is found nowhere in Greek literature except in documents directly or indirectly dependent on Paul.* By the time 1 Peter was written, it had not yet become the general Christian salutation—it is absent, for example, from Hebrews, James, and the Johannine epistles—so that its presence in 1 Pet 1:2 is an indication of direct influence from the Pauline letters. When 1 Peter begins with the name "Peter" but utilizes the letter form in general and the distinctive Pauline epistolary prescript in particular, it is the initial signal that the author is combining the legacies of the two leading apostles now revered by the Roman church (see Introduction, pp. 27-28; 39-43).

First Peter does not merely copy the Pauline formula, however, but uses it as a model to construct a prescript for the letter that—again following the example of Paul—provides a programmatic anticipation of major themes of the following letter. The two verses comprise one carefully constructed sentence, in the titular style without a single definite article (appropriately supplied in English translations):

A. Peter, apostle of Jesus Christ
B. To the elect resident aliens of [the] Dispersion in Pontus, Galatia,Cappadocia, Asia, and Bithynia, [elect]
   1. according to the foreknowledge of God the Father
   2. through the sanctification of the Spirit
   3. for obedience and sprinkling of the blood of Jesus Christ
C. May grace and peace be multiplied to you.

Several items significant for understanding the letter as a whole are to be noted in this structure. The first line claims the apostolic authority of Peter, without elaborating or suggesting that it is contested. After 1:1 this authority is never appealed to directly in the body of the letter (where the author represents himself as a fellow presbyter, 5:1), though the letter throughout presupposes that it authoritatively represents the apostolic faith. "Apostle" means "one sent," and in early Christianity quickly became the key term to designate one commissioned and authorized by the risen Christ to teach and act by his authority. In the New Testament "apostle" is the only term for ministerial office followed by the phrase "of Jesus Christ"—there are no elders, deacons, prophets, or evangelists so designated. Although it is unlikely that Simon Peter had ever been in most of the area addressed, it is assumed that the readers know of Peter and acknowledge his apostleship. This is another mark of the ecumenical perspective of the letter.

The final line adapts the Pauline "grace to you and peace" with only a slight modification in the direction of the Jewish letter formula found in the Greek versions of the Old Testament: "be multiplied" included as in Dan 4:37c LXX; Dan 4:1; 6:26 Theodotian; cf. Jude 2; 2 Pet 1:2. As in Paul's writings, "grace" (10x in 1 Peter) is the absolutely unmerited favor of God made concrete in the Christ-event, the sole ground of the believer's acceptance before God. "Peace," as in the closing benediction of 5:14, is neither merely the lack of hostilities nor a subjective state of tranquillity, but refers to all the blessings—material and spiritual, personal and social—that comprise the good life willed and given by God, practically representing the Jewish *shalom* and a synonym for *sotēria*, salvation.

It is striking that the emphasis in this salutation falls on the middle element that characterizes the churchly identity and status of the addressees, effectively anticipating the ecclesiastical orientation of the body of the letter (cf. Appendix 2: Images of the Church in 1 Peter). The letter is addressed neither to a single congregation nor to the church universal, but (like Revelation written shortly afterward) is a circular letter to the Christians of a large but limited geographical area. The five names apparently represent Roman provinces, not geographical areas, and thus comprise the whole of Asia Minor north of the Taurus mountains. This range formed the natural boundary between most of Asia Minor oriented to the north and west, and the southern coastal strip oriented to Syria and Antioch. The puzzling order in which the provinces are named, separating Pontus and Bithynia that formed one province in the writer's day, is probably best understood as reflecting the (real or imagined) travel route of the bearer of the letter. The messenger from Rome would have landed at one of the ports of Pontus on the Black Sea, made a circuit through Galatia and Cappadocia to Asia, then returned to a port on the Black Sea in Bithynia in order to sail back to Rome.

Theological identity, not geographical location, is the author's concern. The carefully structured elaboration of this segment suggests that the meaning of belonging to the Christian community is the major focus of what the letter has to say. This ecclesiological declaration is included in a proto-Trinitarian framework that presupposes the divine actions that generate the elect community of believers: God's choice, the Spirit's sanctifying acts, and Christ's giving his life's blood. In 2:4-10 it will become clear that God's election of the Christian community depends on God's prior election of Christ. All this is the act of the one God. Since 1 Peter is thoroughly monotheistic and theocentric, the author is thus free to use (proto-)Trinitarian language without compromising his monotheism (cf. Schweizer 1949, 17). The one God responsible for the believer's new identity corresponds to the reader's conversion, which is thought of as a single event, for election, sanctification, obedience, and sprinkling with Christ's blood are not chronological stages, but different metaphors for the one event of conversion.

◊ ◊ ◊ ◊

In the Greek text the first word to the addressees is "elect" (*eklektos;* NRSV: "chosen"). "Elect" belongs to that class of Greek verbal adjectives ending in *-tos* that conceals the act of God as the hidden subject, such as *agapētos* ("beloved," i.e., by God, as 2:11; 4:12) and *Christos* ("anointed," i.e., by God, as 1:1, 2, 3, etc.; 22x in 1 Peter, although the NRSV uses "beloved"). The essential point is that God is the actor who has chosen them (not vice versa). Nothing is made of the point in time when God's electing activity took place, whether in protological, pre-creation times, or at the time of their conversion. The point is their present status as elect (= chosen by God), not the chronological location of God's electing act. First Peter, though smaller than most New Testament writings, uses the term "elect" *(eklektos)* more than any other New Testament document (five of twenty-three occurrences in the New

Testament), and is the only New Testament document in which the election motif forms part of the salutation and is a major theological theme from the outset. "Elect resident aliens" focuses the message of 1 Peter in one phrase characterizing the situation of its readers. The Greek sentence is constructed so that the affirmation of the addressees' election is qualified by three prepositional phrases:

1. They are elect according to the foreknowledge of God (1:2; NRSV: "destined by God"). God's "foreknowledge" *(prognōsis)* of the Christians' election is a form of the same word used of Christ's having been "foreknown" *(proginōskō)* before the foundation of the world (1:20; NRSV: "destined"), and is the first of several connections in 1 Peter that present the destiny and identity of Christians as parallel to that of Christ (e.g., 2:4-5: rejected by humans but chosen by God; 2:20: suffering for doing good). The claim that God has foreknown Christ and Christians is not a matter of speculative mythology about what went on in the heavenly world prior to creation—1 Peter has no interest in such matters, nor does the Bible in general. First Peter here stands in the tradition of Paul, who had interpreted the church as the elect remnant of Israel and who had cited the same Old Testament texts that reappear in 1 Peter (Rom 9:1-33; Rom 9:25 = Hos 1:10; 2:23; cf. 1 Pet 2:10; Rom 9:33 = Isa 28:16; cf. 1 Pet 2:6-8). Paul relates the church's status as God's elect to the divine foreknowledge, predestination, and call, without specifically making election an activity of God before the creation of the world (Rom 8:28-33). The later interpretation of Paul does take this step (Eph 1:4-5; cf. 2 Thess 2:13; 2 Tim 1:9), corresponding to the view prevalent in some streams of first-century Judaism that regarded God's election of the chosen people as having occurred before the foundation of the world (CD 2:7; 1 QS 1:10-11; 3:15-17; 1QH 1:10-20; *Jos. As.* 8:11; *Midr. Ps.* 74:1; 93:3; *Gen. Rab.* 1:5). The affirmation of the believers' election is a way of affirming that the present life and suffering of the addressees is not mere chance, but fits into the eternal purpose of God (see Appendix 1: The Narrative World of 1 Peter), without spelling out a clear picture of when God chose them. First Peter relates the believers' election to the election of Israel as portrayed in the Old Testament

differently from the Pauline tradition, where it is a matter of this-worldly history (e.g., at the Exodus, Deut 7:6-8; Ezek 20:5; Hos 11:1; already in the time of the Patriarchs, Gen 12:1-3; 22:17-18; 26:4; 27:14), rather than a pre-creation act of God in the transcendent world. " 'Election' in the Old Testament refers not to some kind of supratemporal or primeval divine decree but rather to a historical action of YHWH" (Preuss 1995, 1:37). As the continuing community of the Exodus (see on the structure of 1:13-20 below), Christians are incorporated into the history of Israel as the elect and holy people of God. The essential point is that Christians are in the church not merely by their own decision, but by the initiative of God who has called them (1:15; 2:9, 21; 3:6, 9; 5:10; cf. Rom 8:28-39). Election is entirely a corporate matter in 1 Peter, which speaks of an elect people (2:9) but never of elect individuals. As in the case of Israel, election is for service, not to privilege (cf. Rowley 1950, 45 *et passim;* Preuss 1995, 1:80-95).

2. They are elect by the sanctifying power of the Holy Spirit. This refers not to some personal mystical experience, but to the work of the Spirit in the preaching activity by which the readers were converted (1:12). The word for "sanctifying" *(hagiasmos)* is related to the word for "holy" *(hagios),* an essential mark of the people of God. To declare that the readers are elect means that they belong to the holy people of God, that is, not that they are more pious or that they are morally superior to others, but that they have been called to form a distinctive community with a singular mission. To be called "holy" means that they, like Israel, have been set apart for a special purpose in God's saving plan. Like Israel, they are elect for service, not for privilege (Isa 42:1; Amos 3:2).

3. They are elect for obedience to Jesus Christ and for sprinkling with his blood. (So both NRSV and NIV; the Greek may also be understood to refer to Jesus' own obedience and giving his blood.) Election is not for privilege but for obedience, concretely realized in "doing good" (see on 2:14-15; 3:6, 17; 4:19). The imagery of the church as the covenant people of Israel is continued. Both "obedience" and "sprinkling with blood" are covenant language. At Sinai, both the altar (representing God) and the people of Israel

were sprinkled with the blood of the sacrificial animals, joining God and Israel together in a covenant sealed by blood (Exod 24:3-8). God's will was read forth from the Law, and the people responded "we will be obedient." The recipients of 1 Peter are addressed as members of this covenant, now sealed by the blood of Christ (1:19; cf. Mark 14:24 par.).

"Election" is the characteristic biblical designation of Israel as the chosen people of God (e.g., Deut 7:6; 10:15; 14:2; 1 Chron 16:13; Ps 105:6; Isa 43:20-21; 45:4; 65:9). Like other New Testament documents (e.g., Gal 6:16; Phil 3:13; Jas 1:1), 1 Peter considers the Christian community, as members of the renewed Israel, to be the continuing people of God, though the author never uses the terms "Israel," "Jew," or "Judaism." This motif is continued by describing them as the Dispersion (Diaspora), already in the LXX the technical term for Israel scattered among the nations (e.g., Deut 28:25; 30:4; Neh 1:9; Ps 146:2; Jdt 5:19; Isa 49:6). The ecumenical note struck in the opening words of the letter is presupposed throughout and recurs in the conclusion: the Christians of the five provinces in Asia Minor belong to the one people of God scattered throughout the world (5:9), including their fellow-elect sister congregation in Rome (5:13).

The primary overtone in addressing the readers as "Diaspora," however, reflects the social location of the recipients, for the Dispersion of Israel scattered among the Gentiles were noncitizens wherever they were, no longer having a homeland of their own in the land of Israel. While canonical texts such as Nehemiah and Daniel show that Jews of the Dispersion could respond positively to their situation as exiles (cf. also the letter of Jer 29), Diaspora Jews were second-class (non-)citizens wherever they were, often blamed for the ills of society in which they were always outsiders. The *Testament of Asher* 7:2 makes clear the social status the Diaspora Jew could expect, as well as the eschatological hope that gave courage to live faithfully in this sojourner existence: "In the dispersion you shall be regarded as worthless, like useless water, until such time as the Most High shall visit the earth" (cf. Perkins 1995, 12-15).

This aspect of the identity of the people of God is also expressed in the term "resident aliens" of 1:1 (perhaps the best translation for *parepidēmoi;* NRSV: "exiles," NIV: "strangers"; others translate "sojourners," "pilgrims," "aliens." Expressions in contemporary American English such as "transients" or "migrant workers without documents" capture something of their flavor). The term is relatively rare (found only here, 2:11, and Heb 11:13 in the New Testament; only in Gen 23:4; Ps 39:12 in the LXX), but it is paralleled with "sojourner" in 2:11 and in each of the Old Testament references. "Sojourner" (NRSV, NIV: "alien") in these contexts means "resident alien," that is, the person who is not merely a tourist or traveling merchant, but one who lives in the land and is subject to its laws (Lev 16:29; 24:16), yet is not a full citizen and without citizenship rights (Lev 17:15). The term is thus equivalent to the Hebrew *gēr* ("sojourner," "resident alien") that occurs ninety-three times in the Hebrew Bible, being used of the Israelites themselves when they were living as resident aliens in a foreign land (e.g., Exod 22:21; Lev 19:34, where it is related to the love command). The term is also used metaphorically for Israel even when living in their own land (e.g., Lev 25:23, Israel as sojourners in ["their own"] land of which God is the real owner).

First Clement, written from the Roman church about the same time as 1 Peter, likewise uses the verbal form of 1 Peter's term for "resident alien" (*parepidēmeō;* 1:2) to describe the church as such, wherever it is. First Peter does not use the word in the gnosticizing sense of people whose true homeland is the heavenly world and who stand aloof from the affairs of "the world" here below (contra the NIV translation, which twice adds "in the world"), although tendencies in this direction are found in other New Testament documents (Heb 11:13; cf. Phil 3:20). First Peter addresses its readers as "resident aliens" because it identifies them as the continuing people of God of the Bible, and also because it is particularly appropriate to their social status in the five provinces of Asia Minor to which 1 Peter is addressed, where they live a marginalized existence in tension with the hellenistic culture around them. Neither transcendent citizenship in the heavenly world nor their marginal social status as such is the point, but rather historical continuity with the mission and destiny of Israel. Their life is lived on the historical sojourn between creation and eschaton, between conversion and consummation, with their new identity as the people of God who are always in tension with the structures and values of this world and its powers. The perspective is horizontal and historical, not vertical and metaphysical or mystical.

◊ ◊ ◊ ◊

While the letter directly addresses its Christian recipients in biblical language as the chosen people of God, no question is raised by this salutation concerning the relation of the church to empirical Israel. This seems not to be a theological problem to the author. The implied claim "We are Israel" has no counterpart "You/they are not Israel." It is the confessional insider language of self-understanding, not polemical language addressing anyone else. The central issue for 1 Peter is not the relation of the church to empirical Israel, but the relation of the "resident aliens" to their pagan environment to which they once belonged (1:14, 18, etc.). Shall they accommodate themselves to the surrounding culture, resist accommodation, or seek some via media? This is the major concern of the letter, so that the twin exegetical and hermeneutical issues for the modern reader are (1) how to understand the author's instruction to his ancient readers on this issue and (2) how to interpret his instruction for contemporary Christians.

THANKSGIVING (1:3-12)

A new literary unit begins in 1:3 extending through 1:12. The Greek text is one unbroken sentence extending from 1:3 through 1:12, then 1:13 begins anew. In the interest of readability, English translations break the Greek sentence into smaller units: NRSV: six sentences; RSV, NIV, NAB, NJB: seven sentences; JB: eight sentences; NEB: eleven sentences; REB: twelve sentences; TEV and CEV top the list with seventeen and eighteen sentences respectively, by making almost every clause an independent sentence. It is important to note that in the Greek text the ten verses of this unit comprise one extremely complex sentence connected with participial constructions, prepositional phrases, and relative pronouns, constructed with rhetorical skill and subtlety. For example, there is a series of three alliterative alpha-privative adjectives in 1:4, the rhetoric of which is captured by Beare's paraphrase: "*un*touched by death, *un*stained by evil, *un*impaired by time" (Beare 1958, 57-58). The elevated, solemn, and rhythmical language has encouraged some to argue that the section must be adapted from a fixed hymn or liturgical prayer (e.g., Windisch and Preisker 1930), but most scholars regard it as the author's own composition reflecting elements of Petrine tradition. The skillful construction is tripartite, corresponding both to the proto-Trinitarian structure included in the salutation (Father 3-5; Christ 6-9; and Spirit 10-12) and to the body of the letter to follow (Kendall 1986, 113-20). Those who argue for Petrine authorship on the basis of the "secretary hypothesis" (the "ideas" are Peter's but the "language" is Silvanus's) have rarely thought through what this would concretely mean in the composition of such a sentence! Even the "secretary hypothesis" calls for mostly *independent* composition by Silvanus (cf. Schelke 1988, 27).

In the typical hellenistic letter the brief salutation ("A to B greetings") was followed by a brief stereotyped unit expressing a prayer to the gods for the health of the recipient, or a thanksgiving to the gods for their good health. Just as Paul adapted the hellenistic salutation to express his distinctive theology (see above on 1:1-2), so the conventional thanksgiving form was elaborated and deepened so that it was no longer a mere formality, but became a significant theological element in his letters that often provided a theological preface to the letter as a whole (cf. Rom 1:8-17; 1 Cor 1:4-9; 2 Cor 1:3-7; Phil 1:3-11; 1 Thess 1:2-10; 2:13; 3:9-10). This distinctive feature was preserved in some Deutero-Pauline letters of the Pauline school (Eph 1:3-14; Col 1:3-14; 2 Thess 1:3-4; 2 Tim 1:3-5). Paul typically began this section with "I thank God . . ." (*eucharistô*, related to "eucharist"), but once adopted the familiar form of the synagogue prayer, "Blessed be the God . . ." (2 Cor 1:3). Ephesians 1:3 uses this exact form.

First Peter stands in this tradition of Christian letter-writing that had been given its distinctive shape by Pauline tradition. As in 2 Corinthians and Ephesians, the part of the letter corresponding to the usual thanksgiving has been filled by an extended liturgical blessing, but it is epistolary in both form and function (T. Martin 1992, 47-49). As in the Pauline letters, the thanksgiving section is not a formality, but a substantial liturgical-theological unit that lays the theological foundations for the practical instruction to follow. This section that may seem on first reading to be so religiously abstract is actually intended to provide the basis and essence of practical Christian life in society. It is thus altogether in the indicative mood. As is consistently the case in biblical theology, what humans are called to do is a response to what God has already done. In this section the author is not commanding—imperatives begin in 1:13—but declaring and celebrating the saving acts of God.

Attending to the form of this unit allows us to see that here theology is not "taught" or "explained," but celebrated and confessed. The elevated language is not intended to communicate doctrine that can be orthodox or heretical, or that requires rational defense (this is not the meaning of 3:15!). The statement is not speculative, curiosity-satisfying, but is the language of worship and praise, directed primarily not to human beings but to God. "The first and basic act of theological work is prayer" (Barth 1963, 160). This initial paragraph already indicates that the Christian life can involve suffering (1:6-7), and later the author will give concrete instruction about suffering as a Christian (2:19-24; 3:13-18; 4:12-19), but neither here nor elsewhere does the author present an abstract "theology of suffering." The author sees suffering-for-others as the innermost reality of the universe, the nature of God revealed in Christ, the given existence of all who are "in Christ" (see on 2:19-20; 5:9, 12). But he does not explain this; suffering is not an intellectual problem to be resolved, but the givenness of Christian existence to be lived out. Thus to call 1:3-12 the "first doctrinal section" (Selwyn 1947, 121) is to misconstrue the nature of the letter, which does not teach doctrine, but presupposes and communicates a certain understanding of reality determined by the Christ-event. This incredibly rich passage is densely theological without "teaching theology." The Christian imperative is based on a vision of the world and life, "the way things are." This reality is expressed not as metaphysical theory, but as confession of the historical reality of living in a world created and sustained by the God definitively revealed in Christ, and who will bring his creation to a worthy conclusion (see Appendix 1: The Narrative World of 1 Peter).

◊ ◊ ◊ ◊

God is praised for having granted a new, eschatological existence to Christian believers, whose lives are lived in the continuum en route from God's mighty acts in the past to the imminent fulfillment of God's plan for the world. The past/present/future of the Christian life is already expressed in the first subsection of this unit, which looks back to the resurrection of Christ and the conversion of the believer, speaks of the present joyful experience of testing while being kept by the power of God, and forward to the full experience of salvation to be received at the last time (1:3-5; cf. the same structure in Rom 5:1-2, elaborated in 5:3-11).

The perspective is first toward the *past* event of God's act in raising "our Lord Jesus Christ" from the dead (1:3), the basis and means of the believer's own new life, expressed in the language of regeneration. The idea of being "reborn" (or rebegotten; the term is generic) is not widespread in the New Testament, being found outside 1 Peter only in John 1:12-13; 3:3-5; Titus 3:5; James 1:18; and 1 John 3:9; 5:8. In 1 Peter this term is not incidental, recurring again in 1:23, and presupposed in the imagery of 1:14 and 2:1-3. The imagery of "rebirth" corresponds to that of "election," in each case affirming that Christian identity is a result of God's initiative and act, not our decision. God's choice constitutes the elect community; whether or not we are born is not an issue on which we get to vote. Although there are somewhat remote similarities in Jewish language that compare Jewish proselytes to newborn babes, 1 Peter is clearly using the language of regeneration that had long been developed in a variety of hellenistic religions and had already been adopted to some extent by hellenistic Judaism (texts and annotations in Boring, Berger, and Colpe 1995, §§49-50; 109-10; 252-59; 269; 305-6; 351; 363-64; 373; 438).

As elsewhere, the author does not merely take over hellenistic ideas wholesale, but gives them a Christian interpretation. Christians do not become divinized but remain mortal. The Christian does not receive a new immortal nature on the basis of an initiation ritual, but a new life of hope by believing in God's saving act in raising Jesus from the dead when encountered by the word of God in Christian preaching (1:12, 23). The readers did not become Christians by accepting a new theory, by committing themselves to certain ideas and principles, or by joining another worthy cause. Just as God's act in raising Jesus was the divine overturning of all human possibilities, so begetting and birth is an apt metaphor for the conversion process: none of us decides to be born, the initiative is prior to and apart from us, we simply find ourselves having been given life. The old world given us by the socialization "inherited from [our] ancestors" (1:18) is replaced by the new world mediated by the Christian message. To be born again is to receive a new world (cf. 2 Cor 5:17). While for Paul this entry into the new world is conceived in terms of adoption (Rom 8:12-24; Gal 4:4-7), for 1 Peter it is thought of as a real new birth.

The *present* experience of the Christian life likewise has a double aspect. From the transcendent perspective, God is at work in preserving the believer's eschatological inheritance and in empowering the Christian to endure. The incorruptible, undefiled, unfading inheritance is securely preserved by God in heaven, ready for its revelation at the last time. The Christian does not "go up" at death to receive it, but goes forward in history to meet it at the eschatological consummation. While the language of "inheritance" is appropriate to the language of new birth and new home that reverberates throughout 1 Peter (cf. the connection in Rom 8:15-17; Gal 4:6-7), in keeping with the dominant imagery of the new people of God, the primary connotation here is the inheritance that was promised to Israel (Deut 12:9 illustrates scores of LXX instances). Already in Judaism this inheritance had been interpreted eschatologically. Corresponding to God's preservation of the eschatological inheritance, God also keeps the believers by divine power that works through their faith (cf. Phil 2:12-13). This divine/human dialectic is only one example of the theological mode in which the author's mind spontaneously and unreflectively works, very similar to that of Paul.

Christian life in the present is characterized by joy in suffering, and by faith in Christ who though unseen is not only trusted but loved (1:6-9). The joy here described (both v. 6 and v. 8 are indicative not imperative) is not a superficial "feel good," but is a deep, inexpressible joy permeated by the presence and glory of God, that is, it is "in him [God]" or "on the basis of God's mighty acts" (see 1:6). This joy is unforced, is not a matter of cranking it up within ourselves by convincing ourselves to have the "right attitude," but is a response to God's acts of the past, present, and future.

In this initial section the author indicates that to be Christian is to endure suffering (1:6-7; probably also 1:11, see below). The "even if . . ." construction does not mean that suffering is only an optional possibility, since 1 Peter regards suffering as integral to the nature of faith (1:7) and as universal among Christians (2:19-20; 5:9, 12). The suffering referred to is not the mass of everyday problems to which all human life is subject, but the abuse the readers receive because of their faith. Just as gold in its natural state is mixed with less valuable minerals, but is refined by the fire that melts these materials away, so faith is mixed with other less-worthy human aspirations, and is revealed as authentic only in the fire of suffering. The joy of the Christian life is not an alternative to suffering, nor in spite of suffering, but joy in suffering, the depth dimension of the Christian life that is essentially defined by suffering readers who believe and love Christ without having seen him. Since this is the nature of Christian life as such, the author includes himself in those who believe and love without seeing (1:8). There is no implied contrast between the author who has seen and the readers who have not, which would require an additional pronoun *hymeis* to express this emphasis. Just as the "you" of verse 4 is generic for all Christians, so are both of the "you's" of verse 8. Just as the author does not distinguish himself from the readers in the second and third clauses ("you believe," "you rejoice") neither is there any distinction from them in the first clause ("you love without seeing"). Polycarp, a generation later, cites these exact words from 1 Peter, uniting himself with his readers, with no possibility that he is claiming that he has seen but the readers have not (Pol. *Phil.* 3:1). No Christian of the time of 1 Peter, including the author, has personally seen Christ; all Christians trust and love him, and rejoice in the midst of the trials of being a Christian in a hostile society.

The Christian life for 1 Peter has an essential *future* dimension. "Hope" plays an even more decisive role than "faith" for this author, and can serve as the one word that sums up the meaning of the Christian life as such (e.g., 1:3; 3:5, 15). The first imperative of the letter, to which this unit is building, is "hope" (1:13). As in Paul's writings, believers can be contrasted with "[those] who have no hope" (1 Thess 4:13), which is not merely "they don't believe that they will go to heaven when they die," but characterizes the difference between two kinds of life here and now. Human life itself is forward-looking, is stretched out on a temporal line that moves toward the future. Human life is constituted by this movement; to have something to "look forward to" is to have something to live for. To have no tomorrow is to be robbed of today; to be given a future is to be given a present. Thus when the author speaks of the inheritance safely kept in heaven for us (1:4) he is thinking horizontally, not vertically—we do not go to heaven to get it, it comes to meet us at the eschaton (1:13), as the salvation prepared to be unveiled at the last day (1:5), at the revelation of Jesus Christ (1:7), as the goal of our faith, our salvation (1:9). "Souls" here is to be understood biblically as a synonym for "selves," the person's whole being, not in terms of Greek dualism as an immaterial, immortal part contrasted with fleshly existence (cf. 1:22; 2:25; 3:20; 4:19).

Such lists of references illustrate that 1 Peter is permeated with eschatology; it is not a marginal or isolable element with which the author could dispense. Petrine eschatology (like biblical eschatology in general) does not refer to the future in such a way that it can be isolated from the past and present, as though one might say "I'll take 1 Peter's past and present, but not speculate about the future."

Eschatology in this sense is a matter of living in a meaningful history, life in a story-shaped world of which God is the author, not speculation about the end of the world. The eschatological existence of the believer, the "living hope" of which 1 Peter writes (1:3) is not an explanation that someday there will be a resurrection and things will be different, but a celebration that there has already been a resurrection, and things are already different. Such eschatology is implicit in the confession of "our Lord Jesus Christ" (1:3). The Christ is not a great individual, but the promised redeemer of creation and history. "Christ" implies the horizontal line of unredeemed history, and the promise of God to Israel to send one to redeem it. To believe that the Messiah has come is to believe that the ultimate past, the ultimate future, is already manifest in Jesus Christ. The confession projects a picture of the world that stretches from creation to eschaton and defines the whole of history in terms of the revelation manifest in this Christ-event. Thus one cannot reject eschatology but cling to Christology; eschatology is implicit in the confession "Jesus is the Christ." This understanding of biblical hope in 1 Peter is a sharp contrast to the cultural use of the word "hope" as a nice way of saying that something might happen, but probably won't, a "no" that is trying to maintain a positive attitude. In biblical theology, "hope" is the not-yet reality by which one already lives: a small child a day before Christmas, an engaged couple a week before the wedding, a prisoner a year before release.

The author of 1 Peter concludes the thanksgiving by portraying the eschatological existence of Christian believers who live in the climactic time of God's plan for history as the envy of both the biblical prophets and the angels (1:10-12). Again, this conclusion is not a matter of speculative fantasy, but instead plays a practical role. First Peter addresses those who are at the margins of society, reviled and accused. They know how they appear in society's eyes. They need a larger perspective, which the author provides not in psychological or sociological terms of self-esteem, but by helping them see their privileged place in the context of God's plan for history, a privilege they had not achieved but had been granted by God's grace.

The author assumes and projects the understanding that the Old

Testament prophets received God's revelation of the divine purpose to be climaxed at the end of history. He pictures them as not knowing when the time of this fulfillment would be, though God had revealed to them that their prophecies were not for their own time (1:12). This reflects the apocalyptic understanding of prophecy (e.g., Dan 12:5-13; 4 Ezra 4:33-52; 1QpHab), rather than the prophetic understanding, which specifically rejects the view that the prophecies were for some distant generation (Ezek 12:26-28!). The functional point is, what was only sought after by the biblical prophets is now realized in the lives of the Christians of Asia Minor. Likewise the angels, who long to peek into God's secret plan for history, are of lesser rank than Christians, in whose lives this very plan is now being fulfilled. It is not clear whether angels are "good" angels, which would parallel the prophets, or "bad" angels, as is often the case in apocalyptic (e.g., 1QS 3:13–4:14; 4Q Amram; 1 Enoch 6–16). In favor of hostile angels, however, are the following considerations: (1) in the only other reference to angels in 1 Peter is 3:22, they are hostile powers overcome by the risen Christ; (2) the author is heavily influenced by the Pauline tradition, in which angels are uniformly evil powers that attempt to separate us from God, as, for example, in Rom 8:38; (3) specific items of Pauline tradition picture the hostile angelic powers as being kept in ignorance of God's plan that is revealed to Christians (1 Cor 2:8; Eph 3:9-10); (4) the verb for the angels' "longing" (*epithymeō*, sometimes translated "lust") can have evil overtones as in Gen 6:1-6, and as used by the author (3:19-20)—but compare Matt 13:17!

Two further points in this paragraph require comment, each of which has to do with its christological perspective:

1. It is said that the "Spirit of Christ" spoke through the Old Testament prophets (1:11). This could simply be a terminological matter, that is, the author refers to the "Spirit of Christ" as simply a synonym for the Holy Spirit or the Spirit of God. This was done in the Pauline tradition, with which the author is thoroughly familiar (Rom 8:9-10). But more likely the author thinks of the Christ as the One who spans all of history, not only as the one present in Jesus and who will appear at the end of history, but who

was already present with God at creation. He seems to have an understanding of the preexistence of Christ (cf. 1:20), albeit undeveloped, but he is not teaching "doctrine" here. Since he thinks of God as the one definitively revealed by Christ, he can picture the presence and activity of God in terms of Christ (cf. 1 Cor 10:4; Heb 11:26, each of which represents traditions known to our author). He can thus picture the God who spoke through the prophets in terms of the preexistent Christ, a concept that was explicitly developed in the church fathers (cf., e.g., Justin, *Dial. Trypho* 36-38, 55-62, 74, 98-99).

2. The prophets are said to testify in advance to the sufferings of/for Christ (1:11). The debatable issue is whether to translate the preposition *eis* as "of" or "for." In the former case, the prophets are pictured as predicting Christ's own sufferings, that is, the sufferings destined for Christ (cf. both NRSV and NIV). In the alternative understanding, they spoke of sufferings endured for Christ, that is, the sufferings of Christians, including specifically the experience of the readers. Most translators and interpreters incline strongly toward the former view: the prophets predicted Christ's sufferings. Of standard translations, only the REB renders "the sufferings in Christ's cause." The reasons usually given for understanding the predictions as referring to the sufferings of Christ are that this is standard New Testament theology (e.g., Mark 14:49 par.; Luke 24:25-27; Acts 3:18; 1 Cor 15:3), the parallelism between 1:10 and 1:11 (prophets predicted grace for Christians; prophets predicted suffering for Christ), and that "sufferings and glory" are a traditional pair with reference to Christ, as in Luke 24:26, but not for Christians.

On the other hand, however, weighty considerations suggest that the sufferings of Christians are what is in view: (1) The New Testament elsewhere speaks of the prophets predicting not only the events of Jesus' life, death, and resurrection, but the times of Christians (Acts 3:24). (2) The parallelism between 1:10 and 1:11 can just as well be understood to point to the identity between the grace prophesied for Christians and the sufferings prophesied for Christians—especially since 5:12 identifies grace given Christians with their situation of suffering. (3) The whole context of 1:3-12 indicates it is the situation of Christians about which the author is speaking, just as the argument of the whole letter is that the suffering of Christians is integrated into the plan of God, the plan foreseen by the prophets. Furthermore, (4) there would be a certain conceptual awkwardness in having the "Spirit of Christ" at work in the prophets predict his own sufferings. (5) The other two references to Christ's sufferings in 1 Peter use a different construction, the usual genitive *tou Christou* ("of Christ," 4:13; 5:1), in contrast to the prepositional phrase found here (*eis Christon,* "for Christ," i.e., for allegiance to him; cf. *en onomati Christou,* "for the name of Christ," 4:14). (6) The author of 1 Peter uses the preposition *eis* forty-two times in thirty-seven verses, at least sixteen of which mean "for" (see esp. 4:8, 10). (7) The suffering/glory pattern is not only used of Christ (1:21), but also of Christians (1:7; 4:14). (8) The contrast in 1:12 is not between the prophets and Christ, but between their time and the reader's time, which points to the content of their prophecies having to do with the reader's time, not the time of Jesus. (9) The plural "glories" makes more sense with reference to the experience of Christians than that of Christ, where the singular is more appropriate. These considerations lead one to believe that the author's point is that sufferings endured *eis Christon,* for allegiance to Christ, represent the situation of the messianic age, the climactic age of history in which the readers are privileged to live. When seen in this light, sufferings endured for the sake of the Christian cause may be borne with joy, not merely with resignation (cf. 1:6, 8; 4:13).

It is clear that the basis for the kind of life the author will challenge his readers to live is predicated on his convictions about the reality and nature of God. His perspective as a whole is entirely theocentric. Neither eschatology nor Christology are alternatives to faith in God, but expressions of such faith. "God" is the most frequent noun in 1 Peter (39x in 105 vv.). God is not defined metaphysically or experientially, but historically, in terms of God's own mighty acts in history of which the Christ-event is the defining center that characterizes the whole. The one God is Lord of all history, the author of the cosmic story from creation to eschaton.

God is the source and ground of the believer's life of joy-in-suffering. God is the one made known in his mighty acts (2:9). While these are not didactically elaborated, the author's vision of reality that proceeds from God and goes to God is projected as the narrative world presupposed by the whole letter. The actions stated or implied in 1:3-12 can easily be listed and arranged in chronological order, giving the elements of the author's narrative world that become visible in this one sentence, from the time of the biblical prophets through the time of Jesus and the readers' own time to the eschaton.

The fact that this one sentence is so laden with data that it can be fitted into the author's implied narrative world suggests that the letter as a whole is amenable to such an analysis. This has been done at the end of this book (Appendix 1: The Narrative World of 1 Peter), and proves to be a helpful key to grasping the understanding of reality presupposed and projected by this letter, and therefore the basis for the challenge to its distinctive way of life.

◊ ◊ ◊ ◊

Although much of the theology communicated in this section is implicit in the preceding discussion, the following points relevant to contemporary hermeneutical appropriation need to be made explicit:

1. In the author's discourse, the indicative precedes the imperative, as God's act precedes human response. The letter is not a theological treatise, but a call to action. It contains thirty-five specific commands in the imperative mood, plus numerous other constructions that function as imperatives, including seventeen participles usually considered imperatives. Yet this initial section that lays the foundation for the exhortation of the letter as a whole contains not a single imperative! This corresponds to the structure of biblical theology generally. Thus the Ten Commandments are preceded by the announcement of God's act: "I am the LORD your God, who brought you out of the land of Egypt, out of the house of slavery; [therefore] you shall have no other gods before me" (Exod 20:1-3). The imperatives of the Sermon on the Mount are

preceded by the indicatives of the Beatitudes (Matt 5:3-11/5:12–7:27). The structure of Paul's Letter to the Romans has a lengthy presentation of the Christ-centered mighty acts of God as Lord of history (Rom 1–11) as the basis for the "therefore" that begins the Christian parenesis (Rom 12–16; cf. also Gal 1–4/5–6, which has the same structure and the same transitional particle *oun* ["therefore"] at 5:1). First Peter does not begin directly with Christian action and responsibility, which cannot stand on their own, but has preserved this relationship of indicative and imperative as represented especially in the Pauline tradition. The basis for Christian life, ethics, and action is not a theory of self-fulfillment, not the conscious or unconscious adoption of supposed self-evidently true values, ideas, principles, or ideologies, not even the teachings of Jesus, but the kerygma of God's mighty acts centered in the Christ-event. Christians today should seriously ask whether the way of life called for in 1 Peter (and the New Testament generally) can be taken seriously as a valid option for our own way of life apart from the kerygmatic faith on which it is based.

2. The picture of the prophets of Israel not understanding their own prophecies, since they were predictions of what was to happen to Christ or Christians, or both, centuries later (1:11-12), has become problematic for many modern readers. The following theses are suggested as an approach that respects both the ancient text and the integrity of the modern reader in their respective thought worlds.

- The prophets of Israel addressed their own contemporaries, and did not in fact predict the details of events to occur generations later. Their references to the future are almost entirely to the historical future of the hearers and readers of their own time. Some of these turned out to be historically correct (e.g., Ezek 5:5-12; Amos 1:6-8), and some turned out to be erroneous (e.g., Ezek 26:7-14 [cf. 29:7-20]; Amos 7:11 [2 Kgs 14:29]).
- To speak of a "double meaning" of prophetic texts, as though the prophets and their contemporaries understood their preaching to refer to one set of events in their own time, but their preaching in fact had a second-level reference to events in the life of Jesus and the church, is an unnecessary and unsubstantiated apologetic ploy.

- However, most of the Old Testament prophets did speak from within an eschatological perspective. That is, while they addressed their own generation and its concerns, they did so in the light of the ultimate purpose of God to be consummated in the future. Their preaching was not merely good advice or astute political observation, but presupposed the ultimate triumph of God's purpose in the eschatological future. This future was most often thought of as dawning in their own time, that is, it already impinged on the lives of the people they addressed. This is the nature of eschatological preaching, including that communicated in 1 Peter itself.
- Later Christians rightly saw that their Scriptures had a future orientation, pointing to a later time of fulfillment of the eschatological purpose of God. On the basis of their conviction that Jesus was the promised Messiah, they regarded the promises of Scripture as already beginning to be fulfilled in the Christ-event. They read their Scripture, including the prophets of Israel, in the light of the fulfillment in which they already believed, and derived much of the conceptuality and vocabulary in which they expressed their faith from these prophetic writings.

Modern Christians can and should affirm the conviction of 1 Peter and early Christianity in general that the event of Jesus Christ is rightly interpreted as the fulfillment of the hopes for the triumph of God's purpose promised by the prophets of Israel. We need not do this in the same way(s) that early Christians did. Especially, we must be careful not to interpret the Old Testament as part of our Christian Bible in such a way that claims that only Christians can understand what the ancient prophets were saying, that is, that since the Old Testament is actually an encoded book of Christian teaching, neither the prophets themselves, their ancient hearers, nor later non-Christian readers could understand the "real" meaning of these texts. The author of 1 Peter does not reflect on the implications of his confessional stance, but later Christians drew precisely this false conclusion: Israel and Judaism never had a revelation from God, since the Old Testament had always been a Christian book (*Barn.* 4:6-7; 10:12).

BODY OF THE LETTER (1:13–5:11)

The New Identity as the Elect and Holy People of God (1:13–2:10)

This section sets forth the "basic conduct" (Goppelt 1993, 110) of the Christian life, namely hope, holiness, love, and Christian growth as orientation points of the Christian life—orientation points that are grounded in the author's Christology and ecclesiology. While the letter's overall concern is with the concrete issues of the Christian's life within the structures of the world, the author first grounds this in the description of the believers' new identity and what it requires (1:13–2:10), and only then proceeds to specific directions for living as Christians in pagan society (2:11–3:12).

It is clear that 1:13 begins a new literary unit, just as a clear division is made by the direct address at 2:11, with 2:11-12 forming the general introduction to the specific social code that follows. The section 1:13–2:10 develops the theme of the new identity of the readers as the elect and holy people of God. In this section the indicative of God's act begins to evoke the imperative of the believers' response. The basis and essence of their identity in society are declared in a series of indicative statements that alternate with imperatives calling them to abandon their old manner of life and live out their new identity. The section is structured by the series of main verbs in the imperative (hope, 1:13; be holy, 1:15; love, 1:22; grow, 2:2), but the terse commands are preceded by qualifying participles and followed by elaborate indicatives that provide the basis for the imperatives. The indicative of 2:4-10 comes at the climactic structural location that functions as the fundamental indicative for the whole letter (Elliott 1966, 200-201; 215-17; Frankemölle 1990, 43). This dialectic of indicative/imperative is distinctive of the Pauline tradition (Goppelt 1993, 102, documentation and bibliography), and is further testimony of 1 Peter's indebtedness to it. As the imperative degenerates into moralism without the indicative of God's act, so the indicative degenerates into abstract speculation unless it is made believable by being concretized in actual life.

While it may be possible to discern major subdivisions (e.g., 1:13-25/2:1-10), the train of thought of this entire section is so tightly woven together that it is perhaps better to treat the whole section as one unit, within which the following subunits can be discerned on the basis of a series of direct commands in the aorist imperative:

1:13 Hope
1:14-21 Be Holy
    (17-21 Christological Grounding)
1:22-25 Love
    (23-25 Kerygmatic Grounding)
2:1-10 Grow
    (4-10 Ecclesiological Grounding)

Corresponding to the climactic concluding unit that addresses the readers as the people of God, this section throughout applies to Gentile converts the whole exodus experience of Israel: former slaves are freed by the mighty act of God, are redeemed by the blood of the lamb, have been made participants in the divine covenant within which they have pledged their obedience, and are presently underway through a series of testings and harassments toward their promised inheritance, becoming like Israel a holy people and royal priesthood. As Israel in the wilderness longed for the fleshpots of Egypt, Christians are now tempted to long for their former social life. The section contains echoes of the Passover, God's ransoming of Israel, God's demand to Israel at Sinai: "be holy," as well as allusions to disobedience and the golden calf (cf. Brown 1984, 77-78; Brown 1997, 709; Michaels 1988, 52-53).

The Command to Hope (1:13)

The NRSV's "prepare your minds for action" is more literally "gird up the loins of your mind" (KJV), reflecting the stance of the Israelites as they ate the first Passover "[with] their loins girded," that is, ready to travel (Exod 12:11; cf. Luke 12:35; "loins" also used figuratively in Eph 6:14). The flowing garments common in the ancient Mediterranean world were tightened about the waist in preparation for work or travel (e.g., 1 Kgs 18:46). The initial command is thus something like "roll up your (mental) sleeves," to prepare for disciplined intellectual work. The beginning of their historical pilgrimage is a matter of hard thinking, but not something they are to figure out for themselves; it is a response to the word of God that comes through preaching, that is, through the church's communication of the gospel.

The second command is "discipline yourselves," the same word as 4:7; 5:8. The three occurrences in the Pauline tradition (1 Thess 5:6, 8; 2 Tim 4:5) are usually translated "be sober," the opposite of confused intoxication. The idea is "stay sober, be well balanced, self-controlled." The hard thinking the author calls for, the hard ethical decisions he will call on them to make, cannot be handled by those who equate religious thinking with the bland fuzziness of a confused mind (cf. on 4:7).

With regard to their Greek form, the first two commands are not grammatically imperatives, but the first two of seventeen participles in 1 Peter usually considered to function as imperatives (though this has been recently challenged, cf. Martin 1992, 90-91 and *passim;* Krodel 1995, 45-46; Achtemeier 1996, 117 and *passim). The first "true" imperative in the letter is the command to "hope."* This command stands at the key transitional location at the beginning of the body-opening, and thus is not one instruction among many, but signals the theme of the whole letter (Martin 1992, 70).

Can one person command another to hope? Is hope something that one can do in response to a command? Here as elsewhere in 1 Peter, the imperative is related dialectically to the indicative. Authentic hope can only be a response to God's act (1:13 presupposes 1:3; the "therefore" *[dio]* of 1:13 presupposes the indicatives of 1:3-12). As the first indicative statement after the epistolary salutation is the declaration of God's act that generates hope (1:3), so the first imperative calling for human response is the command to hope. Since God *has* acted, definitively and eschatologically, Christians can live a life of hope that is not illusory self-confidence or merely striving for a positive attitude.

"Hope" is seen here not as one quality among others in the Christian life, but as the comprehensive term that summarizes

Christian existence as such, corresponding to "faith" in Paul's writings. First Peter's concept of hope is at the furthest pole from either the selfish Christian otherworldly pietism expressed as "think about your heavenly reward," or pop psychology's "positive thinking." Christian hope is not a bland optimism, but can name its basis and make it concrete in a changed life (Brox 1979, 75). In this context, the imperative "hope" means to live out fully the life of hope you have been given between Christ's resurrection and the eschaton; to live in this meaningful history as a journey into God's future, the God who is creator and redeemer; to live in this creation → consummation history in which the definitive Christ-event has already happened.

J. N. D. Kelly's more literal rendering than either the NRSV or NIV is helpful in portraying the author's meaning: "set your hope completely on the grace being conveyed to you at the revelation of Jesus Christ" (Kelly 1969, 64). "Revelation" is always eschatological in 1 Peter (cf. 1:5, 7; 4:13). The grace here is eschatological, as in the liturgical cry of *Did.* 10:6—"Let grace come, and let this world pass away." The preposition "on" *(epi)* points to the ground of hope, not its object or content. The idea is not that Christians are to hope *for* the return of Christ, but that based *on* this promise they can live a life of hope. The NRSV is misleadingly ambiguous. The hope is not for what Jesus Christ will bring (at the *parousia*), but for the grace Christians will receive when at the eschaton God fully reveals Jesus Christ. "Jesus Christ" is not the subject but the object (of *God's* action). Again, 1 Peter's Christology is theocentric. While the focus is on the full revelation God will execute in the future, both the present participle "being born" *(pheromenen)* and the use of "grace" (10x in 1 Peter, usually of the believer's present experience) indicate that hope is not only future but a present reality by which one lives (Hort 1898, 67). "The grace-bearing return of Christ already casts its shadow back onto the present" (Achtemeier 1996, 118).

The Command to Be Holy (1:14-21)

First Peter 1:14-16 is one sentence, with "you" (readers) the understood subject, and "be holy" in the imperative mood, the main verb. The sentence is then qualified by five subordinate adverbial clauses:

Be holy (15c)
    (14a) . . . as the obedient children of God you in fact are
    (14b) . . . by nonconformity to your previous life (your values held in "ignorance")
    (15a) . . . corresponding to the Holy One who called you
    (15b) . . . in your whole manner of life
    (16) . . . in obedience to Scripture.

Verses 17-21 then begin a second complex sentence, which continues the grounding of the holiness of the Christian life in christological affirmations taken from Christian tradition.

Live your lives in a certain way (1:17b)
    (1:17a) . . . since you invoke God the impartial Judge as Father
    (1:17c) . . . in fear (of God)
    (1:17d) . . . during the time of your sojourn
    (1:18-20) . . . since you know that you have been ransomed/redeemed by the blood of Christ
    (1:21) . . . since all this was God's act, the intention and result is that your faith and hope are in God.

Although the sentence is in the form of a command to the readers, being holy is not something they can achieve on their own (cf. the command to hope, in the preceding verse). They are already constituted as the holy people of God by God's own act of choosing them (1:1) and by the sanctifying act of the Holy Spirit in their conversion (1:2; "sanctify" is the verbal form of "holy" = "make holy"). Again, the imperative rests on the indicative, "be what you are," or better "show yourselves in your daily, public conduct to be what you in fact have been made by God's act."

"Holiness" belongs inherently to God alone. "The Holy One" became a name for God in the Old Testament, used forty-five times, especially in the Isaiah tradition (e.g., 1 Sam 2:2; 2 Kgs 19:22;

Job 6:10; Ps 71:22 and often in the Psalms; Isa 1:4; 5:19-24 [6:1-5]; 40:25; 60:9, 14; Jer 35:7; 51:5; Hos 11:9). In the rabbinic period, after the sacred name "Yahweh" had become too holy to pronounce, it was often replaced by "the-Holy-One-blessed-be-He," the whole phrase functioning as the divine name. Etymologically, the word "holy" originally meant "separate," "different," "other." When applied to God the word took on the connotation of the Wholly Other, the One who is Creator over against all else as creation. It was then filled with moral and ethical content corresponding to the character of God. God is the Near and Compassionate One, so "holy" does not connote remoteness or aloofness (Hos 11:9!), but God is still the Incomparable One (Isa 46:9), the Unfathomable, Mysterious One who is ultimately Other than all creation. The holiness of God points to God's active power. That which is holy is charged with an ultimate energy that may be dangerous, like electricity, a power that calls for insulation and that may not be approached casually (cf. Exod 3:1-6; 19:7-25, and the rules in Leviticus for coming to terms with God's holiness).

What belongs to God becomes holy by association (e.g., Spirit [Ps 51:11], name [Lev 20:3], covenant [Dan 11:30]). God chooses people and things and separates them for his saving purpose. God removes them from the realm of the ordinary and communicates to them something of his own holiness. Thus, the Temple (Ps 5:7), the priesthood (2 Chron 23:6), the Levites (2 Chron 35:3), Jerusalem (Neh 11:1), and the land of Israel (Zech 2:12) are holy. But especially, God's people Israel have been constituted a holy people by God's having chosen them, delivered them, and entered into covenant with them (Deut 7:6; 28:9 *et passim*). Although the author is thoroughly steeped in Pauline tradition, it is striking that neither here nor elsewhere does he use the typical Pauline expression "saints" (i.e., "holy ones") for the church (Rom 1:7; 1 Cor 1:2, etc.), but develops the understanding of holiness in his own way (cf. Appendix 2: Images of the Church in 1 Peter). Nonetheless, the readers are commanded to "be holy." The challenge is to live in the midst of the world as the distinctive people of God, bearing witness in word and manner of life to the mighty acts of the God who has set them apart (2:9).

1:14a: . . . As the Obedient Children of God You in Fact Are: When the readers are addressed as obedient children, "obedient" reflects the covenant language of 1:2 and the obedience inherent in belonging to God's covenant people (cf. 1:22). "Children" does not connote immaturity, but reflects the Semitic idiom in which "sons of" or "children of" indicate the category to which one belongs and the character one possesses (cf. the related Eph 2:2), as well as continuing the metaphor of the new birth into the family of God of 1:3 (cf. 1:23). Unthinking obedience is not called for (1:13), but rather the obedience appropriate to those who belong to God's covenant people and God's family.

The author writes as a pastor (5:1-4) addressing a hurting, harassed community. It is remarkable that he does not consider mere survival their top priority, nor does he consider it sufficient to minister to their personal hurts in a way that focuses on their individual needs. He does not hesitate to address the readers in terms of their mission, in a way that transcends their personal needs without denying them. The church is not called to be a narcissistic or esoteric community, but to seek bridges across which the Christian message, in word and deed, can address those still in the unbelief from which the readers have been delivered (cf. Brox 1979, 255).

1:14b: . . . By Not Being Conformed to the Desires of Your Former Ignorance: Holiness means being different. When translated into social terms, this becomes nonconformity. What this concretely means is yet to be discussed (cf. 2:11–3:12), but here, is expressed in the same general parenetical terms found in Rom 12:2, the holiness of the people of God that means nonconformity to their previous life. The readers are addressed as former Gentiles who had previously lived in futile ways inherited from their ancestors (1:18), for example, those who had been socialized to accept a false view of the world and life within it. They had formerly lived in darkness (2:9), had previously practiced idolatry (see on 4:3), and first became believers in God when they became Christians (1:21). Even if, as pagans, they had practiced a sophisticated monotheism, the author considers them to have first become believers in the true God when they accepted the Christian faith. The perspective adopted by the author does not encourage the readers to look *out* on *others* in anything like a "holier than thou" attitude, but to look *back* on *their own* former way of regarding what is real and important. The contrast is not with contemporary nonbelievers, but with their own previous selves. The "ignorance" thus refers not to information, but to their previous world and its values, just as "desires" is a neutral word *(epithymeia)* that is not inherently evil (the NIV here adds the interpretive word "evil" not in the Greek text). The point is not a moralistic or pietistic one that the readers had previously lived an "evil" life by social standards, and now lived a "good" life by those same criteria, but that they have been reborn into a new world, and must not live by the old world into which they had been socialized by their ancestors (1:18). One's character is shaped by the understanding of the world one assumes to be real. Holiness is to live by the new reality, not the old one now seen to be false.

1:15a: . . . In Your Whole Manner of Life: The holiness of the people of God is not to be achieved either by withdrawing from the world (as at Qumran, which also saw itself as the holy people of God of the end time, and used some of the same biblical texts as the basis for its life on which 1 Peter relies), or by confining holiness to a separate area of individualistic, internal spirituality. The believer's whole life is the arena in which God's holiness is to be manifested. "Conduct" *(anastrophē)* is a key word for 1 Peter (1:15, [verb form 1:17], 18; 2:12; 3:1, 2, 16), in each case referring to the public, engaged life of the readers. Precisely what this means in actual practice is yet to be spelled out (2:11–3:12); but when details are given, they will be from within the perspective that is now being developed of holy nonconformity to the prevailing standards of the world, standards that have now been left behind by rebirth into the family of God.

1:15b: . . . Corresponding to God's Holiness and God's Call: The Greek of verse 15a can be translated either "as the one who called

you is holy" or "corresponding to the Holy One who called you."
While the latter translation is preferable and does not require
adding words presumed to be understood in the Greek text, the
basic meaning is the same: the author makes explicit that Christian
holiness is derivative, and is to correspond to God's own holiness.
As the Holy One, God does not determine his relations to the world
on the world's own terms, but by the divine standard. Holiness thus
cannot mean antiworld orientation, since God is not antiworld, but
an orientation to the world's creator and redeemer. As God has
revealed himself in Christ as the One who acts on behalf of all
people and for their welfare, even at the cost of God's personal
suffering, so the Christian's holiness must be engaged with the world,
not withdrawn from it, and it is for the sake of the world, not merely
in a presumed superior contrast to it. Contemporary Christians might
be less hesitant to adopt the term "holiness" as basic to Christian
existence if they understood it in 1 Peter's biblical sense.

1:16: . . . As the Scripture Says: Although the author's mind is
saturated with Scripture, which he reads from a christological
perspective and works into his statements allusively and perhaps
even unconsciously (cf., e.g., Isa 52:3 in 1:18 below), his first clear
reference to Scripture is an explicit quotation (Lev. 19:2; cf. 11:44-
45; 20:7, 26). Like the rest of his citations, it is from the LXX, and
as always, though originally addressed to Israel, he appropriates it
as directly addressed to Christian readers. The modern reader might
be surprised that it is from Leviticus, generally neglected in contemporary "mainline" Christianity, just as many present-day readers
would be surprised to learn that Jesus' citation of the command-
ment to love one's neighbor is taken from Leviticus—the same
chapter as here cited by 1 Peter (Lev 19:18; cf. Mark 12:31 par.).
We need not be surprised. Leviticus was the "Priests Manual"—
Torath Kohanim in rabbinic terminology—and the author understands the church to be a priestly community (2:9 etc.). The citation
is from a subdivision of Leviticus known as the Holiness Code (Lev
17–26) which, in contrast to the rest of Leviticus, understands all
Israel, and not only the ordained Levitical priests, to be priests to
God for the sake of the world (see on 2:9). The author wants his

readers to understand that the kind of holy life to which he calls them as the people of God is grounded in Scripture.

1:17-21: Based on God's Redeeming Act in Christ: Verses 17-21 form one complex Greek sentence, structured like the previous one around the imperative of verse 17c as the main verb (*anastraphête*, "live your lives in a certain way") with four qualifying phrases and clauses:

> Live your lives
> > in reverent fear
> > as those who invoke the impartial Father as Judge
> > as those who have been redeemed from their futile past by the blood of Christ
> > as those who have come to trust in God through Jesus Christ.

Most scholars see a traditional formula cited in 1:20, signaled by the solemn liturgical tone and balanced antitheses, while some see all of 1:18-20 as hymnic or creedal material, claiming that more is cited than is directly relevant to the point. A few have adopted Bultmann's argument that 1:18-21; 2:21-25; and 3:18-22 are all elements of a single complex of "Christ hymns" (Goppelt 1993, 114, 207-10, 247-50 for details and bib.). While it is virtually certain that the author incorporates earlier liturgical formulae, attempts to reconstruct them in detail generally have not been convincing. The complex sentence is replete with traditional and profound theological imagery, including as its longest segment the christological grounding of 1:18-20, but its purpose is not didactic, to explain theology. The structure makes clear that Christian life, not abstract thought, is the focus. The main verb *anastropheō* is cognate to *anastrophē* of 1:15, continuing to point to the believer's life as a whole, including especially its public dimensions, as the arena where faith and hope become real. The life they now live (*paroikia*, "exile" NRSV; "as strangers" NIV) is that of "sojourners" or "resident aliens" (*paroikoi*; see on *parepidēmoi* of 1:1; the two terms are equated in 2:11). Though they formerly belonged to the culture and its values that had been inherited from their ancestors (1:18), they are now outsiders in this society as the result of their response to the gospel. This passage reflects the language of Israel's redemption from Egypt, where they had been *paroikoi* in a country of high culture (Deut 23:7), but had been delivered (*lytroō*, same word as 1 Pet 1:18) from slavery by God's mighty act. The author gives an ironic twist to this traditional language: the readers once themselves belonged to the high hellenistic culture and its values, but have been ransomed by God's act of deliverance to live a new life as outsiders in their own country!

The "empty way of life" (1:18 NIV) from which they were redeemed was "handed on from their ancestors," that is, it represented the world into which they were born and for which they were socialized to accept as real, the world of conventional values they now regard as "futile" (1:18 NRSV). The old world was not obviously false or blatantly sinful. The word for "inherited" (*patroparadotos*; 1:18) is a positive word in the hellenistic world, representing the means by which cultural values were transmitted, having something of the same overtones as our "heritage." The readers have been given a new world by being born again, by the word of God, that is, given a new narrative world by accepting the good news of the mighty acts of God as constituting the real world within which they live a new life (see 1:23 and Appendix 1: The Narrative World of 1 Peter).

This life is to be lived "in reverent fear" corresponding to the Holy One. "Fear" is not cowardice or lack of trust, but honoring God as God, not becoming too casual or cozy with the Creator (4:19). Paul too had pictured pre-Christian life as those who have no fear of God (Rom 3:18 citing Ps 36:1), and connected holiness and the fear of God (2 Cor 5:10-11; 7:1). Such reverent fear is not only not incompatible with calling upon God as "Father" (1:17), but in the ancient world was inherent in this invocation. Father-language for God was found in both pagan and Jewish religion in the first century, but had received a new perspective in the Christian community. While the author gives no indication of personal acquaintance with Jesus' own *abba* prayer (cf. Mark 14:36), like other second-generation Gentile Christians he would have been acquainted with this tradition alive in the Pauline churches (Rom

8:15; Gal 4:6). Christians are to live lives of reverent fear as those who in their prayers invoke God as "Father" (the lack of article with "father" indicates it is used adverbially, "fatherwise"), remembering that God is the One who judges all impartially, not by their theology but by their lives. Their status as God's elect (1:1) and God's children (1:3, 14; 2:2) does not imply favoritism (Amos 3:2). Like Paul, the author finds no conflict between salvation by grace and judgment according to one's life (Rom 14:10; 2 Cor 5:10). Since the word for "work" is in the singular (cf. Phil 2:30; 1 Thess 5:13), judgment is according to one's life as a whole, not according to one's "works," that is, individual deeds.

The new life of the believers is grounded in the good news that they have been ransomed from their old life by God's mighty act in Christ. Three items are to be particularly noted about the author's presentation of this traditional structure:

1. He begins with the blood of Christ, interpreted as the ransom that delivered the readers into their new life. Although one statement in the Gospels expresses this theology (Mark 10:45//Matt 20:28), 1 Peter does not base this aspect of his theology on the saying of Jesus, but on the ransom imagery of the Old Testament (cf. Introduction, pp. 35, 39-40), where "ransom" can mean freeing from Egyptian bondage (Exod 6:6; 15:13) and Babylonian exile (Isa 51:11; 52:3). First Peter alludes specifically to Isa 52:3 in making the point that Christians are redeemed with the blood of Christ more precious than silver or gold. And since the author will shortly refer to Isa 53:7, which pictures the Servant as the lamb who silently suffers for others (2:22), the Christ as the Passover lamb is already in view. In first-century Judaism (though not in the Old Testament), the Passover lamb had already been interpreted as a sacrifice for sins. First Peter clearly affirms the atonement theology of the early church according to which Jesus died to mediate God's forgiveness and reconcile sinful human beings to God (see 2:24; 3:18), but that is not in view here. The "ransom" of Jesus' blood does not here deliver us from the guilt of sin, but from the old way of life, as another expression of the Exodus-imagery that forms much of the metaphorical framework for this section (see above on structure of 1:13–2:10).

2. "Blood" terminology, though alien to many modern readers, permeates biblical language, and must be understood within its own framework of biblical theology. "Blood" is a shorthand way of saying "life." It was a maxim of the biblical world that "the life is in the blood," so that "blood" and "life" are virtual synonyms (Gen 9:4; Lev 17:11; Jon 1:14, etc.). To say Jesus gave his blood for us is to say he gave his life, himself, for us. Further, the concept of sacrifice, by which the blood/life of an animal is given to the deity as an expression of gratitude, a release of power, an atonement for sin, while alien to most modern readers, was intrinsic to the ancient world, both Jewish and pagan. Christians interpreted the death of Jesus in sacrificial terms from the earliest days, especially in the Pauline tradition to which 1 Peter is closely related (e.g., Rom 3:21-26; 1 Cor 15:3; 2 Cor 5:21).

A deep theological problem was inherent in the Christian adoption of this category to interpret the meaning of Jesus' death: it appeared to make the death of Jesus a three-party transaction in which the innocent Jesus was sacrificed (or sacrificed himself) in behalf of sinful humanity to appease a holy God. This perverse theology of the atonement, in which God is pictured as demanding someone's blood before forgiveness is granted, not only falsely objectifies the language of confession, but betrays a low Christology that is hesitant to identify God and Christ. Yet the New Testament language of atonement consistently presupposes a two-party transaction, the Holy God and sinful humanity, in which God himself, and not a third party, suffers for human sin (e.g., John 1:1, 29; 2 Cor 5:19). "Ransomed with the . . . blood of Christ" pictures what God did for us, not what Jesus did to appease God. This means that the tendency of the New Testament to identify God and Christ, to use God-language of Christ, is not metaphysical speculation but the expression of the church's conviction that God, not a lesser being, is the one present and active in the Christ-event, including the Crucifixion (cf. on 2:21-25 below, pp. 122-23). The incipient "Trinitarian" elements already present in the New Testament (cf., e.g., 1:2 above) and elaborated at Nicea and Chalcedon were thus not mere abstract speculation, but directed to something implicit in the Christian confession.

3. The theocentric orientation of 1 Peter as a whole is clearly expressed in the sentence before us, which on the surface seems to be thoroughly christological, but in which God is the hidden subject throughout: God is the Father who judges all impartially; God is the Holy One to whom "reverent fear" is appropriate; God is the one invoked in prayer; God is the one who ransomed the readers from their past futile life; God is the one who provided the Passover lamb whose blood signaled their redemption; God is the one who foreknew/destined Christ before the foundation of the world; God is the one who manifested/revealed Christ in the eschatological times in which the readers live; God is the one who raised Christ from the dead and glorified him. This crescendo of God's mighty acts, some of which are expressed by the "divine passive," is climaxed by the declaration that all this happened so that their faith and hope might be in God (1:21). "God" is the hidden subject in the title "Christ" (= the anoint*ed* one, i.e., by God). This "christological" section begins and ends with God-language. Christological language does not answer the question "Who was Jesus?" but the question "Who is God?" (Ogden 1982). The subject modulates back and forth, so that "God" and "Christ" are not two distinctive topics; to talk of God is to talk Christology; to make christological statements is to talk about God. Thus the Bible's language for God can now be used directly of Christ (2:3), and the antecedent of relative pronouns can be either "God" or "Christ" (cf. on 1:23-25; 2:21-25; 4:11). This has important implications for those efforts to translate statements about God in biblical Greek and Hebrew into gender-neutral English statements in which masculine pronouns can be used for "Christ" but not for "God," forcing a decision about whether God "or" Christ is the antecedent that the biblical text may not have intended (cf., e.g., Luke 1:15-17; John 3:16; 1 John 1:6; 2:1-6, 26-29; Rev 1:1).

The Command to Love (1:22-25)

1:22: The third imperative of this section (which follows 1:13, the command to hope; and 1:14-21, the command to be holy) is the command to love. Since Jesus made the love command supreme (Matt 22:34-40; Mark 12:28-34; Luke 10:25-28; John 13:34;

15:12, 17), one might expect an eyewitness of Jesus' ministry to appeal to Jesus' teaching, but here as elsewhere the command is given as a part of general Christian parenesis, with the same set of associations made by Paul (holiness; living as brothers and sisters in the family of God; Rom 12:10; 13:8; 1 Thess 4:3, 4, 7, 9). Like the New Testament in general, 1 Peter uses two different Greek words as synonyms, *philadelphia* (related to *philia*) and *agapē*. A popular but nonscholarly modern exegetical tradition has developed to the effect that the Greek words *agapē* (noun) and *agapaō* (verb) represent a special kind of unconditional love distinct from *eros* and *philia*. In reality, however, *agapē* and its cognates were used in the ancient world, as in modern Greek, for all kinds of "love," selfish and unselfish, sensuous and unsensuous, just as is the case with the English word "love" (cf. *agapē* in e.g., Eccl 5:9; Jer 2:25; Luke 6:32; 2 Tim 4:10; 2 Pet 2:15). The special quality of Christian love is not a matter of Greek vocabulary but of christological content: the caring, self-giving, unconditional love revealed in the life and death of Jesus. Love so understood is not a feeling (despite some translations), but an action.

First Peter affirms that when the readers were converted they entered not merely an institution or organization but a church where loving care for each member is given to all and required of all. Their entrance into this community is called "having purified your souls"—the perfect participle points to a past event the effects of which continue into the present. "Souls" is a synonym for "persons" or "selves," as in 3:20 and consistently in 1 Peter. "Purified" echoes the biblical word found thirty-four times in the LXX, used of the consecration or sanctification of priests, Levites, Nazarites, and the people of Israel as a whole. The word is used in the LXX almost exclusively for ritual purity, the kind of cultic holiness necessary for priests and the Temple. First Peter uses it in a spiritual but real sense of the Christian community that, as a whole, has been sanctified as a priesthood to God, a spiritual house, where spiritual sacrifices are offered (see on 2:5). Thus what Christians do is to be done from "pure" hearts (so NAB; cf. NRSV margin). The word "pure" is not found in all manuscripts, and thus is not included in some translations. (Metzger 1975, 688, indicates the majority of the Committee that produced our standard Greek New Testaments agreed it is original.) "Pure" *(katharos)* in this Petrine context retains its cultic overtones; in the LXX it is often used as a synonym for "holy" *(hagios)*. The Christian priestly community is to be pure (holy), but its purity is not ritual but a matter of the heart. (This connotation is thus different from Matt 5:8, where the emphasis is on singleness of heart and integrity, as in Gen 20:5; Ps 50:12.)

The readers did not achieve this purity by strenuous moral effort, but received it as an element of their new birth, which made them members of the "brotherhood," the family of God (cf. 1:3, 14, 23; 2:1, 17; 3:8; 4:8; 5:9) in which family love *(philadelphia,* literally "brotherly love," 1:22) prevails. When they were converted, they did not receive a list of high ideals they were to strive to live by as individuals, but a new world (see on 1:23) and a new community. The love here commanded is for "one another," that is, it is the norm for relations inside the Christian community (cf. John 3:34; Rom 12:10; 13:8; often in 1 John). While in 1 Peter, Christian love is by no means confined to insiders, readers must not rush too quickly to make the point that God's love, and therefore the Christian's, must be directed to everyone, especially the outsider who does not return it. That is indeed the nature of Christian love, and it is expressed elsewhere in 1 Peter (see e.g., on 2:8-9; 3:9). Yet it is also important for believers who are going to be asked to suffer for Christ's sake and, like Jesus, for the sake of outsiders who do not return the love, to know that they belong to a community that loves and accepts them, that they are not called to be heroic individuals but members of a family that cares for and supports them. "Love your enemies" is conspicuously absent here, where the focus is on the development of the loving support of a Christian family. The goal of sanctification and obedience is here neither personal perfection nor making the social order more just, but love in the family of God.

This love should not be sentimentalized or romanticized. "See how they love one another" was said by outsiders of ancient Christians not as a compliment, but with resentment and suspicion of those who had been charged with "hatred for the human race" (cf. Tacitus, *Annals* 15.44; Tertullian, *Apology* 39; cf. Lucian's sneering comment in *Death of Peregrinus* 13: "Their first lawgiver persuaded them that they are all brothers and sisters," and Minucius Felix, *Octavius* 9.2: "They know one another by secret marks and insignias, and love one another almost before they know one another . . . they call one another promiscuously 'brother' and 'sister.' "). A Christian community such as the readers of 1 Peter could be tempted to turn their love exclusively to each other, as did the Qumran community, whose "Manual of Discipline" urged members to "Love all the children of light and hate all the children of darkness" (1QS 1.10). First Peter specifically resists yielding to this pressure from outside to see themselves as others see them, and calls his readers to orient their lives according to their own faith rather than by cultural perceptions. Thus the love command here is more than a "catechetical cliché" (*contra* Kelly 1969, 79).

1:23-25: Verse 23 is the conclusion of the sentence begun in 1:22, providing the indicative kerygmatic grounding for the imperative of verse 22. The challenge to Christian love and faithfulness is not mere moralism but is grounded in the reality of the believer's new birth effected by the word of God heard in Christian preaching (cf. on 1:3, 14; 2:2). The readers have been given a new life, a new world (cf. Appendix 1: The Narrative World of 1 Peter). The new life is not a matter of developing innate qualities. Nor is immortality a natural property of human beings—only God is by nature immortal (Rom 1:23; 1 Cor 15:53-54; 1 Tim 1:17; 6:16)—but is the gift of new life through the gospel (cf. 2 Tim 1:10). In 1:3 the new birth was by the resurrection of Jesus Christ; here it is through the word that is inseparably bound to this event and mediates it to the believer (Schweizer 1949, 43). The new birth is not a matter of experience that can be verified empirically—the attempt to observe and document it reveals only the world of "flesh" that is passing away. Rebirth is not a matter of experienced feelings, but of the divine word (1:23–3:1), the same word of God by which the world was created (Gen 1:1; Ps 33:6, 9; John 1:1-3; Rom 4:17), the word that endures forever when the temporal world of our physical birth has passed away (Isa 40:6-8). The religious verbiage should not dull our senses to the amazing declaration: when Christian missionary preachers came into the backwoods provinces of the addressees and preached their sermons using whatever conceptuality and theologies they employed to express the Christian message, the readers were confronted by the same word of God by which the world was created. The initiatory divine word corresponds to human obedient response (1:22); God's gift and human responsibility are two aspects of the same event of conversion (cf. Phil 2:12*b*-13).

There is a terminological similarity to the "Logos spermatikos," Stoicism's "seminal reason" that permeates the universe (although 1 Peter's word for seed is *spora*, found only here in the New Testament, not *sperma* as in 1 John 3:9 and the Synoptic seed parables, the two words belong to the same semantic field). We thus have here a good illustration of a New Testament author using imagery and vocabulary common in the hellenistic world but in a different sense better oriented to his Bible and Christian tradition (cf. John 3:3-5; Jas 1:10-11, 18; 1 John 4:7-8, which also connects the love command to new birth). This kerygmatic grounding of the new Christian life is based on a key text of Scripture, which is immediately cited.

This unit contains 1 Peter's second explicit Scripture citation (Isa 40:6-7, 8-9). Like other motifs in this section, this biblical passage was traditional Christian parenetic material (cf. Jas 1:10-11, with which there is no literary connection). It is appropriately chosen by the author, however, not only because it expresses the temporal/eternal contrast between the divine word and human culture, but also corresponds to the exodus motif that dominates the section as a whole. Deutero-Isaiah had originally addressed those leaving Babylonian exile, who were en route toward their true homeland as participants in a "new exodus." First Peter's appropriation of this imagery corresponds to that of the Qumran covenanters, who also understood themselves as the community of the second exodus and relied heavily on the imagery of Isa 40 (Goppelt 1993, 105), and is another point of contact between 1 Peter and early Palestinian tradition.

As always, the author basically follows the LXX text, which differs somewhat from the Hebrew (40:7*bc* is missing!). The one significant difference from the LXX is that 1 Peter has "Lord" *(kyrios)* for the LXX "our God" *(theos)*, a change that blurs the distinction between Christ and God (cf. 1:11—it is the word of Christ that is heard in the Old Testament prophets—and 2:3, where *Kyrios* of Prov 33:9 [= Yahweh] modulates from "God" to "the Lord Jesus Christ" [cf. 1:3], and cf. 3:15 where "Christ" is inserted to make clear the Old Testament's "Lord" is understood christologically). Again (cf. on 1:16) the author perceives no hermeneutical gap to be bridged, but assumes direct continuity between Old Testament Scripture and Christian readers. As Christ spoke through the prophets (1:11), so the author leads the church to hear their Bible as speaking directly to/about them. His hermeneutic, about which he offers no explicit reflections, seems to be expressed in Rom 15:4, a text, along with Romans as a whole, that stands in the background of 1 Peter.

The Command to Grow (2:1-10)

The chapter division here is unfortunate, since 2:1-10 is the concluding literary unit of the first major section of the letter 1:13–2:10 (cf. above discussion of structure, and Introduction, p. 47). While it is clear that 2:1-10 is a unified composition, its exact internal literary structure is less clear, as indicated by the fact that various editions of the Greek New Testament have divided the sentences differently, with even more variety in English translations. The following division in the Greek makes most sense in terms of syntax. First Peter 2:1-5 is one sentence. Placing a period at the end of verse 3 is awkward, since verse 4 is linked to it with the relative clause to make verses 1-5 into one compound sentence with two main verbs ("long for" and "you are being built"). Verse 6 is one sentence, an explicit citation from Scripture. Verses 7-10 are two sentences, contrasting the response and status of unbelievers (7-9) with believers (9-10).

While the syntax is indistinct, the rhetorical effect of the passage as a whole is compelling, ringing the chimes on a plethora of metaphors that evoke a kaleidoscope of images portraying the readers' new identity. Thematically, the section is composed of two subsections that cut across the actual syntax (thus most translations rightly follow the thematic division rather than actual sentence structure), picturing Christian growth toward eschatological salvation (2:1-3) and Christian identity as the elect and holy people of God (2:4-10).

2:1-3: Like 4:3, 2:1 reflects the form of a "vice catalogue," a common element of early Christian ethical exhortation especially prominent in the Pauline tradition (cf. Rom 1:29-31; 1 Cor 5:10-11; 6:9-10; Gal 5:19-21; Eph 4:31; 5:3-5; Col 3:5, 8; 1 Tim 1:9-10; 6:4-5; 2 Tim 3:2-4; Titus 3:3; four of the five words are found in Rom 1:29-31, in the same order). Some of the terminology is also found in the parenesis of the Dead Sea Scrolls, so that here as elsewhere 1 Peter reflects the author's drawing upon the reservoir of early Christian tradition (cf. Jas 1:21), particularly his characteristic combination of Pauline and Palestinian tradition.

While this means that the particular items on the list are conventional, not necessarily reflecting the particular faults of the addressees, the author's selection is not random, but focuses on the attitudes and behavior that destroy community: malice, deceit, phoniness, envy, slander (*katalalia*, literally, "talking down" other people). The list is thus not composed of general clichés exhorting the readers to "be nice," nor is it yet specific instruction about social ethics (these come later), but is aimed specifically at the internal life of the church as those who have been born anew into a new household and whose ethic cannot be privatistic.

It is thus likely that baptismal imagery is reflected in the opening participle translated "rid yourselves" (NRSV, NIV) or "laying aside" (KJV) (*apothemenoi*, literally "lay aside," as when one takes off clothing). The Christian's entrance into a new life was sometimes symbolized in early Christianity by taking off one's old clothes, entering naked into the baptistery, and emerging on the other side to don new garments (cf., e.g., Rom 13:12; Col 2:12; 3:8-10). These baptismal overtones are reinforced by addressing the readers as "newborn infants" (2:2) again not a random metaphor, but continuing the preceding imagery (cf. 1:3, 14, 23). The considerable baptismal imagery, here and elsewhere in 1 Peter, does not mean, as was once often thought, that the letter was originally a baptismal sermon or liturgy for new converts (see Introduction, pp. 37-38). Rather, the presence of baptismal overtones emphasizes that the meaning of being a Christian as having-been-baptized continued to play a role in the self-understanding of Christians struggling to come to terms with their role in society. First Peter is not addressed to a group of new converts within the church, but to the churches of the five provinces of Asia Minor as a whole, most of whom were not newly baptized. As Paul in Rom 6:1-14 appeals to the fact that the readers have been baptized (long after their actual baptism) as a foundational element in their ethical decisions, so 1 Peter continues to refer to the status of believers as those who have been born/begotten anew as basic to their understanding of themselves as Christians in a hostile society. Baptism, conversion, and entrance into the household of faith was not a passing event that could be left behind in the past, but continued to be crucial in the believer's Christian life.

The vice list does not lead to a contrasting list of virtues (as e.g., Gal 5:16-23), but to a command to long for nourishment by the same word that gave them new birth. This is the main verb of the sentence, and like the corresponding verbs of the preceding sections, is an imperative (1:13, "hope"; 1:15, "be holy"; 1:22, "love"). The command is to "long for" (NRSV) or "crave" (NIV) the "pure spiritual milk" that gives them life. Literal babies, of course, do not have to be commanded to do this; they instinctively know that their life depends upon it. But the readers of 1 Peter need to be reminded that just as their entrance into the household of faith was a matter of divine begetting and birth, so their continued growth is not something they can generate themselves, but depends on life-giving nourishment. While the term used *(logikon)* is related to the term for "word" *(logos),* it may mean "spiritual" or "metaphorical" in a more general sense. In this context, however, the "spiritual milk" must be the divine word that brought their new life into being and continues to nourish it (cf. 1:23, 25; 2:8). First Peter does not restrict the word of God to Scripture (cf. 1:25). The nourishment that sustains the kind of Christian life the readers are called to live in a hostile society is the word of God that comes through the Bible, the church's teaching and preaching, the church's witness in word and deed to God's mighty acts (2:9). It is by the word that the new creation, the new world to which they belong, is communicated and made real (cf. Appendix 1: The Narrative World of 1 Peter).

Christians never outgrow this. The picture of Christians as babies longing for their mothers' milk means they can never be satisfied, must always be hungry. In this world, they never arrive; they are always en route. In contrast to Paul and the Paulinists, Christian maturity is not an ideal to be realized in this life (cf. 1 Cor 3:1-17, which has much of the same imagery as here; but in Paul "milk" is used in a disparaging sense, as in Heb 5:11–6:2). For 1 Peter, the divine "milk" of the word of God is something Christians must never outgrow. Our being "filled full" is a matter of eschatological salvation (2:3; cf. 1:5, 9). Just as God's acts in the past are seen in seamless continuity with the present Christian reality, so present Christian life and eschatological consummation are seen as of one piece. "Salvation is seen not as a last-minute rescue operation from the outside but as the fitting consummation of a process already at work in and among Christian believers" (Michaels 1988, 91). This is a different way of conceiving the same reality Paul writes about, using some of the same imagery in a different way (see on 5:10).

In verse 3 the author's thought moves to Ps 34 (LXX Ps 33), which is often present to his mind as he composes this letter, and to which he will explicitly return in 3:10-12. The psalm as a whole, which speaks of divine deliverance and vindication to harassed believers, must have seemed particularly appropriate to the readers' situation. It has even been suggested that the whole of 1 Peter is a homily on this psalm, providing both structure and content (Bornemann 1919). The author's language about receiving the milk of the word of Christ reminds him of a specific text with which he concludes this exhortation: since they have already tasted the goodness of the Lord, they must continue to long for the spiritual nourishment he provides. "Lord" in Ps 34:8 referred to Yahweh. As often in the New Testament, the LXX translation as *kyrios* facilitated the early Christian understanding of the word as referring to Christ, as the following context makes clear in the present instance. The author also may have been drawn to this text since the word for "good" is *chrēstos,* which, though written differently, sounds exactly like "Christ" *(christos)* in hellenistic Greek, thus facilitating a serious pun: "The Lord is Christ/good." Taken as "The Lord is Christ," the psalm text affirms the basic Christian confession, which in Asia Minor was already being heard as a contrast to the cultural "creed" promoted by advocates of the Roman civil religion: "The Lord is Caesar." We may have a subtle anticipation of the issue to be faced squarely in the next section: what is the relation between those who confess Christ as Lord *(kyrios Christos)* and those who live by the cultural code *(kyrios Kaisaros)?* Before addressing this issue directly, the author concludes this section with a crescendo of images elaborating and confirming Christian identity.

2:4-10: This passage brings the whole unit begun at 1:13 to a powerful climax, forming the conclusion of the first major part of the letter. It echoes themes already introduced in the opening greeting of 1:2 and elaborated in the thanksgiving of 1:3-12, with "the continuing people of God in history" as the underlying motif that dominates the whole. The new identity of the readers, given by the word of God that came through Christian preaching by which they were reborn and continue to be nourished, is that of the elect and holy people of God.

While earlier form critical studies proposed that this passage is essentially a quotation from an early Christian hymn (Windisch and Preisker 1930, 158; Selwyn 1947, 268-81), more recent scholarship has concluded that the unit is structured and composed by the author himself, integrating various elements of earlier Christian traditions (Elliott 1966, 129-45). Some elements in this section bear striking similarity to traditions prevalent in both rabbinic Judaism and the Qumran community, for example, the combination of the same Scripture texts, their eschatological and messianic interpretation, and, at Qumran, the self-understanding of the community as a new temple where spiritual sacrifices are offered (cf., e.g., 1QH 6:25-28; 1QpHab 12; 4QpPs37 2:16; 1QS 5:5-6; 7:5-10; 8:4-10; 9:3-9; cf. Michaels 1988, 96). Likewise, this section is replete with similarities to the Pauline tradition. To name only a few examples:

the combination of "milk" and "building/temple" images (cf. 1 Cor 3:1-17); "spiritual sacrifices" (Rom 12:1/1 Pet 2:5; cf. already *logikon* in 1 Pet 2:2); Christ as the foundation (1 Cor 3:11).

Especially striking is the same combination of Old Testament texts as in Rom 9:25-33, using the same form of text that differs both from the MT and the LXX (Isa 8:14; 28:16; Hos 1:6-9). While the differences from Paul in both detail and application preclude a slavish direct dependence on Paul, as though the author had only the Pauline letters before him, such items as the combination of texts noted above are better explained on the view that the author writes from a context in which his own view had been shaped in part by having heard Paul's letters regularly read in worship (cf. Schelke 1988, 61-62). In the postulated setting of Rome in the 90s, this would have been the case, and it has had its effect on the author's own theology.

Unlike Paul, however, the author incorporates the texts from the Old Testament as though they spoke directly to his situation. In its original context, the rejected stone of Ps 118:22 was Israel, rejected by the nations, but accepted by God and now receiving great honor, but 1 Peter understands it to refer directly to Christ. While Paul agonizes over the relation of Israel and church (Rom 9–11), and appropriates Israel's Scriptures only secondarily as referring to and addressing the church, the passage before us is an excellent example of 1 Peter's view and practice throughout, whereby the seamless continuity between the people of God in the Bible and his own church situation allows him to hear the texts as directly addressed to the church, without allegory, typology, prophecy/fulfillment, or any such hermeneutic. This was not possible for Paul in his time and place, but a generation later, the (apparently Gentile) author of 1 Peter betrays no awareness of a problem of relating the church of his time to the Israel of the Bible or non-Christian Jews in his own setting.

The author cites the Old Testament frequently and often alludes to it without any indication that his material is from the Bible. He is obviously saturated with the biblical text himself, and addresses his readers as though such a familiarity may be presupposed with them as well. When such familiarity is presupposed, it is sometimes assumed that both writer and readers were Jewish. But in this case the readers are certainly predominately Gentile, and the author is most likely a Gentile Christian himself. The presupposition of intimate familiarity with the Scriptures by no means implies exclusively a Jewish author or readers. A point of communication, evangelism, and hermeneutics is involved here. How much of the Bible the readers actually knew, we have no way of knowing. It is likely some of the allusions were lost on them, as they are on the modern reader, whether Jewish or Gentile. Yet the author knows the Old Testament and Jewish traditions, thinks and writes from this background, and projects it upon his readers, whether they in fact have it or not. This is also what Paul did (cf., e.g., 1 Corinthians and Romans!). Neither was overly concerned to use only imagery and textual allusions that could certainly be presupposed in the readership. Modern interpreters sometimes consider this poor communications theory, but it may be the opposite, as well as good theology and evangelism. The author lives in the narrative world provided by the Scriptures, and assumes it is the only real world (cf. Appendix 1: The Narrative World of 1 Peter). By writing from within this assumption, he tends to instill it in his readers, whether or not they catch all the nuances. "One becomes what one is addressed as" (Berger and Luckmann 1966, 165).

One of several points of independence from Paul is that Ps 34, which plays no role for Paul, is in the author's mind throughout his composition of 1 Peter (cf., e.g., 3:10-12, the longest quotation in 1 Peter, and the citation in 2:3 just preceding).

◊ ◊ ◊ ◊

Three key themes are developed in this crucial section: (1) the rejection/election parallel between Christ and Christians, which leads to (2) an explication of the elect status of Christians in a plethora of seven ecclesiological images, which leads in turn to (3) the Christian mission of worship and testimony.

Christ/Christians Parallel: The parallel between Christ and Christians, which will play a major role in the author's understanding of Christian ethics in a hostile world (2:21 etc.), is introduced for the first time. Both Christ and Christians are "elect" (2:4, 6, 9; cf. 1:1) and "honored" (cf. 1:7; 2:4, 6, 7). Christological affirmations are not speculative statements about Jesus, but illuminate and provide the basis for the readers' own Christian existence. Just as the readers are rejected by society in general, so Christ was and is rejected by people in general (2:4). The author is not thinking only of the Jewish leadership's rejection of the historical Jesus (cf. Mark 12:1-12 par., where the same text from Ps 118:22-23 is cited), but of the continuing rejection of Christ by human society. (The term "rejected" is a Greek perfect participle, like "crucified" in Mark 16:6; 1 Cor 2:2; cf. Gal 3:1.) Being rejected and crucified was not an episode in the career of Jesus that was put behind him by the Resurrection. He continues through history as the Rejected One, modeling the present status of his disciples. "The builders" who put aside the stone that turns out to be the cornerstone for the building they are attempting to construct are not Jewish chief priests, scribes, and elders, but people in general. The fundamental contrast is not between Jews who reject and Gentiles who accept (cf. Rom 9–11), nor even between believers who accept and unbelievers who reject, but between human rejection and divine vindication. This rejection from the human side has already been reversed by God's vindication.

Making use of a collection of three "stone" texts that had already become traditional, the author understands the rejected-but-vindicated stone to be both Christ and the Christians. What has already happened to Christ at the Resurrection will certainly happen to Christians at the eschaton. The reader's life is understood in terms of the divine salvation history, and can be assured that the dishonor they now experience will be transformed into honor, an honor they already experience as the elect and holy people of God. Thus while verses 4-6 interpret the Scriptures to parallel the experience of Christ and Christians, verses 7-8 contrast the status of those who believe in the rejected stone with the unbelievers who stumble over it. Christ is pictured as a building stone placed in the path of humanity in general, so that one is either incorporated into the holy temple of God with Christ as the cornerstone, or one does not recognize it and stumbles over it. Since the Christ-event is the definitive event of world and personal history, there can be no neutral stance toward it.

In verses 9-10 the author returns to his portrayal of the status and honor of the Christian given by God, appropriating a kaleidoscope of biblical imagery for Israel to describe the status conferred on believers. "Honor" in 1 Peter is not a matter of "status" or "self-esteem" as these are popularly understood, but is reinterpreted in terms of Christology and eschatology. This in fact reverses the popular understanding of "honor," both for the ancient honor-shame culture and for contemporary readers (cf. 1:7, 19; 2:7, 17; 3:7). The key verse 2:8 should be translated "But the honor to you," reflecting both the honor and elect status of Christ in 2:7 (*entimos* of Christ is cognate to *time* of Christians) and the eschatological vindication already present for Christ but still to come for Christians (1:7). Their new status remains a nonstatus in the eyes of the world; their security is neither visible to empirical observation nor a matter of the heart. It is not found in "feeling good about themselves" and "having a sense of self-worth," but is a turning away from themselves and finding the meaning of their lives in their incorporation into God's saving plan for history and the elect and holy people of God.

The Elect Status of Christians, Explicated in Seven Images: This passage presents one of the most dense constellations of ecclesiological imagery in the New Testament. They are to be understood within the context of the extensive variety of images for the church that permeates the letter as a whole (see Appendix 2: Images of the Church in 1 Peter). Each of the seven images is taken from the Bible, was originally applied to Israel, and designates the church as the continuing people of God in history, "fostering [their] self-consciousness as 'Israel' " (Michaels 1988, 96).

1. As heirs of Israel, the readers are addressed as "living stones" who are being built into a spiritual house (2:5). "House" *(oikos)* is used elsewhere in 1 Peter only in 4:17, where Christians are the household of God. Thus some interpreters understand the "house" of 2:5 to be the "household" of 4:17 (cf. NRSV, NIV). In 2:5,

however, the context indicates we have temple imagery. Even in 4:17 the image is linked to Ezek 9:6, a temple context, so the temple idea is also present in 4:17.

The church is pictured as the temple of God, composed of Christians as "living stones." However, there is nothing here along the lines of "each of you is a stone, which, when placed together, make a temple." If the author has such an individualistic concept of the church, he misses a good opportunity to express it, since the metaphor is amenable to such use. Nor is there any allusion to the "rock" imagery of Peter's name. There appears to be no reflection of Matt 16:16-18 in 1 Peter at all. Note that "stone" is applied to Christ and Christians (not to Peter), and that "rock" is used as a synonym of "stone" in 2:8, with no hint of awareness that any of this is related to an ecclesiological role of Peter indicated by his name.

2. As heirs of Israel, the readers are addressed as a "holy priesthood" or "royal priesthood" (2:5, 9). The latter term could be translated as "a royal house, a body of priests," depending on whether one takes the Greek term for "royal" as an adjective (so most) or noun (e.g., Elliott 1966, 50-128; Kelly 1969, 98). The image of Exod 19:6, used for Israel as a whole, is here applied to the church as a whole. The later issue of whether there is a special order of priests within the church, or whether every individual is a priest, is not here in view. The point is that the Christian community as a whole plays the role of the continuing people of God in history, which includes being a priestly community on behalf of the world.

3. As heirs of Israel, the readers are addressed as a "chosen race" (2:9). "Chosen" is often translated "elect," and is applied to both Christ and Christians (1:2; 2:4, 6, 9; 5:13). Like the biblical language of election and predestination in general, this is the confessional language of the insiders who want to give praise to God for their being included, rather than taking credit for their own salvation. Only rarely does such confessional language praising God for choosing insiders stray into objectifying language that can be understood as making God responsible for the rejection of outsiders (cf. Mark 4:10-12; Rom 9–11; 1 Thess 5:9; Jude 4). Even such texts are not intended to "explain" the act of God in excluding outsiders, but are directed to believers. First Peter only touches on

the status of unbelievers in passing, as a foil for the status of believers that he is elaborating. Thus exegetes should be wary of "explanations" of the text that either defend God's "horrible decree" of double predestination (Augustine, *Anti-Palagian Writings;* Calvin, *Institutes* XXI-XXIV, and their later interpreters) or that attempt to explain that God has decreed only that those who "disobey" shall "stumble," but has left the choice of whether to obey or not in human hands (so Best 1971, 106 and many others; rightly rejected by Grudem 1988, 107; Schrage 1993, 85). The author of 1 Peter attempts no explanation at all, but lives within the Pauline stream in which each person is responsible, but everything is still finally in God's hands (cf. Phil 2:12-13).

4. As heirs of Israel, the readers are addressed as a "holy nation" (2:9). In the LXX the term for "nation" *(ethnos)* in the plural refers to the Gentiles, and is contrasted with Israel as the people *(laos)* of God (cf., e.g., Exod 19:5; Deut 7:6). But in the singular the term can also be used for Israel (e.g., Gen 12:2; Exod 19:6).

5. As heirs of Israel, the readers are addressed as "God's own people" (2:9). "People" *(laos)* is the common word for Israel in the LXX, from which our term "laity" is derived. The phrase translated "God's own" (NRSV) or "belonging to God" (NIV) does not contain the word "God," but renders a Greek phrase that literally means "for [a] possession" *(eis peripoiēson)*. Since it is not a LXX phrase but is found exclusively in the Pauline tradition in eschatological contexts (Eph 1:14; 1 Thess 5:9; 2 Thess 2:14; cf. Heb 10:39), the phrase here could be another indication of the still-to-come divine vindication of the believers' present hidden identity (so Michaels 1988, 92-93, who renders it "a people destined for vindication").

The list of honorary titles is summed up and concluded by applying two designations taken from Hos 1:6, 9-10; 2:23 (also used in a similar context by Paul in Rom 9:25):

6. As heirs of Israel, the readers are addressed as the "people of God" and

7. as those who have "received mercy" (2:10).

In Hosea, the contrast was between unfaithful Israel rejected by God and the renewed eschatological Israel accepted by God. First

Peter applies this to the Gentile past of the readers, who have now by the divine mercy been incorporated into the continuing people of God. The final word is one of divine initiative and mercy. The readers' identity is established not by their own deed, but by God's choice and effective call.

The Christian Mission of Worship and Testimony: Like the Israel of the Bible and history, the church as the people of God is called into being not for its own sake, but as an expression of the divine mission to the world, and is itself charged with a mission. The gift becomes a responsibility.

As a holy priesthood, the church offers spiritual sacrifices (2:5). This expression, another point of contact with Paul's Letter to the Romans (12:1), is not made specific (e.g., in terms of the Eucharist, which is never mentioned in 1 Peter), but refers to the total life of the Christian community, including its public worship, as a priestly sacrifice to God. Already in the Old Testament, and especially in later Judaism (not only by groups alienated from the temple or after its destruction), Israelites and Jews had expressed the insight that true worship of God is not (only) a matter of animal sacrifice, but the spiritual sacrifice of prayer, praise, study, repentance, and righteous living (Ps 4:5; 49:14; 50:13-14, 23; 51:9; 59:30-31; 141:2; Isa 1:11-17; Hos 6:6; Mic 6:6-8; 1QS 9:3-5). This understanding, of course, was linked to the fairly widespread ideas that the true temple was spiritual, formed not by a physical building but by the community of worshipers themselves (1QH 6:25-28; 1QpHab12; 1QS 5:5-6; 8:4-10; 9:3-9; 4QFlor 1:1-7; 4QpPs37 2:16) and that the people as a whole, and not (only) a separate class of ordained priests constitute a priesthood (Exod 19:6; Isa 61:6; 2 Macc 2:17; Jub. 16:18; 33:20; T. Lev. Gk frag 67; Philo, Sobr. 66; Abr. 56). Rather than contrasting Christian "spiritual" sacrifice with Jewish "material" sacrifice, this passage illustrates that 1 Peter stands within a particular stream of Jewish tradition itself.

The worship life of the Christian community, in both its liturgical and everyday forms, though directed to God is already a testimony to the world. But the church also has a mission more directly oriented to the world: in word and deed to proclaim God's "mighty acts" (*arētas*; 2:9). This term, which is still related to the praise of God and is not without a vertical orientation, refers to God's acts in history, not to divine qualities (cf. Isa 43:21 LXX, reflected in this passage). As the readers are a "chosen race" and a "holy nation" not on the basis of nature, genetics, or social standing, but by the act of God, so their testimony to the world is not a matter of general truths or principles, but the declaration of God's saving acts in history, from creation to eschaton (cf. Appendix 1: The Narrative World of 1 Peter).

The author addresses readers who must decide how to live as faithful Christians in the midst of a suspicious and hostile society. He has responded to this need not by immediately giving a list of specific "do's and don'ts," but by presenting, on a grand scale, a historical understanding of the readers' new identity "in Christ" and the basic orientation it calls for: hope, holiness, love, and nourishment in the divine word that sustains Christian existence. This theological grounding has not been randomly presented, but with a view to the specific calls to Christian action that are about to begin, but which could not be addressed until the readers' identity was established. Who you *are* is basic to what you are to *do*. Of the thirty-five direct imperatives in 1 Peter, only five have been met so far (1:13, 15, 17, 22; 2:2). The emphasis is about to shift, as, on the basis of the indicative of God's act and the believers' new identity, specific responses are given to the question of "How, then, should we live?"

Christian Existence and Conduct in the Given Structures of Society (2:11–3:12)

A new unit begins at 2:11, indicated by the direct address "beloved," the hortatory "I urge you" signaling the transition from the more indicative part to the more parenetic part of the letter (cf. Rom 12:1, where the same word [*parakaleō* "I appeal to you" "I urge you"] serves the same function at the same structural point in the letter). The unit that begins here concludes at 3:12, with the "finally" *(to de telos)* of 3:8 signaling the conclusion of a subsection, and the scriptural citation 3:8-12 functioning as conclusion to the preceding instruction on the pattern already established

(1:24; 2:9-10). The author's subunits within 2:11–3:12 are not sharply marked, but the structure appears to be:

2:11-12 General introduction (to all).

2:13-17 General instruction: subordination to the given social structures, illustrated by respect for governmental authority.

2:18-25 Specific instruction to slaves, modulating into christological affirmations that provide a model for all.

3:1-7 Specific instruction to wives and husbands.

3:8-12 General instruction to all, concluded with extensive Scripture citation.

At 3:13 the author then begins afresh with a deepened discussion of unjust suffering.

The author addresses the readers' Christian responsibility in society in the context of their particular situation. In Asia Minor at the end of the first century, as in the ancient world generally, religion did not belong to the privatized sphere of individual lives, but was an integral aspect of the life of community. Every public occasion, festival, business or guild meeting, and private social gathering had religious rites integrated into it that Christians (and Jews) could only regard as "lawless idolatry" (4:3). The readers had been converted to a new faith that required them to withdraw from participation in the public and family religious rites of their community. When they did this, "as [they] were bound to do, . . . they ceased to be members of the community in any effective sense; the old ties of social relationship were broken" (Beare 1958, 102; this may be overstated with regard to slaves, who had little choice). Their religious convictions made them subject to the charge of antisocial behavior or worse: atheism, hatred of humanity, treason, lack of patriotism. Thus the network of connections of race, people, and nation that had formed their previous community was broken, and they found themselves to be like "sojourners and resident aliens" within their own previous community. This is the point of the address with which this section begins, as it was of the concluding metaphors of the previous section (2:9-10). The readers are given a new social code giving them instructions for continuing their life within a society that is now suspicious and critical of them.

Hermeneutical Approach: Six Principles

These instructions are problematic to modern readers. Before we consider the details of this instruction, it is advisable to consider approaches by which they may be heard and understood in their own context and how (or whether) they may be appropriated as instruction for Christian life today. Some contemporary Christians, wishing to respect the authority of the Bible, attempt to follow the instructions literally—as did the advocates of slavery in early-nineteenth-century America. Other modern readers (perhaps the majority) are puzzled, embarrassed, or resentful that 1 Peter instructs citizens, slaves, and wives to be subordinate to those who are above them in the social structure, raising no questions about the validity of the structures and institutions themselves. Let it be clearly said: This biblical text does instruct people to be subject to governing authorities, slaves to be subject even to harsh masters, wives to be subject to their husbands. The following comments are not an effort to "get around" or "water down" what the Bible clearly says, just as they are not an attempt to paint biblical instruction in dark and repressive terms we may then use as the foil for our own more liberal ideologies. There are a number of considerations, however, that facilitate our hearing the text's own agenda in its own terms, rather than coopting it as grist for our own mill either positively ("we must do it because it's in the Bible"; "family values") or negatively ("we must reject it as part of biblical patriarchy and imperialism").

1. The Text Is to Be Interpreted Historically as a Letter
   (Not An Essay)

Historical Perspective: It is important to interpret 1 Peter in general and 2:11–3:12 in particular as a *letter*. The text before us is not a programmatic essay on "the state," "slavery," or "the role of women." We have before us a letter instructing Christians in a particular situation on how they should (in the author's view) fulfill their Christian calling within the structures of society assumed to be given. While the structures themselves are not challenged, neither are they justified, and *unjust* suffering can happen within them. The question addressed in 1 Peter is not whether the Roman Empire, the institution of slavery, or the patriarchal family should exist, but how Christians in Asia Minor at the end of the first Christian century should live out their faith within these given social structures (cf. Selwyn 1947, 104; Goppelt 1993, 172; Brox 1979, 139). The letter allows the modern reader to see a *specific application* of the kerygma mediated by the Pauline/Petrine tradition in a particular situation, a social situation different from that of the modern reader. We modern readers must make our own decisions on how to apply this kerygma to our situations. We decide *for* ourselves—there are no specific instructions for our time in the Bible, here or elsewhere—but we do not decide *by* ourselves. We can learn something by listening with a sympathetic ear to the instructions of our ancestors in the faith as they struggled with translating the apostolic faith into concrete attitudes and actions in their situations. This is the meaning of historical study of the Bible from a theological perspective.

The "Household Code": One dimension of the historical situation in which this text was composed was the prevalence in the hellenistic world of tables of household duties, known since Luther as "Haustafel" (singular) or "Haustafeln" (plural). While it is probably not the case that 1 Peter takes over and modifies a specific household code, it is likely that both author and readers were aware of such codes, and that the text before us was both composed and read in the light of the pervasiveness of such codes. To perceive the text in its original context, the modern reader needs to be aware of the influence of such codes on early Christian literature.

Already in the fourth century BCE Aristotle had discussed social responsibility in terms of master/slave, husband/wife, father/children (Aristotle, *Politics* 1.1252a 7-9, 24-28; 1252b 9-31; 1253b-1254a). This discussion, in form and content, became a topos repeated for centuries, being especially prevalent in the late–first century CE (cf. Balch 1981, 33-38, 51-59). The *Haustafel* became common. It is surprising that the Old Testament and Palestinian

Judaism, though concerned with the household and the state, disregarded the household code. Hellenistic Judaism, on the other hand, adopted and adapted the *Haustafel* as a means of ethical instruction (Crouch 1972, 74-119, 147; Best 1971, 30-31).

Paul, a hellenistic Jew turned Christian, did not utilize the *Haustafel* form, though he is concerned to translate the gospel into family and civic life (cf., e.g., Rom 13; 1 Cor 7; Philemon). The *Haustafel* first emerges in Christian literature in the Deutero-Pauline literature, and is found thereafter in a spectrum of documents otherwise mostly confined to the Pauline stream of Christian tradition (Eph 5:22–6:9; Col 3:18–4:1; 1 Tim 2–3; 5:1–6:3; Titus 2:1-10; *Barn.* 19.5-7; *1 Clem.* 1.3; 21.6-9; *Did.* 4.9-11; Pol. *Phil.* 4.1–6.1). It is striking that when the *Haustafel* enters the Christian stream, even though the patriarchal order continues to be presupposed, instruction is given in terms of mutuality and not merely hierarchy. This is explicitly the case in the Colossian and Ephesian *Haustafeln,* and implied in the others, including 1 Peter. In the Christian literature, slaves, women, and children are addressed as persons in their own right, not merely as subjects to masters, husbands, or fathers.

The instructions in 1 Pet 2:11–3:12 are thus not merely ad hoc formulations by the author of how he thinks Christians should live, but reflect his own adoption and adaptation of material from a lively Christian discussion that had preceded him, a discussion of which both he and his readers were aware. The modern reader should keep in mind that in this section 1 Peter is not formulating new rules for Christian conduct, but is offering his own adaptation of a development that had already had an extensive and varied history.

2. The Text in Its Entirety Is Directed to "All"

Just as the whole letter was addressed to all the churches in an extensive area (1:1), so this section 2:11–3:12, including the instructions to slaves and wives, is addressed to the whole church. The texts in 1 Peter addressed to specific groups are framed by texts addressed to the whole community (2:11-17; 3:8). But this address to "all" also permeates the middle section that on the surface appears to be addressed only to slaves and women. Before slaves are addressed directly, the whole community is reminded that they are all free in Christ, all slaves of God (2:16). The direct address to slaves of verse 18 immediately modulates into generalizing instruction to "one" (*tis*, v. 19), just as the direct address "you" (vv. 20-21) modulates into the inclusive "we" and "our" (v. 24). The christological grounding in verses 21-25 clearly relates not just to slaves, but to the community as a whole. What is said to slaves in 2:18-25 is said to all in 3:13–4:11. The conclusion of the letter (4:17-19) applies to all what is here applied to slaves, and the general demeanor commended to wives in relation to their husbands is intended also as a model for the church as a whole in its relation to worldly authorities in general (cf. Michaels 1988, 171 and commentary on 3:1-6 below). The whole community stands under the command to mutual love and respect (1:22; 2:17). As the author concludes the section containing the celebrated "in his steps" text (2:21), the reader has already quite properly forgotten that formally it is addressed "only" to slaves, and has rightly understood it as being addressed to all Christians (cf. Michaels 1988, 135).

Since 2:13–3:7 doesn't cover all cases and classes, instructions to slaves and wives are to be taken as *illustrative*. It is not as though there is nothing here for bachelors, widows, divorcées, children, or employees. The whole community is to learn from what is said to slaves and wives. This corresponds to the indirect communication inherent in the letter form as such, especially in the case of a pseudonymous letter. The reader, ancient and modern, overhears "Peter" instructing slaves and wives, but the message is to all.

3. The Text of the Whole Letter Is Oriented to the Weak and Vulnerable; It Sees the World from the Underside

Why pick on slaves and wives? The question is asked from a society in which things are mostly seen from the upper side. But 1 Peter is addressed to a church that saw the world from the underside, where the church as such, whatever the previous status of its members, now is marginalized and is, as a whole, in a weak and vulnerable situation with regard to the power structures of society. Thus the situation of the church as a whole and the

Christian life as such can be addressed in instructions to those who most clearly represent social weakness and vulnerability.

The slaves and women here addressed have already made a courageous decision to join a despised foreign cult that is not the religion of their non-Christian masters and husbands. That is, they have already shown that they are *not submissive*. Their profession of the Christian faith can itself be seen as a form of social protest. It can also be that they simply believed the gospel to be true, and were prepared to take the consequences. This makes them a model for the church as a whole.

4. The Text Does Not Merely Command Docility, Submission, and Obedience, but Sub-Ordination

What is called for here is not mindless robotic obedience or servile cowering that denies one's own identity and sense of worth, which is provided not by status in society but by rebirth and incorporation into God's saving plan for history as members of the holy people of God (1:3–2:10). The key word is "be subordinate" (*hypotassō*; 2:13, 18; 3:1, 5, 22; 5:5), related in both Greek and English to the word for "order" *(tassō, taxis)*, a broader and more flexible word than *hypokoē,* "obedience." To be subordinate is to fit into a given order; insubordination is to rebel and refuse to fit in.

First Peter accepts the view of the Bible as a whole that God the creator is the God who brings order from chaos (Gen 1–2; cf. "order" *[taxis]* for the fixed courses of heavenly bodies, Judg 5:20; Hab 3:11 LXX). The Pauline tradition in which 1 Peter stands emphasizes that God the creator is a God of order (e.g., 1 Cor 14:33, 40). First Peter's own emphasis on God as creator includes the implication that order itself is from God (2:13; 4:19). But there is no way to have order without having suborder, that is, without fitting into the given order. It is a sociological truism that no society can exist without some form of subordination, without its members fitting into a given structure (Simmel 1950, 181-303). First Peter presents a picture of the world in which God has subordinated the transcendent world to Christ, with angels and authorities subject to him (3:22).

Order Is from God. Order as such is from God the creator; but no particular order is from God. European theologians of the past generation who resisted the Nazi regime and then had to come to terms with the Soviet regime were in situations analogous to that of the author and readers of 1 Peter, and found that the Petrine texts did indeed address the realities of their daily task of being faithful to God while living in a hostile and suspicious social structure. The author of 1 Peter does not divinize the established social order (contrast Rom 13), just as he does not demonize it (contrast Rev 13). "God remains the creator even of our fallen world" (Barth 1957, 308). God the Lord of history from creation to eschaton is the God of order, but the states and social institutions that have developed in history to express this order are not as such the divine order. Order is a historical (not ontological) entity. In this fallen world, formed by the "futile ways inherited from your ancestors" (1:18), an ordered world must be a selfish world. Thus "all forms of community life, the best and the worst alike, stand equally under the judgment of God" (Bultmann 1924, 42). The socialization process of every family, clan, tribe, city, state, and nation is geared to transform the inherent selfishness of every human being into a selfishness oriented to the larger social unit rather than the individual. But since this larger social unit is always only a segment of the human community defined by boundaries of tribe, race, nation, class, and ideology, this necessary process of fitting into the given social order also inevitably develops an us/them orientation. The price of having order rather than chaos is to have a society geared toward selfishness. "In its reality the state is always organized selfishness" (Brunner 1947, 460), always oriented inwardly to "us" rather than outwardly to "others/all," always held together by violence or the threat of violence. The social orders of this world make human life possible, and as such are the gift of God. Some orders are better than others—vastly better—but no particular order can claim to be from God.

Within this fallen world, the orders of society and the social demand to conform to them are socially transmitted, for example, by the language and symbol system of a given society. One is born into a given social structure with its confirming language and symbol system. This means that when a new community arises, with a new vision of reality projected and transmitted by a new language and symbol system, this constitutes a threat to the old world (cf. Petersen 1985, 53-63). The faith of early Christians such as the author of 1 Peter was expressed in a view of the world in which God the creator is lord of the whole of history of which Christ is the defining center. They understood this view of creation-to-eschaton history not as a subjective projection but as representing the real world (cf. Appendix 1: The Narrative World of 1 Peter). Those who play institutional roles in the social order of the present fallen world know themselves charged to maintain the symbol system that validates it, and recognize that the Christian message presents them with a different world (Acts 17:6). The authority of the emperor and governors, the institution of slavery, the patriarchal family, all represented the Roman standard in the hellenistic world. To oppose it, to destabilize it, is unpatriotic and disruptive, precisely because this questions the *order* of the world.

First Peter's instructions in 2:11–3:12 should be seen within the context of the tension created by a community that knows it lives by a different vision of what the "real world" is like than that projected by the social order around it. How do those born anew relate to the orders of the world into which they were originally born? As the continuing people of God situated in this world, they are not to make an exodus from the world, withdrawing Qumran-like from the normal social world. They are not to retire from social obligations and cultivate their own interior spiritual life. They are not to ignore the world as they contemplate the imminent end of history. Rather, just as the exodus community had social rules (e.g., the Pentateuch's covenant code of Exod 20–23), so the new people of God are given instructions on how to live responsibly as Christians within the given structures of society.

There is thus a profound dialectic involved in 1 Peter's instructions. On the one hand, they must not conform to the old world, its values and its structures, as indicated by all the preceding part of the letter establishing their identity as the holy people of God distinct from the world. "Don't conform" is the fundamental theological message of 1:3–2:10 (cf. especially 1:14 and its relation to Rom 12:1). Thus when the instructions of the present section emphasize Christian responsibility to be subordinate, to respect the given order, to fit in, they cannot be properly understood except as in dialectical tension with the larger context identifying them as those who do not fit in and cannot. The exhortation to fit in is given by and to congenital "misfits" who have been given the freedom and responsibility to choose. If they heed the instruction of this letter and choose to "fit in" as a dimension of their responsibility for the Christian mission, their choice is an expression of their freedom rather than an alternative to it.

5. The Text Is to Be Understood in Its Wider Theological Context

The social code of 1 Peter must be understood not only within its own larger theological context, but within its larger stream of tradition and presuppositions. First Peter stands in the Pauline stream, presupposing but not parroting the Pauline kerygma of justification, freedom, and equality. First Peter does not develop the Pauline theology as doctrine, but presupposes it as the basis for practice. The Pauline understanding of justification by faith is not a theological doctrine to be elaborated theoretically, but is the basis for declaring that all Christians are free, all are slaves. As those who are already freed and accepted before God, their identity does not depend on the social status others attribute to them. They are freed from obsession with their self image to place their lives in the service of the Christian mission (cf. Rom 6; 1 Cor 8–10). That husbands and wives are coheirs of the grace of life presupposes the reality of Gal 3:27-28, and sets them free to live in accord with the social structures of their situation for the sake of the church's mission.

Even if one disagrees with the view advocated here, that 1 Peter stands in the Pauline tradition and is to be understood as presupposing it, it is still the case that for the modern reader the witness of the Pauline kerygma is presupposed. Whether or not Paul's understanding of the kerygma, justification, and Christian life as expressed in Romans and 1 Corinthians was current for the author and his readers in Asia Minor, they form part of the canonical context within which our own interpretation of 1 Peter is to be worked out.

While not the primary factor, it is the case for 1 Peter as it was for Paul that their eschatological perspective inhibits thinking in terms of reforming society (for Paul, cf. 1 Cor 7; for 1 Peter, cf. 4:7). First Peter is thoroughly eschatological, with "hope" as a synonym for Christian existence as such (1:3 etc.). While the author resists the temptation to allow eschatology to cut the nerve of social responsibility, it is also the case that when one expects the present order to pass away shortly, as did both author and readers of 1 Peter, there is little motivation to attempt to change the present social order.

6. Mission, Not Sub-Mission, Is the Focus of This Text

In the commentary below we will note that the Christian mission is not the only motive introduced for adhering to the instructions in the social code. But the Christian mission to outsiders, not internal troubles or concerns, is the primary motivation for Christians to live by the social code here presented. The point is not social conformity as such, as though that were a virtue in itself, but "to live a life in accord with social custom to the extent that it is possible without compromising their faith, so as not to give more offense than is necessary" (Achtemeier 1996, 194). The instructions of 1 Pet 2:11–3:12 are directed to a church that is not oriented to looking inward to its own sense of status and self-esteem, but outward to the Christian mission. The whole section is prefaced with a concern that Christians so live that outsiders who now speak evil of the Christian community will come to glorify God (2:12). The challenge is to remove a false stumbling block, so that people may decide for or against the truth of the Christian message without being put off by (their perception of) the cultural forms associated with it. To be good citizens subordinate to the civil authorities is to silence the objections of outsiders, that is, it is in the service of the Christian mission (2:15). By voluntarily living in accord with the patriarchal family structure, wives may win over husbands who have not been won by preaching to them (3:1). Members of the people of God on pilgrimage through history must take responsibility for the community's witness to the mighty acts of God (2:9). This evangelistic, missionary orientation is probably the explanation for the absence of instructions to children traditional in *Haustafeln* (cf. Eph 6:1-3; Col 3:20). In the social situation to which 1 Peter was directed, it was hardly possible that Christian children could be called upon to relate to non-Christian parents as a dimension of the evangelistic witness of the church. Throughout, the emphasis is on mission, not on *sub*mission. As in the example of Christ (2:21-25), submission is for the sake of mission.

General Exhortation to All (2:11-12)

This brief transitional section is theologically very important. The address "beloved" is rare in non-Christian hellenistic literature, but common in the New Testament epistles (30x), especially in the Pauline (12x) and Johannine streams (6x). The phrase connotes not only that they are beloved by the author and other Christians (as 1 Thess 2:8), but by God (as Rom 1:7); "dear friends" (NIV) is inadequate. "Beloved," like "resident aliens and sojourners," reminds them of God's act and their place as God's elect people (see on 1:1), contrasting them with "the Gentiles"—although ethnically they themselves are Gentiles. Just as the problem always faced by the Jewish Diaspora was how to maintain Jewish tradition, practice, and testimony in an environment dominated by Gentiles, so the Christian author now faces the specific social responsibilities of the Christian people of God in the Gentile world (cf. Martin 1994, 156).

The turn toward social responsibility marked by this paragraph includes a shift in terminology. The vocabulary analogous to Qumran and Palestinian Judaism virtually disappears from this point on (Goppelt 1993, 154; he has overemphasized this valid point, for there are reflections of Qumran tradition in the later sections also, e.g., 5:1-5). The life to which they are called is no longer characterized primarily by the biblical vocabulary of holiness, but by the hellenistic categories of "good works" and "doing good," expressed in the hellenistic vocabulary of "desires of the flesh" that war against "the soul." Although the language is that of hellenistic dualism, the underlying thought is that of the biblical anthropology affirmed by Paul. "Soul" is not the "true inner self," in contrast to "evil flesh." The author's perspective, in contrast to hellenistic

anthropology, is made especially clear in 4:2, where "human desires" are contrasted with "the will of God." It is not the case that
one "spiritual" part of a person, the "soul," is contrasted with the
"fleshly" part. Here as elsewhere in 1 Peter, the soul is the whole
person (cf. 1:24; 3:18; 4:1-2), and the evils warned against are not
carnal but a matter of one's demeanor as a whole. "The point here
is more the notion that the Christians are caught in a war of
cultures, not in a war within themselves" (Achtemeier 1996, 176,
n. 51). The readers' pagan neighbors malign them as criminals and
adherents of a foreign superstition (cf. Tacitus, *Ann* 15:44; Sue-
tonius, *Nero* 16:2). Just as Jews had been challenged to do in the
past (*T. Naph.* 8:4), so Christians must demonstrate by "good
works" that this is not the case (cf. Matt 5:16). We should not too
easily suppose that it was always a matter of immoral Romans
resentful of the righteous lives of Christians. Moral Romans sus-
pected Christians of immorality. "Abstaining from passions of the
flesh" means not only "don't go back to the old life," but "live *up*
to Roman morality."

The "doing good" here called for (a key term in 1 Peter) is not
mere personal piety, but an active missionary role (cf. 2:15) that
will eventuate in their present detractors not only changing their
minds about the Christians, but glorifying God. "Doing good" here
means right conduct as judged by the norm of the Christian mission,
"doing right." It is not clear whether the "day of visitation" (cf.
NRSV margin) pictures a this-worldly conversion of contemporary
critics, or the eschatological judgment in which present unbelievers
will find mercy. It is clear from this preamble that the instructions
on social responsibility are oriented outwardly toward the ultimate
good of others, not inwardly to personal piety or communal purity.

Instructions to All on Attitude to God, the State, and Each Other
(2:13-17)

The section begins with a comprehensive command for the
readers to be subordinate to every "human creature." Subordination does not mean blind obedience, but rather finding and responsibly exercising one's proper role within a given social structure (see
above). The phrase translated "human institution" (NRSV) or

"authority instituted among men" (NIV) is literally "human crea-tion/creature" (cf. Achtemeier 1996, 179-80), a combination of words unique not only to the New Testament but to all literature. While the word translated "creation" can be used for human activities such as the founding of a city, institutions themselves were not designated by this term. Since elsewhere in the Bible "creation" always refers to God's act, and since God-as-creator is important to 1 Peter (4:19), it is better to see the phrase as referring to the structures of society as part of God's creation, yet in such a way that they are not divinized (cf. the introduction to 2:11–3:12 above). They are to be elements of the historical process of which God the creator is Lord. The institutions of history are human institutions, therefore changeable, not ultimate, not part of an order of creation fixed by God. The orders are established by humans-as-creatures, part of the history of which God is creator and Lord, and therefore historically conditioned and not ultimate. The world is understood not from itself and its own claims, but from the God who is revealed in Christ. Christians can in good conscience respect and fit into them without considering them ultimate, and can still maintain a critical distance because only God is to be wor-shiped/feared. Christians can "fit in" as free persons who at the same time are servants of God (2:16). The call to be subordinate is not despite the reality of their freedom in Christ, but on the basis of it; precisely because they are free, they can be instructed to exercise their own responsible decision to fit into the given struc-tures of society. They are subordinate to governmental authorities, including pagan Roman rulers, not as a strategy, compulsion, compromise, indifference, transcendent superiority, or resignation, but as an aspect of Christian service ("for the Lord's sake," 2:13) to the God who has called us (like the *prophets*) as "slaves of God." Karl Barth, who had resisted Hitler and Nazism, in the years after World War II counseled faithful Christians in the German Demo-cratic Republic to accommodate themselves to their Marxist sur-roundings. Responding to the question of whether Christians in East Germany could take the loyalty oath to the officially atheist Marxist state, Barth replied with a clear "yes." " 'Loyalty' to this established order means honest readiness to recognize its existence and to take one's place in it . . . [it] does not mean approval of the ideology. . . . The First Epistle of Peter, I should think, is a portion of the New Testament that today is read with special attentiveness in the East German Republic by all who want to be true Christians" (Barth 1959, 49, 67-68).

First Peter here understands the freedom of the Christian life in Pauline terms, in which freedom for human beings can never be absolute, but represents a change of masters that excludes both libertinism and servility (Rom 6:15-23; 1 Cor 7:21-23; Gal 5:13-14). There are also numerous points of contact with Paul's exhortation in Rom 13:1-10, including not only specific concepts but also exact vocabulary (more apparent in the Greek than in most translations): "every soul" (Rom 13:1/1 Pet 2:11), "be subject" (Rom 13:1/1 Pet 2:13), "authority" (Rom 13:1/1 Pet 2:14 ["emperor," "governors"]) "no authority except from God" (Rom 13:1/1 Pet 2:13 ["human creation"]), emperor as supreme (same word, *hyperechō*, Rom 13:1 "governing"/1 Pet 2:13 "supreme"). Both Rom 13 and 1 Peter declare that rulers punish only the evil and those who do good have nothing to fear, both speak in the eschatological context of coming judgment, both appeal for submission for the sake of conscience (Romans) or the Lord (1 Peter), both command that honor be given to those to whom it is due, and regard love as the supreme command.

While reflecting Paul's instruction in Romans, which were also current in the Roman church from which 1 Peter writes, 1 Peter also has elements distinctive from Romans, especially his omission of Paul's declaration that the government authorities have been instituted by God, and that whoever resists them resists God (Rom 13:1-2). The emperor is not to be dishonored, despite his claims to divinity, but is to be honored, as are all human beings as part of God's creation. But only God is called Lord *(kyrios)* in contrast to the emperor as part of the "human creation" (2:13). Likewise, while all people are to be honored, only God is to be feared (2:17; cf. 1:17; 2:18; 3:2, 6, 14, 16). In the concluding paraphrase of Prov 24:21 in which the Old Testament text had used the same verb with respect to God and king, 1 Peter pointedly uses "fear" only of God.

Instructions to Slaves (And to All) (2:18-25)

The author now comes to the "household code" tradition proper, in which instruction to the whole church is given in the form of commands to slaves, wives, and husbands (for general hermeneutical perspectives, see above). The New Testament household codes are distinctive in addressing slaves as those who are humans in their own right, with their own responsibility, just as are their masters. While there are some precedents in hellenistic Judaism and Stoicism that affirm the equality and full personhood of slaves (e.g., Philo *Spec. Leg.* 2.67-68; 3.137), no pre-Christian household codes address slaves directly. All New Testament household codes directly address slaves as responsible members of the inclusive Christian community. However, in contrast to other New Testament household codes, 1 Peter presents no analogous instructions to masters (cf., Eph 6:9; Col 4:1). This is not because there were no Christian slave owners in all of Asia Minor (cf., e.g., Philemon!), although most of 1 Peter's addressees probably did belong to the lower strata of society. Rather, the situation of Christian slaves of unchristian masters here addressed was symbolic of the situation of the church as a whole, which was marginalized and vulnerable.

The situation of Christian master and unchristian slave, though it sometimes existed, was both rare and unrepresentative of the circumstances of all Christians in Asia Minor. Slaves were often thought to be pilferers, liars, and irresponsible in their assigned duties and were sometimes abused on the assumption that this was so. This perspective was now applied by society to the Christian community as a whole, who were often unjustly insulted and accused. Despite misunderstanding and maltreatment, the readers are instructed to continue in doing good.

The section is thus paradigmatic for the whole Christian community, which has been addressed as "slaves" *(douloi)* who are nonetheless "free" (2:16). The particular social class instructed here is addressed as "household slaves" *(oiketai)*, in part because *Haustafel* tradition is here directly used, but also because of the overarching metaphor of the church as the household of faith.

Slavery in the hellenistic world must not be thought of in terms of the deplorable circumstances represented by slavery in the southern United States in the pre–Civil War period. People became slaves by being born to a slave woman, by selling themselves or being sold into slavery to satisfy a debt, or by military conquest. Racism was not a factor. Many slaves had managerial positions, and were better educated than their masters. One could not necessarily distinguish slaves and free in a crowd in the marketplace. It is not the case that there was always a wide gap between the status of the slave and the free person, nor that slaves were always badly treated, nor that all slaves wanted to be free (Bartchy 1973, 37-120). But neither should the picture be romanticized. Slaves were without most rights, from the legal point of view were considered property rather than persons, and were sometimes abused. When 1 Peter speaks of unjust suffering, the slave is the model for a social reality.

The reality of unjust suffering is not explained, excused, or justified. There is no call in 1 Peter to defend or perpetuate injustice. Yet slaves are instructed to fit into the given social system, and not only to endure unjust suffering, but to do good. In contemporary North America most Christians have a kind of freedom, power, social status, and influence that not only makes it impossible for us to translate this instruction directly into our own situation, but makes it difficult to hear it as ever having had any validity in its own time and place. We are rightly reluctant to encourage those who are suffering injustice to continue to do so. At this point it may be helpful to hear this text from the perspective of those Christians in the former German Democratic Republic while the Iron Curtain was still in place. Like the household slaves addressed in 1 Peter, they had no power, and many of them had no desire to change the social structure itself. The question was how to live a faithful Christian life within the given social conditions. The exposition of 1 Peter by Fritz Neugebauer, an East German New Testament scholar and pastor of that period, rightly understands this text not as a call to sink into passivity. It was and continues to be not a matter of either suffering or acting, but of suffering as action. In 1 Peter, those who suffer are called to action—not revolution, not revenge, but "doing good." The exhortation is not to endure suffering even to death—the situation is not that extreme (contrast

Revelation)—but to hold fast in doing good. "In fact the danger for those who suffer injustice is that they cease to do good, that they either do nothing at all, or do the wrong thing" (Neugebauer 1987, 129). Many contemporary Christians in China, South and Central America, and other parts of the world can still hear these texts with ears more attuned to their original setting, and can help their brothers and sisters in North America and Europe to hear them afresh.

The author of 1 Peter chooses this point, precisely in the midst of instruction purportedly directed to the most beleaguered and vulnerable group in society, to introduce his most profound discussion of the motivation for such a Christian life. He does not explicitly repeat the missionary motive that frames the whole (see above), and does not base his appeal on the likelihood that patient enduring of unjust suffering by the slave will win the master over to the faith. Pragmatic reasons, even noble evangelistic and missionary ones, are missing here. Just as Jesus did not suffer silently as a strategy, so slaves and the Christian community at large are not encouraged to think that by innocent suffering they will win over their bad masters.

Rather, the author speaks of the fear of God (2:18 continues the thought of 2:17), by which he does not mean servile fear or the threat of divine punishment, but as in 1:17 and 3:2, the worshipful reverence of living one's life before God. One thinks through one's responsibility in the given situation in the light of living before God, not merely before the court of human opinion. This is the meaning of "consciousness of God" (2:19). Thus the difficult sentence of 2:19 is translated in a variety of ways in modern translations, but is best rendered literally: "This is grace from God" (so Goppelt 1993, 190, 195-200; Brox 1979, 127). The idea that unjust suffering gains "credit" before God, on the analogy of Luke 6:32, is at the farthest pole from the author's thought. He stands in the Pauline tradition in which unjust suffering for the sake of Christ is understood as a gift from God (cf. Phil 1:29, which uses a form of the same word for grace, *echaristhē*). The statement is not made casually. The author will conclude his letter by declaring that the theme of the whole letter is that the situation of unjust suffering in which the Christians of Asia Minor stand is in fact the grace of God (5:12). Such a paradoxical and scandalous affirmation is not commonsense wisdom. It is immediately grounded in a profound christological declaration that constitutes the theological center and fulcrum of the letter. As elsewhere, the life to which Christians are called (2:21) is not based on commonsense empirical observation of the world understood in terms of itself, but only on the basis that the Christ-event has indeed happened and that the world must be understood from that perspective. Unjust suffering is not just a strategy in 1 Peter. It is inherently right, as revealed in Christ. The nature of God and the universe embraces unjust suffering. This is the polar opposite of saying that Christians may cause, contribute to, or excuse unjust suffering. But when they are called upon to endure it, they can do so as grace from God, as was the cross itself (2:19-20; 5:12).

This is declared to be true not on the basis of the author's own experience or insight, but on the basis of Scripture as already interpreted in Christian tradition. The text of 2:21-25 has often, and rightly, been understood as a traditional Christian hymn adapted to the present context by the author, sometimes as part of a larger hymnic composition also found in 1:18-21 and/or 3:18-22. That 2:21-25 is not composed ad hoc, but is the adaptation of traditional material, does seem clear from the presence of relative clauses, from the shift from second to first person, and from the horizon of the piece that seems to go beyond the immediate parenetical point. As we shall see, the last item may be exaggerated, but 2:21-25 does seem to be adapted from a traditional hymn or creed—which, however, can no longer be reconstructed in detail.

◊ ◊ ◊ ◊

The passage pictures Christ as the suffering servant of Isa 53. The details and vocabulary do not come from historical memory of what happened during the trial and crucifixion of Jesus, nor from the author's adoption of Pauline theology, but from the Scripture. Contrary to popular opinion, Isa 53 was not immediately adopted by earliest Christianity as a vehicle for expressing Christian theology of the atonement. It is here interpreted more extensively, and more specifically, than in any other New Testament passage (1 Pet 2:22/Isa 53:9; 2:24/Isa 53:5, 11; 2:25/Isa 53:6, 10; cf. Schelke 1988, 83; Goppelt 1993, 208-10). Although Paul too regards the death of Jesus as an atonement for human sin, and cites texts from Isa 52:13–53:12 (Rom 10:16; 15:21), Paul does not bring these together: he never uses texts from Isa 53 as support for his understanding of atonement. Conversely, 1 Peter does not here have the Pauline understanding of sin. The vocabulary of sin in this passage is taken from Isa 53, not from Paul, and does not focus on the atonement as the divine response to universal human sinfulness, but on sin as particular acts of wrongdoing that Christian slaves, and Christians generally, are tempted to perpetrate in response to the bad treatment they are receiving. Although the author of 1 Peter appears to have read Romans, 1 Pet 2:21-25 is not derived from reflection on Paul's doctrine of sin as expressed in Romans. The eight occurrences of "sin" vocabulary are oriented in a different direction than Pauline theology (cf. 2:20, 22, 24 [2x]; 3:18; 4:1, 8, 18).

The passage presents a profound christological grounding for Christian slaves responding to unjust suffering with patient endurance and doing good rather than retaliating, as a model for the Christian life generally. Christ himself is the example for this (2:21). The word translated "example" *(hypogrammon)* refers to the sketch, tracing pad, or outline used to teach children to write the alphabet. It is thus a guideline to be used in one's own composition, not a mechanical pattern to be duplicated. Similarly, to follow in someone's steps means to move in the same direction they are going, rather than a matter of reproducing details (Kelly 1969, 120; Schelke 1988, 81). Thus the call to adopt Christ as example is not analogous to "a child's placing foot after foot into the prints of his father in the snow" (so Davids 1990, 110), but more like making our own creative adaptation of a pattern. It was common for hellenistic moral philosophers to present themselves as examples of their own teaching, a pattern followed by Paul (e.g., 1 Cor 4:16; 11:1; 1 Thess 1:6; cf. Perkins 1994, 121). The readers were likely aware that both Peter and Paul had suffered for the faith, but the author of 1 Peter holds up only Christ as example. The manner in which Christ bore unjust suffering is the model for Christian slaves and Christians generally.

It is important to see the profundity of the Christology involved in this example. Since it is Christ who provides the example, it is not merely an idealistic model to be followed as though it were somehow inherently right. As the noble Maccabean martyrs suffered unjustly, they denounced their persecutors and promised divine vengeance (e.g., 4 Macc 8:12–9:25). Why not adopt their example of courageous resistance and denunciation of injustice rather than that of Jesus? The answer is not a matter of choice on the basis of commonsense wisdom, but of the ultimate revelation of God's nature revealed in the Christ-event. For the author of 1 Peter, Jesus is more than a human example to be imitated; the Christ-event is the saving act in which God both acts for the salvation of humanity and reveals the depths of the divine nature. The christological framework within which the example of Jesus is set is thus not extraneous material that happened to be related to the hymnic tradition adopted by the author, nor does it a represent a speculative christological penchant, but is rather the central reason he is drawn to it in the first place. "Jesus suffered as an example" and "Jesus suffered for others" are two sides of the same *christological* coin.

The suffering of Christ for sinful humanity (2:21, 24) is a revelation of the nature of God, so that *God*-language is used of Jesus. The section concludes (2:25) by applying to Jesus the biblical imagery of God as the divine shepherd (Jer 23:3-6; 31:10; Ezek 34:11, 23-24; 37:24; Job 20:29; Wis 1:6), as happens in other late New Testament texts (John 10; Heb 13:20). Throughout 1 Peter, language about Christ modulates into language about God and vice versa, so that "Lord" is used indistinguishably of Christ or God. Thus the "Lord" is the "living . . . God" (1:23), but in the same context the "word of the Lord" is the Christian message (1:25). In 3:15 the "Lord" of the Isaiah quotation referring to God has become "Christ as Lord." In 1:8 love for *Christ* stands in place of love for *God*. In the immediate context of the passage here discussed, the readers are charged to be subject to every "human institution" "for the Lord's sake" (2:13); the reader should not ask whether this refers to Christ or God, for the two images flow together in the author's theology. This means that in 2:21-25 the suffering of Christ for others is not a matter of three parties, God/Christ/others, in which *Christ* suffers so that *God* can be merciful, but is a two-party transaction: in the suffering of Christ, God is present and active (cf. pp. 84-85, 90, 152 on 1:17-21, 23-25; 4:11). This means that Christ's suffering is a revelation of the nature of God, the God who suffers on behalf of others. When the author of 1 Peter charges his readers to endure unjust suffering, he is not dragging in extraneous theology that happened to be incorporated in the hymn he is quoting, but he is asking them to do this on the basis of the ultimate truth of the universe as disclosed in the cross of Christ. This also clarifies why, in contrast to the other elements of the social code, the missionary motive appears to be missing. While there is no explicit missionary reason invoked in the section directed to slaves (contrast 2:12; 3:1-2), the theological center of the section affirms that the orientation "for others" is at the heart of the universe, made known in Christ. Love that does not retaliate but breaks the spiral of violence is the ultimate nature of things. Acting not in one's own interest, but for the sake of others, is not merely following the example of Jesus, but is in step with the nature of God. This is why the author can say that to endure unjust suffering for the sake of others is grace from God and can consider this the theme of the whole letter (2:19-20; 5:12).

Those who are not enduring oppression might well be wary of commending patient suffering for the sake of others, for the sake of the church's mission, to those who are enduring unjust social discrimination, deprivation, and oppression. But in 1 Pet 2:13–3:12 we do not have someone who belongs to the oppressor class advising the oppressed to endure their lot on the basis of the example of Jesus. The author too speaks from the underside of society, speaks from "Babylon" (5:13) in the name of the martyred Simon Peter. But even that is not the basis of his appeal. He believes the Christian kerygma that such a life manifests the reality of God's love that is oriented not to self (self-esteem, self-vindication, self-worth, self-image), but to others.

The author does not take credit for being able to live such a life. Those who do so are called by the divine initiative (2:21), and though once straying sheep, they have been brought back (passive voice 2:25, as TEV) by/to their divine shepherd who has given his life for the sheep.

Instructions to Wives, Husbands (And to All) (3:1-7)

It would be grossly anachronistic to approach this text with sensitivities formed in another cultural situation. The exegetical task is neither to defend the cultural presuppositions of the author and his readers, nor to impose ours upon them, but to understand the text in its own context. (For general hermeneutical approaches, see above, pp. 104-13.) The two fundamental questions are (1) What does the author charge Christian wives in his context to do? and (2) On what basis?

◊ ◊ ◊ ◊

The instruction is to "fit in" to the given social order. On the term translated "accept the authority" (NRSV) or "be submissive" (NIV), see above on subordination *(hypotassō)*. The opening "in the same way" (3:1; *homoiōs*) is paired with the identical word addressed to husbands in 3:7 (cf. also 5:5), and relates 3:1-7 to the general command to all Christians in 2:13 (q.v.). The point is not that women should be submissive in the same way as slaves, but that wives and husbands, like slaves and Christians in general, should fit into the given structures of society.

In this case, the patriarchal family is in view. There was some variety in family structure in the hellenistic world, which included households managed by women (Balch 1981, 139-42 and passim; Osiek and Balch 1997, 54-74 and *passim*). The typical and preferred pattern from the Roman point of view, however, was the patriarchal household ruled by the *paterfamilias* (head of the family). Romans were suspicious of deviation from this pattern, being especially nervous about the freedom of women as practiced, for example, in Egypt and promoted by the Isis cult, which encouraged women to engage in public processions, wear loud clothing, and in general call attention to themselves. Romans commonly viewed these actions as violating customary standards, while those of the upper class regarded such displays as a violation of patriotism and public decency. Christians as such were already suspect for having joined the new "foreign superstition," and wives who had joined without their husbands were probably considered especially insubordinate. Plutarch, a contemporary of 1 Peter, had expressed the common view that husbands determine the religion for the family, and that wives must acknowledge and worship only his gods, and not participate in "outlandish superstitions" (*Mor., Con.* 140D).

In such a situation, 1 Peter gives Christian wives the same instructions as to other Christians: show respect for the given social order, fit in. They are not commanded to be subservient to men in general, but to respect the authority of their husband in the patriarchal household. Their dress is not to call attention to themselves as in the cults of Artemis and Isis, but is to be the standard dress of housewives. (N.B.: the instructions of 3:2-3 are completely conventional, with many parallels in the hellenistic moralists [cf. Balch 1981, 101-2]). For modern women in North America to adopt this as "biblical teaching" for their own conduct would make them stand out from the general cultural scene—the precise opposite of the original intent of the text. Similarly, the contrast between internal beauty and external adornment was standard fare in the hellenistic moralists (as also in the Bible; cf. 1 Sam 15:7), not particularly a matter of feminine virtues. So also the "meek and quiet spirit" is not restricted to women, but is the character of the Christian life as such (cf. Matt 5:5; 11:29; 1 Cor 4:21; Gal 6:1). First Peter requires "gentleness" of all, not only of women (*prautēs*, 3:16, a form of *praus* in 3:4).

In looking for an illustration of this point appropriate to Christian wives, the author cites Sarah's addressing Abraham as "Lord" (LXX of Gen 18:12, where "my husband" = "my Lord," "Sir"). Here he is stretching a point both because the case is not analogous—Abraham was not the unbelieving husband of a believing wife—but also because in the same text Sarah was hardly the paradigm of the servile housewife, but was laughing out loud. The author chooses Sarah because in hellenistic-Jewish tradition she was the ancestor of women proselytes, and can function as the model for the Christian wives of 1 Peter's readership who once were pagans but now, as members of the holy people of God, have become Sarah's daughters. The image of Sarah also is appropriate to the readers' social status as "sojourners and resident aliens" (1:1; 2:11), which was always the status of Abraham and Sarah. Again, 1 Peter posits a direct continuity between the biblical people of God and the contemporary Christian community as those who "hope in God."

The people of God are charged with a mission, to bear witness to God's mighty acts, to win others to the faith (2:9). The instruction to Christian wives is placed within this framework of the evangelistic missionary task of the people of God. If their husbands have not been won by the verbal proclamation of the Christian message, they may be convinced by the Christian conduct of their wives. Like all Christians, the wives of unbelieving husbands are to manifest fear of God, that is, worshipful awe of God, in the way they live their lives (3:2; cf. 2:17-18), but are not to fear what the culture in general fears (3:6). The instructions are a call to courage, not servility; they are concerned with responsibility, not status. The challenge is given to women who have already courageously committed themselves to a faith not shared by their husbands. The acceptance of such instruction requires persons who are secure in their own acceptance by God, on the basis of the faith articulated in 1:3–2:10, 21-25. Christian wives are called to manifest in their own situation the same "manner of life" (*anastrophē*; 3:2) and "doing good" (*agathopoieō*; 3:6) that are the responsibility of all Christians as such (*anastrophē*; 1:15, 18; 2:12; 3:1, 2, 16; *agthopoieō*; 2:15, 20; 3:6, 17; cf. *agathopoiia*; 4:19).

In 3:7, the author turns briefly to church members who are in the socially dominant role: the husbands in Christian households. The husbands' responsibility, as seen by the author, is not merely to accept the dominant role assigned him by society. While the social structure itself is not challenged, the husbands are instructed to live with their wives no longer merely in terms of cultural expectations, but "according to knowledge" (*gnōsis,* only here in 1 Peter). This phrase probably does not mean merely "show consideration" (NRSV) or "be considerate" (NIV), but refers to knowledge of the Christian faith as articulated in 1:3–2:10, 21-25, in contrast to their previous lack of such knowledge (cf. 2:15, unchristian *agnōsia* contrasted with Christian *gnōsis*). In the Pauline tradition in which the author is embedded, such knowledge means concern for the weaker, more vulnerable members of the group (1 Cor 8:1-13). Their new faith calls upon them to respect ("honor") them as coheirs of the gift of life, with "life" referring both to eternal life as eschatological salvation and to everyday human life. Concern with "honor" was common in hellenistic culture, but the command for the husband to honor the wife is uniquely Christian. Though the social structures do not encourage it, within the Christian community husbands are to respect their wives as coheirs of the life received by both wife and husband as grace. Christians must relate within these social structures in such a way that does not provoke misunderstandings among outsiders.

Since the husbands addressed are Christians who have Christian wives, here no explicit missionary motive is given for the husbands' conduct, no suggestion that by considerate conduct the Christian husband might win over a nonchristian wife to the faith. In contrast to 3:1-2, there were probably very few cases in which the husband had become Christian without the wife's joining him in the Christian community. Nonetheless, the way in which the Christian family conducts itself in a hostile environment is considered throughout to be a matter of Christian witness to the world, not merely a matter of internal rights, roles, and relationships. The concluding motivation, "so that nothing will hinder your prayers," is therefore probably not merely a matter of individual or familial piety—either the husbands' or the wives'—but, like the domestic code in general, has the wider community of faith in view. A community cannot be in right ("vertical") relation to God when it does not attend to right relationships within itself and its stance to the wider world ("horizontal"). The outward, missionary view permeates the whole. Thus the concluding reference to prayer, like 2:11-12 above, cannot mean "cultivate the inner life." Today it is the case that "One could spend a lifetime tinkering with one's soul—more time alone, more retreats . . . more self-improvement, more searching for one's center—and at the end have no record of self-denial in the quest for the other's good, no risky investment in altering the oppressive conditions under which others live, no voice raised in the public forum of conflicting values. Religious self-centeredness is seeking to save one's life and that, even if it is called spirituality, is finally fatal" (Craddock 1995, 42).

Concluding Instructions to All (3:8-12)

The expression "finally" introduces the conclusion of the subsection begun at 2:11, with "all of you" forming an *inclusio* with the repeated "all" of 2:13-17. The address returns explicitly to the community as a whole, which has been implicitly addressed in the preceding instructions to slaves, wives, and husbands. The list of irenic qualities Christians are to manifest in their hostile situation represents the solidarity of a community charged with a mission to the world, not the individualistic ethic common to hellenistic moral instruction. The nonretaliatory orientation reflects both Synoptic tradition of Palestinian origin (cf. Luke 6:28/Matt 5:44; *Did.* 1:3-5) and the instruction of the Pauline tradition (Rom 12:14, 17; 1 Thess 5:15), but is closer to the latter (cf. the chart in Michaels 1988, 174). This point is not only crucial for the question of authorship, but for interpretation of the letter as a whole: for the most part the Petrine author grounds his message in the cosmic Christology of Paul, but even on those rare occasions when he presents instruction that also appears in the Gospels, "Peter" is still closer to Paul than to the Gospels.

Although there are related sayings in the Gospel tradition, it is striking that here as elsewhere the author does not support his teaching with sayings of Jesus, but with a text of Scripture (the longest such citation in 1 Peter). Psalm 34 (LXX 33) is important to the author, reflected not only here but in 2:3. It was apparently important in the Roman church from which 1 Peter originates, since the same passage is cited in *1 Clem.* 22:2-6. Originally a wisdom tradition based on life experience and oriented to practical living in this world, the psalm is here understood kerygmatically in terms of the Christ-event. "Life" here is not only everyday life, but as in 3:7 refers to the eschatological gift of eternal life. The "for" added to the quotation in verse 10 grounds the instruction not in commonsense instruction that can stand on its own but in the author's own theology. As the abuse to which Christians are subject is primarily verbal, they are warned against replying in kind, and as previously instructed are urged to meet suspicion and false charges with positive "doing good." Since Christians have been marginalized by a hostile society that misunderstands them, their temptation is to accept their status as those who "don't belong," and to opt out, adopting the mentality that turns over "the world" to nonbelievers, while withdrawing into a "spiritual" realm from within which they respond in disdain and personal hostility. Christians cannot do that because the world they accept as real is not defined by the cultural values and structures of their opponents, but as the world of God the creator who has appeared within it as self-giving love for others (see Appendix 1: The Narrative World of 1 Peter).

As in 3:7, the worship life of the community, through which it is related to God, is a paramount motivating factor for maintaining proper relationships with other people, both inside and outside the Christian community. The divine ear that hears prayers also attends to how Christians speak to each other and to outsiders.

Responsible Suffering in the Face of Hostility (3:13–5:11)

The text of 3:13 both begins afresh and is in continuity with the preceding. In this section the progression of thought is not neatly linear, but neither is it merely rambling. The author's discourse spirals back around over all the main themes in 2:11–3:12, but at a different level. Verses 13-17 begin to deal more specifically with unjust suffering, which is grounded in the christological traditions of 3:18-22. These are then specifically applied to the Christian life in 4:1-6, followed by the eschatological parenesis and doxology of 4:7-11. The overarching theme that becomes ever more specific is that Christians are called to endure unjust suffering not merely as a superficial *imitation* of Christ, but as a genuine *participation* in God's act in Christ (4:12-19). The body of the letter concludes with an exhortation to specific groups and then to all (5:1-11). As elsewhere, the perspective is theocentric, God is the actor, with Christ as willingly subordinate to God in both death and resurrection. The section throughout is shaped with a consistent parenetic intention. In this wider context, the christological hymn/tradition of 3:18-22 is seen to be not a fragment of interesting or bizarre speculation, but a profound testimony to the outward, "for others" dimension of God's saving act in Christ.

Suffering for Doing Good (= Doing Right) (3:13-17)

Structurally, 3:13-17 seems to be a parallel to 2:11-12 (q.v.), each providing a general introduction to their respective more specific subsections. The rhetorical question with which verse 13 begins seems to imply the answer "do good and you won't have to suffer." This sounds naive only within the framework of commonsense wisdom, for both the community's experience and the author himself document the reality of unjust suffering (see on 1:6, 11; 2:19-23). The author is not speaking within the horizon of human wisdom, however, but against the background of the narrative world of which the Christ-event is the defining center (cf. Appendix 1: The Narrative World of 1 Peter). These words are thus not a trivializing of the readers' actual experience, nor are they a commonsense bit of wisdom strategy to avoid harassment and persecution, just as they are not part of a preliminary letter written before the persecution became intensive. But neither are they to be spiritualized in the sense that the hostile world can harm the body but not the soul (differently Matt 10:28). The kind of spiritualizing dualism in which the believer withdraws into the recesses of one's own heart, while turning the world over to the powers of evil, is precisely what the social ethic of 1 Peter wants to avoid. Rather, what we have here, as in the traditional saying of Jesus it echoes (Matt 5:10; cf. the other beatitudes of Matt 5:3-12), is the eschatological paradox that both proclaims the eschatological security of those who do God's will and provides a positive framework for continuing to do good in this world. The author has the positive view that the rulers of this world recognize the good as practiced by Christians and do not punish it (2:14) and that good conduct will win over the revilers and unbelievers (2:12; 3:1-2).

The author also has the realistic view already validated in the readers' experience that doing good sometimes provokes a dangerous response. The two verbs in this section referring to unjust suffering are in the rare optative mood, more literally translated as "but even if you should suffer for doing what is right . . ." (3:14), and "if it should after all be God's will that you suffer for doing good . . ." (3:17). This grammatical construction does not connote a remote future possibility, as though persecution had not already occurred, for indeed it has, as both writer and readers know. But the persecution is not constant, organized, or official, as already illustrated in the discussion of 2:13-17 above (cf. Introduction, pp. 33 and 43-44). It was a matter of discrimination, ostracism, verbal abuse and harassment, employment and commercial disadvantages, and suspicions that could lead to accusations before unfriendly courts. All these are real possibilities at any time for the readers, similar to the situation of racial and ethnic minorities in many modern contexts. It is this real but sporadic nature of the persecution that is indicated by the optative mood (Achtemeier 1996, 231).

The readers' temptation is to keep a low profile, to accept the culture's evaluation of their religious commitment, for example, to be ashamed (cf. 4:14-16). Honor and shame were important aspects of life in first-century Mediterranean culture. But the Christians of Asia Minor have already been reminded that they will never be put to shame (2:6 citing Isa 28:16). They are so to live that their detractors will be put to shame (3:18), if not in the present when they see the error of their accusations, then in the eschatological reversal of the final judgment (2:12; 4:5).

The readers always are to be prepared to respond to those who question them about their common lifestyle that seems so strange and threatening to their neighbors (3:15-16). Christianity is not to be mistaken for a mystery cult with secrets to conceal from the uninitiated. Its ordinary members, all of them, are to be prepared to explain who they are and why they live as they do. The "defense" (NRSV) or "answer" (NIV) is literally "apology" *(apologia)* in the sense that would be developed by the second-century defenders of the faith, but the word has not yet become a technical term. It could include hearings before the courts, but in this context refers to the broad spectrum of settings in which Christians are likely to be misunderstood and need to present a coherent explanation of what they are about, and what is the nature and basis of their hope. All Christians, not only teachers and leaders, have this responsibility. In contrast to the dominical saying of Luke 21:14, they are not to wait until the situation is upon them and depend upon charismatic help for an answer, but are to think through the meaning of their faith and its relation to public life, and be prepared to respond intelligently when asked.

How should the readers respond? Not with hostility and retaliation, but with gentleness (*prautēs,* cf. 3:4) and fear (of God, as 2:17-18; 3:2). The Christian's "fear" (reverent awe before God's holiness) is oriented to God, not to worldly threats and powers (3:16 vs. 3:14). The world is not to be responded to on its own terms, but in terms of the God revealed in Christ. This, and not mere individualistic self-righteousness, is the meaning of the good conscience (3:16) with which Christians respond.

The motive for such a reasoned and restrained response to unjust suffering is expressed only indirectly. While it is presupposed and reflected only incidentally, the assumption about the nature of reality functions as the powerful motivation on which one can habitually act. Three such facets of the Christian view of the believers' situation in the world emerge in this context:

1. "You are blessed" (3:14). As in the beatitudes of the Synoptic tradition (Matt 5:3-12/Luke 6:20-22), "blessing" refers not to a subjective psychological state ("happiness") but to an objective soteriological reality that is a reversal of how things appear to be. As elsewhere, the author confirms his statement not with an allusion to what was once said by Jesus, but by a loose quotation from Scripture reinterpreted within the Christian framework (Isa 8:12).

2. Your good manner of life is "in Christ" (3:16). The phrase "in Christ" or some variation thereof ("in the Lord;" "in Jesus;"

"in the beloved;" "in him;" "in whom") is found in the New Testament 165 times, only in Paul's Letters and in the literature influenced by him. When 1 Peter uses the phrase "in Christ" (here and 5:10, 14), this is a clear indication of direct or indirect influence by the Pauline tradition. Though a strange phrase, the author uses it as though it were familiar to his readers. "In Christ" signals the incorporation of Christians into the whole historical reality of which the Christ-event is the center (cf. Appendix 1: The Narrative World of 1 Peter). Christians can willingly endure unjust suffering because they participate in the reality of Christ, the paradigm of divine suffering-for-others.

3. The concluding comment that it is better to suffer for doing good than for doing evil, though a commonplace of both hellenistic and Christian moral instruction (e.g., Plato, *Politics* 285E; 1 Cor 9:3; 2 Cor 7:7), is here lifted to another plane by incorporating it within the "will of God." This expression from 1 Peter does not connote case-by-case that particular situations are willed by God, but points to the whole creation-to-eschaton scheme that represents the divine will for the world. Within this framework of thought, "doing good," even if misunderstood and eventuating in unjust suffering, is not a platitude but a pointer to God as creator and redeemer of all. Thus all three motivating comments point the reader to the comprehensive narrative world in which the thought of the whole letter is embraced (see Appendix 1: The Narrative World of 1 Peter). This is also true of the following christological tradition.

Christological Grounding (3:18-22)

Just as 2:18-20 required the christological grounding of 2:21-25, so 3:13-17 requires the christological grounding of 3:18-22. Without this christological presupposition, what 1 Peter has to say simply cannot be understood. The author would seem to be presenting a challenge to an unrealistic life in a fantasy world. Thus whether the narrative world projected by the letter throughout is taken to be real or not is the fundamental question on which its ethic must stand or fall.

Many contemporary readers would echo Martin Luther's declaration that "This is a strange text and certainly a more obscure passage than any other passage in the New Testament. I still do not know for sure what the apostle means" (Luther 1967, 113). Yet the primary meaning is clear, both to Luther and to us: Christians are called to endure unjust suffering for the sake of others (3:17; cf. commentary on 2:11–3:6). This central thrust of the passage stands regardless of how the problematic elements of the tradition quoted in 3:18-22 are understood. This view is grounded not logically but christologically: Christ suffered for others (3:18). Christians are related to the Christ-event not only as an example to be imitated, as in 2:21-25, but by being incorporated into this event by baptism (3:21). Patient endurance of the harassment and marginalization inherent in their outsider status is to be seen as of a piece with Christ's suffering for others, itself a central element in the divine mission to the world. But suffering is not the last word: Christ was vindicated, and his suffering had cosmic, eschatological effects (3:22). Christians too will be vindicated at the last judgment (4:5-6), and therefore cannot return to the old life from which they have been delivered by their baptism (4:1-4). The point is pastoral and hortatory, not speculative and dogmatic. The author is not interested in teaching information about what happened to Jesus in the transcendent world after his death, but in grounding the call to discipleship in the Christ-event—hence the repeated "you" of direct address (3:18, 21; 4:1).

Overlapping and Interlocking Issues: Verses 18-20 speak of Christ's going to preach to the disobedient spirits in prison and verse 22 of his going to heaven where angels, authorities, and powers are subject to him. The interpretation of this text involves making decisions on a number of overlapping and interlocking issues:

1. Should the interpreter attempt to fit this text into a general dogmatic schema constructed from a variety of sources, as though it were data for systematic theology, or should the focus be entirely on the historical meaning of the text in its original setting?

2. Is 3:18-22, or parts of it, composed of a hymn, creed, or fragments of such material, or is it all composed by the author for this occasion?

3. Does the proclamation of the gospel to the dead in 4:6 refer to the same event as 3:18c-20, or does 4:6 refer to an unrelated event so that the two texts are to be interpreted independently of each other? Since 4:6 itself can be understood in more than one way, if the two texts are interpreted interdependently, the possible meanings of 3:18-22 are expanded even more.

4. When did Christ go to preach to the spirits in prison? Does the repeated "having gone" *(poreutheis)* of 3:19 and 3:22 refer to two trips or one? If two trips are postulated, does the former one refer to the time between Jesus' death and resurrection (as in the later Apostles' Creed)?

5. How did Christ go? Does the Greek phrase that begins 3:19 (*en hō,* "in which" NRSV; "through whom" NIV) indicate that it was as a disembodied spirit that Jesus preached to the spirits?

6. Where is the prison in which Christ preached? Is it located in the realm of the dead, thought of as *under the earth* (as in the case of both the Hebrew Sheol and the Greek Hades), or in the regions *between heaven and earth,* as in various apocalyptic and later Gnostic cosmologies?

7. To whom did Christ preach? Were the "spirits" the heavenly beings of Gen 6:1-6, or their offspring, or both? Or were they human beings, either those in the world of the dead or those alive in Noah's day? If to human "spirits," was it to all or only to the righteous? Was the proclamation to the flood generation alone (if so, why precisely these?), or to the flood generation (either spirit-beings or humans) as representatives of all the pre-Christian dead?

8. Where should one look for illumination on the thought world here presupposed? To the mystery religions of the hellenistic world, in which there were numerous descents of divine beings to the netherworld? Or to Jewish apocalyptic writings in which Enoch's announcement to the spirits in prison played a major role?

9. Why did Christ go to preach to the imprisoned spirits? Did he announce his own victory, and hence their condemnation, or was the proclamation one of salvation or the possibility of repentance?

10. A final issue is whether or not we have sufficient information, either from 1 Peter or elsewhere, for an adequate understanding of these allusory references. We must remember that we

are reading a real letter, and that it is characteristic of letters to presuppose a matrix of connections in its historical context, well known to its writer and readers, but obscure to later readers no longer privy to information inherent in the situation (cf. Brox 1979, 169-70). First Peter is a letter not written to us. But it is a pastoral letter. The hortatory point is clear, as is the appeal to Christology as its ground. The details of the christological grounding may have to remain obscure to us.

Result: Main Views in the History of Interpretation: The combinations of the variables listed above produce a large number of possible interpretations. Even to list them all, identified with their major proponents, is a labyrinthine project requiring many categories, subcategories, and cross-references, as illustrated by the lengthy monographs devoted to this text (Reicke 1946; Dalton 1965; cf. also Selwyn 1947, 313-62). It may be a helpful oversimplification to divide this grand spectrum of interpretations into three major types that have emerged in the history of the church's dialogue with Scripture, each of which contains variations and nuances:

1. After his death but before his resurrection, Christ preached the gospel of the salvation he had provided to the human spirits in the world of the dead, thus making available the possibility of salvation to those who had lived before Christ. In this interpretation both 3:19 and 4:6 were understood to mean that Christ preached to the dead between his own death and resurrection. This interpretation, already found in the *Gospel of Peter* in the second century, and advocated especially by the Alexandrian theologians Clement and Origen in the late–second and early–third centuries, fit in with the developing Apostles' Creed, which added the "descended into hell" clause in the Fourth Formula of Sirmium in 359. This interpretation also opened the door to the notion of a "second chance" after death and to the possibility of universal salvation, a view advocated by Origen.

2. Augustine, partly in opposition to the Alexandrian view, interpreted this text to mean that the preexistent Spirit of Christ

preached through Noah to the wicked generation that perished in the flood (cf. 1 Pet 1:11). Christ's descent to Hades was affirmed on the basis of the Creed, but was understood to be an affirmation of the reality of Christ's own death, and did not involve any preaching activity (about which the Creed, of course, is silent). First Peter 3:19 was unrelated to this creedal affirmation. First Peter 4:6 was referred by Augustine to Noah's generation, which was spiritually dead when he preached to them, and thus unresponsive.

3. After the beginning of historical study of this text in modern times and the rediscovery of the text of *1 Enoch,* the "spirits in prison" were identified with the fallen angels of Gen 6, often referred to in *1 Enoch, Jubilees,* and other Jewish apocalyptic literature. In this literature, these evil angelic spirits were responsible for the evil of the flood generation, and their spiritual offspring continued to trouble the earth. Although the angelic spirits hoped to be released to continue their evil activity, Enoch was sent by God to announce their irrevocable doom. In this view, the crucified and risen Christ, as an aspect of the events of his exaltation to divine sovereignty, announced his victory to the transcendent powers, who were now subject to him. In this view, 3:19 and 4:6 are not necessarily related, so that 4:6 may be understood within a different framework.

Positions Adopted in the Exegesis: With no attempt in this brief discussion to list supporting evidence, refute alternate views, or document which scholars argue for which interpretations, I will indicate the choices I have made on the issues listed above that undergird and provide the framework for my own interpretation:

First Peter should be interpreted historically, on its own terms, with no effort either to fit it in with views expressed elsewhere in the canon or in later Christian theology, but also with no compulsion to interpret the text so as to conflict with other biblical and theological affirmations.

The author did not compose 3:18-22 ad hoc; it contains hymnic or creedal material familiar to his readers (but unfortunately not to us). Several attempts have been made to reconstruct the hymn, the most elaborate of which is M. E. Boismard's expansion of Rudolf

Bultmann's reconstruction, combining it with 1:20 as Bultmann had done. The hymn reconstructed by Boismard has Christ for its subject:

> Destined before the foundation of the world
>> manifest at the end of times
> Put to death in the flesh
>> made alive in the spirit
> Evangelized to the dead (from 4:6)
>> gone into heaven
> Made subject to him: angels and authorities and powers.
>> (as translated in Best 1971, 136)

Such precise reconstructions have not found widespread support. I regard the author's composition of 3:18-22 as based on a traditional hymn, but his adaptation has made recovery of the precise original impossible (in contrast to the situation with other New Testament hymns such as Phil 2:5-11; Col 1:15-20; and 1 Tim 3:16). Verses 18 and 22 are clearly traditional material. Verse 19 may also be from the hymn (as printed in Nestlé [27]), but many scholars attribute it to the redactional composition of the author.

This hymn was not written to form part of a discursive argument in a letter, but, like other early Christian hymns, to celebrate the cosmic victory of God in the Christ-event (cf. Phil 2:5-11; Col 1:15-20; 1 Tim 3:16). Such hymns, however, were not written and sung merely to express Christian subjective emotions, but had a didactic and hortatory orientation (Eph 5:19; Col 3:16; cf. Heb 13:15). All such hymns that have been preserved portray the victory of Christ on a cosmic scale. There are no songs about Jesus' teaching or mighty deeds on Galilean hills or in Judean synagogues: it is the universal sweep of God's saving act that is celebrated in song and liturgy. Like their counterparts in Israel's psalms (e.g., Pss 46, 48, 98), the mood and intent of such songs communicate the celebration of God's mighty victory, not interest in speculative theology. First Peter's resonance with the psalter is seen not only in its employment of Ps 34 (33), but in the allusion to Ps 110 in this very passage. One must thus first picture the way in which the song originally communicated its meaning in the context of worship, in such a manner that made it available for citation here in an allusory or fragmentary way as an evocative background for the appeal to Christian living that is the main point.

Verse 19 refers to Christ's triumphal proclamation to the angels, authorities, and powers that are now subject to him (3:22), and is to be interpreted independently of 4:6, which refers to Christians who have died. The proclamation of 3:19 was made at the time of Christ's death, resurrection, and exaltation, but the interpreter should not attempt to locate the transcendent geography or chronology more precisely. Jewish apocalyptic ideas, especially as found in *1 Enoch,* illustrate the religious thought world in which the original hymn was composed. Such christological hymns as Phil 2:5-11 were used often enough in the worship of churches in both Rome and Asia Minor that the author of 1 Peter could presuppose familiarity with their meaning and imagery.

◊ ◊ ◊ ◊

In 2:21-25, the manner in which Christ suffered was presented as an example for the Christian to follow, and the picture was altogether the this-worldly picture of Jesus' conduct during his Passion. In 3:18-22, the cosmic victory of Christ is not one that can be imitated on the human level, just as his "[suffering] for sins once for all" (3:18) was unique. Nonetheless, the christological picture has a double relevance for Christian life: (1) just as Jesus' suffering was vindicated by God (3:22), so the Christian whose suffering is presently despised will finally be vindicated (4:5-6); and (2) Jesus' suffering was not a matter of egocentric first-the-cross-then-the-crown selfishness, but was for others, "the just for the unjust" (3:18; "the righteous for the unrighteous" NRSV). Though the Christian's suffering is not in the same category as the redemptive suffering of Jesus, the "for others" dimension of Christian conduct pervades this section just as it has the preceding one (see on 2:13–3:12). Like the suffering of Jesus "in order to bring you to God," that is, to reconcile sinful humans with God by providing access (cf. Rom 5:2, utilizing a form of the same word *prosagōgē*),

Christian suffering is set here in the context of the evangelistic mission of the church.

"Put to death in the flesh, but made alive in the Spirit" is a rhythmical part of the quoted hymn fragment. "Flesh" and "Spirit" do not refer to two "parts" of Christ's being, but, as elsewhere in 1 Peter, to the two realms of existence of the crucifixion/resurrection event. "Flesh" is the this-worldly empirical sphere; "spirit" is the transcendent world of God. The meaning is that Jesus was put to death by human beings in the this-worldly sphere of the "flesh," but was vindicated by God in the transcendent world of "spirit." Jesus is pictured as passive in both cases: he was subject to the human powers of this world that put him to death, but God acted in the transcendent world to raise him from the dead and install him as Lord over all transcendent powers (3:22; cf. Phil 2:5-11).

The phrase *en hō* ("in which" NRSV; "through whom" NIV) does not refer to the Spirit, but should be taken as an adverbial conjunction "when," "at that time," as elsewhere in 1 Peter (cf. 1:6; 2:12; 3:16; 4:4). The "spirits in prison" do not refer to deceased human beings, but to the evil angelic spirits of Gen 6:1-6, later understood as the demonic powers behind the world's systemic evil. Though their influence is still felt, they were imprisoned by God awaiting their condemnation at the Last Judgment. The myth is elaborated in *1 Enoch* 10:4-5, 11-14; 91:15 and is reflected in the New Testament (cf. 1 Cor 6:3; 2 Pet 2:4; Jude 6). Enoch was sent to these spirits to announce their doom. It is not clear whether Christ is also pictured as proclaiming their ultimate condemnation, or whether the redemptive act of God in the Cross and Resurrection is pictured as extending even to the rebellious evil spirits (cf. Eph 1:10, 20-23; Phil 2:5-11; Col 1:15-20; Rev 5:13). Although the author's intent is not to speculate on the doctrine of universal salvation, the possibility that the hymn to which he alludes evokes this picture should not be resisted. The readers may have known the Enoch tradition, in which the spirits are condemned, but it is more likely that they knew Colossians or Ephesians or both, or the Pauline traditions incorporated in them, in which the hostile spirits are reconciled (Eph 1:10; Col 1:15-20). Contrary to the theology of some later interpreters, it is not the case that a picture of ultimate universal grace to all would cut the nerve of the courageous resistance to which 1 Peter calls his readers, as though there is no motive for Christian faithfulness if all are finally redeemed anyway (*contra* e.g., Achtemeier 1996, 261). The motive for endurance is not selfish eschatological reward, but the revelation of God in the suffering Man for *Others*.

The modern reader may be puzzled by what appears to be a jump to the time of Noah, the reference to the ark and the threatening waters, but once one sees the connection to the evil spirits of Gen 6 and the Enoch myth that lies behind the imagery, the association is natural. The author follows this lead because he sees a parallel between the few righteous souls saved in the ark and the smallness of the Christian community in comparison with the pagan culture of his own time. But statistics are no indication of right. It was the few who were vindicated by God then, and thus it will be in the reader's present situation.

The imagery of Noah's time also allows the author to insert the only explicit reference to baptism in 1 Peter (3:21). The waters of baptism correspond to the waters of the flood in that they represent the decisive break with the old world. The pattern of thought is analogous to 1 Cor 10:1-6, where the deliverance at the Red Sea is taken by Paul as a typological reference to baptism, and which also uses the imagery for parenetic purposes: the water decisively separated them from their enslaved past. As in the case of Paul's letter, the point in 1 Peter is not exegetical but hortatory: Christians can no more return to the old ways they once shared with the surrounding culture (cf. 4:1-4) than Noah and his family could return to the world judged and destroyed in the flood.

Baptism is not merely an external ritual that removes dirt from the body, but neither is it a matter of a "good conscience" in the individualistic, subjective, modern Western understanding of "conscience." In 1 Peter (cf. 2:19; 3:16), "conscience" is not merely a personal subjective untroubled feeling that what one is doing is right, but is the critical and responsible ability to decide, one's "discerning self-knowledge" (Goppelt 1993, 268), a human potential that may be either good or bad. It is good and godly when this human ability is subjected to the Christian gospel, so that this critical and responsible human capacity is oriented to and empowered by the Christ-event. This is what happens in baptism, when the believer is incorporated into Christ and becomes "in Christ" (cf. on 3:16 above). Thus while there is little direct reference to Rom 5–6, and 1 Peter lacks the developed doctrinal emphases of Paul, the main line of thought is the same: Christians cannot go back to the old way of life because in baptism they have been incorporated into Christ, the story of the Christ-event has become their own story, and they do not merely imitate, but participate in Christ's sufferings (4:13). This line of thought had apparently been reflected upon in Rome; compare Heb 10:22, which relates baptism, washing, and conscience. The precise meaning of the word in 1 Pet 3:21 translated as "appeal" (NRSV) or "pledge" (NIV) is not clear, and thus whether the "good conscience" is the basis for baptism or its result is ambiguous. The statement may be related to the questions asked baptismal candidates on the occasion of their baptism. In any case, individuals do not create their own "good conscience" but receive it in relation to baptism. Yet there is no magic in the baptismal act itself. It is not baptism per se that saves, but God's act in the resurrection of Christ mediated through baptism.

Whatever the traditions used by the author may have originally meant, his own meaning in this cryptic section is clear. It is not informational or doctrinal as such, but pastoral and evangelistic. Just as Christ suffered unjustly but was eschatologically vindicated by God, so it is with the Christians, who are now enduring unjust abuse but are soon to be vindicated at the eschatological judgment (4:5-6). In neither case, however, is the final victory merely personal and egocentric. Christ's suffering won the victory over the cosmic powers and brought them into subjection to him as exalted Lord. His Passion and death were not meaningless, but neither was their meaning a matter of his own well-being; his suffering was oriented outward, to the whole cosmos. So also the Christians' suffering is not merely for their own later reward, but encourages participation in the "for-others" orientation of the Christ-event, which finds its meaning within the larger context of the church's mission of witness and service to others. Johannes Hamel, pastor to university students at the University of Halle in the Soviet-dominated German Democratic Republic in the years after World War II, often had Bible classes of more than a thousand students. Hamel repeatedly appealed to 1 Peter, which he found to speak directly to the situation in which he and his congregation were called to exercise Christian faith. "The fundamental question is this: does the Christian Church in the Marxist world hear and acknowledge her own gospel in its own sovereignty and in all its dimensions? . . . Does the church deny the sovereignty of God over everything? . . . Or does the Christian Church proclaim publicly and privately, in small and in great things, that all powers and principalities are already overcome and imprisoned through the resurrection of Jesus Christ?" (Hamel 1959, 85).

Application to the Christian Life (4:1-6)

At 4:1 the author returns explicitly to his main theme: as Christ has suffered in the flesh (= died), Christians are to equip themselves with the same insight/intention as Christ. The thought is also found in Paul's writings (cf. Phil 2:5), but the word translated "insight" or "intention" *(ennoia)* is found only here and in Heb 4:12 in the New Testament. However, the word is used twice in *1 Clement*— once again illustrating the late-first-century Roman world of Christian thought in which the author's language is at home. It is not clear whether the statement "whoever has suffered in the flesh has finished with sin" applies to Christ, Christians, or both. The context and the indefinite "whoever" suggest that it embraces both Christ and Christians, but not as a general moralizing platitude. Rather, as Christ's suffering made a decisive end of sin, so the Christian's own suffering (and participation in Christ's suffering) makes an end of sin in a different sense. The sinless Christ (2:22) suffered to bring the reign of sin to an end. Christians, who participate in Christ's suffering and death because they are baptized, and whose own sufferings are part and parcel of the Christ-event that is now their own story, have finished with sin in

143

the sense that they can never return to their old way of life. The integral connection between Christ's death that brought the controlling power of sin to an end, and the Christian's way of life that must put sin behind it, was a principal element of Paul's thought (Gal 2:19-20), and was continued in Rome as his letters were collected and read there, not only by 1 Peter but by Hebrews (cf. Heb 9:28).

The author wants to warn against the very real temptation of returning to the values of the old life, which he characterizes as "human desires" in contrast to the will of God. What at first might appear to be a somewhat rambling, moralizing bit of exhortation, on closer examination turns out to be a carefully structured parenetical section climaxing in the perfectly balanced 4:6, a construction utilizing the Greek conjunctions *men . . . de,* which parallels and contrasts the human and divine realms. The construction is striking in Greek, and retains its character even in a literal English translation:

"hina			
[men]	*krithôsi*	*kata anthrôpous*	*sarki*
[de]	*zôsi*	*kata theon*	*pneumati"*

"in order that
on the one hand   they may be judged by human standards
    in the flesh, [but]
on the other hand   they may live   by God's standards
    in the Spirit" (AT).

The two realms of this human world and the transcendent divine world are not arranged vertically, in Platonic or Gnostic fashion, but on the horizontal line of history that corresponds to the author's narrative world projected by the letter as a whole (see Appendix 1: The Narrative World of 1 Peter). These two parallel streams of history continue in the readers' present experience. As this grand scheme of redemptive history applies to the believers, all time is divided into two by their conversion: "the time that is past" (literal translation of 4:3; cf. ASV "the time past," REB "time enough in the past") and "the rest of the time" (RSV). The pre-conversion "time that is past" is characterized by "flesh" (4:1, 6), "human desires," (4:2) and "doing what the Gentiles like to do" (4:3), in contrast to "the rest of the time" which is characterized by "the will of God." The readers previously belonged to the old world where people are judged by human standards, and are tempted by the social pressures upon them to return to it. These two lines of history converge at the imminent eschatological judgment, in which those who presently revile will give account to the judge of all, and Christians who have already died will be vindicated (see on 4:6 below).

The "rest of your earthly life" (4:2 NRSV) does not refer to the brevity of human life generally, but to the time prior to the parousia, expected to occur in the readers' lifetime (4:7). They have been born anew to a living hope (1:3), separated from the old world and its values by baptism (3:20-21), and must not return. The plurality of old desires is also contrasted with the singleness of the will of God (4:2). They are now to live a focused, centered life, devoted to one goal: the will of God (cf. Pss 86:11; 119:113; Matt 5:2; 6:22; Luke 9:62; 10:42; Phil 3:13; and Kierkegaard's "Purity of heart is to will one thing" [not one *more* thing]). Their rebirth to a new life did not mean an adding of Christian responsibilities to their previous commitments, but a subsuming of everything under the one lordship of Jesus Christ.

The author, who like his readers is probably ethnically a Gentile himself, understands the Christian community to be in continuity with Israel, and speaks of non-Christians as "Gentiles," (4:3; cf. 2:12) and the "human desires" he warns against as "what the Gentiles like to do." The six-membered list climaxing in "lawless idolatry" does not mean that the author has personal knowledge of particular ethical practices of the population of Asia Minor. Like other vice catalogues, including the author's own previous list (2:1; cf. comment above), the terminology is more or less stock language, reminiscent of such lists also used by Paul (e.g., Rom 13:13-14; Gal 5:19-21). Yet it is not merely a matter of stereotyped catalogues of sins. The activities here refer particularly to the practices of civic and religious festivals, the community celebrations and social activities of business and professional guilds—in short, to the social world in which the readers were once active participants. Their new faith had caused them to withdraw from much of this social scene, and they are now criticized and reviled by those who were once their associates, who cannot understand this new commitment and its consequences in the lifestyle of its adherents. In the understanding of the author, pagan verbal abuse of Christians modulates into blasphemy against God (v. 4).

This brings him to the thought that Christians need not respond in kind to those who revile the holy people of God (and thus God himself, in the author's view), since all, living and dead, shall shortly stand before God as judge and render account (4:5). Both context and language are reminiscent of Paul in Rom 14:7-12, though in Romans the application was to intrachurch relationships rather than response to outsiders. The judgment to come is both universal and imminent, and will reveal God's justice to all. Outsiders who now call the church to account for their "antisocial" behavior (3:15) will soon face an eschatological turning of the tables: "Those who now ask questions will have to come up with some answers of their own" (Michaels 1988, 234).

The meaning of the preceding (4:1-5) is clear enough, but the concluding v. 6 statement is extremely obscure. In the past it was often understood as part of the same complex of thought as 3:18-19, identifying the dead to whom the gospel was preached with the "spirits in prison" to whom Christ preached. Thus Christ preached the Christian gospel to the dead of past ages, so that they could be judged on the same basis as those now living—on their response to God's act in Christ. The current majority scholarly opinion identifies the "spirits" of 3:19 with the "fallen angels" of Gen 6, and distinguishes them from the "dead" (humans) of 4:6 (cf. above comprehensive discussion). Many recent interpreters adopt the solution argued extensively by William J. Dalton (Dalton 1965) that the reference is to Christians to whom the gospel was preached, but who have since died. Their non-Christian detractors taunt the Christian community that some of their members have died ("been judged in the flesh"), but the believers are urged to remember that they live in the spirit. That is, all, living and dead, will stand before God in the imminent last judgment, and then it will be seen that those Christians who have died are in fact not judged but vindicated in the transcendent spiritual world. On this reading the text is not mere speculative mythology, but expresses a pastoral concern analogous to 1 Thess 4:13-18. Dalton sums up the meaning according to his interpretation:

"For this is why Christ was preached to those who have since died . . .

in order that . . .

though judged in the flesh in the eyes of men

they might live in the Spirit in the eyes of God."

(Dalton 1965, 270-72)

Dalton's very detailed argument, while persuasive and attractive in the main, is not without special pleading. A variation on this view has been argued by Ramsey Michaels according to which the believers of all generations were actually "Christians before the coming of Christ" (Michaels 1988, 237-42). It was these Christian members of the people of God, who lived and died before the earthly advent of Christ, to whom the gospel was preached during their lifetime by the preexistent Spirit of Christ active in the Old Testament saints (cf. 1:11; 3:5). Though their own generation rejected them, they can be judged [and vindicated] on the same basis as Christian believers of the writer's own generation. In favor of this view is its affinity with the letter to the Hebrews (cf. 4:2; 11:25-27) and *1 Clement,* which saw the Old Testament believers as forming one community and sharing the same faith as later Christians (*1 Clem.* 9-12, 17, 31-32 all a development within the Roman church of Paul's thought in Rom 4:1-25).

Norbert Brox, on the other hand, despairs of fitting 4:6 into any known early Christian theological construct, and considers it to be a fragment of another mythical picture, unrelated to 3:19, in which the dead of past ages had the gospel preached to them after they had died (Brox 1979, 196-201). Once again, the visible tips of icebergs of lost early Christian traditions remind us that we are reading an ancient letter, whose readers understood the allusions familiar in their own situation, to which we no longer belong. Christian duty, the hortatory point, is clear quite apart from the meaning of the attached mythical fragments. Yet neither here nor in 3:19-22 do we have a "magnificent digression" (Michaels 1988, 224). Even if the meaning of the details is forever lost, such glimpses of the framework of early Christian theology show that the author does not restrict his affirmation to the needs of the moment. The Christ hymns and their accompanying imagery present a larger panorama than our everyday concerns. God's deed in Christ is larger than our immediate need (so Craddock 1995, 61). Alternatively said: our real need, whether we so express it or not, is to belong to something bigger than the way we articulate what we perceive as our immediate needs. Our need to belong to something bigger than ourselves is addressed, and perhaps even revealed to us for the first time, in the larger-than-life pictures of a redemption that spans the universe and the ages, even if the pictures that attempt to express it are fragmentary and obscure to us later readers.

Eschatological Parenesis (4:7-11)

This paragraph concludes the section that began at 3:13 by shifting the focus from the theme that has dominated the unit—unjust suffering at the hands of outsiders endured for their sake and as a testimony of the truth of the gospel to them—to the internal life of the Christian community itself. In 1 Peter's own terminology (2:17), the perspective now briefly shifts from "respect everyone" to "love the family of believers" (Michaels 1988, 244). This does not, however, represent a fundamental change of theme or lapse into self-centeredness, for the call to endure unjust suffering is not a matter of individualistic fortitude but of participation in a Christian community of mutual love, support, and service to each other. Like Christ and the suffering servant of Isa 53, the community is called to suffer on behalf of the world, and it must be able to do so. Hence it needs to be a community of mutual love and support as an aspect of its mission to others. Thus in this section, the relation to outsiders does not explicitly appear, and the two poles around which the discussion proceeds are the community's relation to God (4x in 10-11) and their relation to each other (3x in 8-10). We have seen that a major theme of the preceding argument is the Christian calling to witness to others by enduring their jibes, discrimination, and insults without retaliation, and doing it for their sake. This missionary theme of suffering-for-others is not forgotten, but it is not mere selfishness to remind the community of faith of its need to nourish its own life together. Here we see the household of faith as a matter of practice, not doctrine.

◊ ◊ ◊ ◊

As in the christological section above, concrete practical instruction is placed within a universal framework, with the nitty-gritty of the historical present surrounded by an eschatological declaration that the "end of all things" is near (4:7) and a doxology that glorifies God "in all things" (4:11). Neither here nor elsewhere in the letter is eschatology a didactic theme in itself, but is an expression of the Christian hope that permeates the letter as the presupposition of the Christian life (see on 1:3-12). Although the author takes the nearness of the end seriously (continuing the thought of 4:5), there is here no "interim ethic," no otherworldliness, no apocalyptic demonizing of the opponents, no explaining that the present troubles are the necessary "tribulation" before the end. Rather, there is a call to serious and clear-headed thinking, and to spiritual discipline that facilitates the life of prayer—the very opposite of eschatological fanaticism. Worship requires clarity and discipline, not muddled, excited thinking; prayer is not "opiate" or escape, but an expression of clear vision that sees the world as it actually is (cf. Appendix 1: The Narrative World of 1 Peter). Neither does the instruction promote a private spirituality, but the worship life of the community, which is very important to the author (3:7, 12).

The command to love one another (4:8) is thus not the moralizing inculcation of a Christian virtue, but the necessity for life together in the Christian community. Christian love (*agapē*, synonymous with the *philadelphia* of 1:22, q.v.), means "caring," self-giving care for the other, as opposed to selfish not-caring. The opposite of Christian love is not hate but indifference. Life and work together in the Christian mission require that people look away from their own rights and concerns, that they not be too easily offended by the foibles of their fellow Christians, lest the mission to which the church is called be neglected. "Not every emotional and psychic bruise can be given attention; otherwise all the church's energy for mission and witness would be burned up in damage control" (Craddock 1995, 68).

The love command is considered supreme, "above all" (4:8), as in analogous contexts in the Pauline tradition (1 Cor 13:1-13; Rom 13:8-10; note the context in each case). Again, it is striking that "Peter" does not support the priority of the love command by appealing to sayings of Jesus (Mark 12:28-34 par), but by citing a Scriptural text that had already become proverbial in Christian tradition. "Love covers a multitude of sins" is a free rendering of the Hebrew text of Prov 10:12. Since the author elsewhere consistently quotes from the LXX, here he is probably repeating a current proverb also found in Jas 5:20, *1 Clem.* 49:5, and *2 Clem.* 16:4. The idea found in some Jewish and Christian traditions that deeds of love help to atone for ("cover" before God) one's own sins (cf., e.g., Luke 7:47) is far from 1 Peter, who cites the proverb to encourage the readers to "cover," i.e., not notice and call attention to, the sins of their fellow Christians (cf. 1 Cor 13:5). That Christians can contribute to the atonement for their own sins by deeds of love is alien to the fundamental theological perspective of 1 Peter (2:21-25; 3:18), but that Christian love disregards the faults of others is a firm instruction in the Pauline tradition familiar to the Roman church (Rom 13:8-10; *1 Clem.* 49:5, which cites the same proverbial text with this meaning).

The particular acts of hospitality in which such love becomes concrete (4:9) refer not only to the charitable manner in which Christians opened their homes to each other and to needy strangers in general (cf. Matt 25:35, 38, 43; Rom 12:13; Heb 13:2), but in particular to provision for traveling Christian preachers and teachers, without which the Christian mission could not have existed (cf. Phlm 21-22; Mark 6:10-11; Matt 10:11-16, 40-42; Acts 16:15; 21:7, 17; 28:14; 2 John 7-11; 3 John 7-8; *Did.* 11-13). The *Didachê* passage shows that such openness was subject to abuse and exploitation, and the context in which 1 Peter's urging to show hospitality "without complaining" (4:9) was heard.

In this context, the mention of the gifts that each Christian has received (4:10-11) is also intended to emphasize their purpose in strengthening the Christian community. The discussion reflects not only the distinctive vocabulary of Paul—"gift" is *charisma,* a term found only in Paul and in literature dependent on him—but the main lines of the Pauline understanding of the church. Every Christian has received a gift, there is a variety of gifts, and the gifts are not for individual self-aggrandizement but for edification of the Christian community as a whole. Yet 1 Peter does not merely repeat the Pauline teaching of 1 Corinthians and Romans: here the gifts are repeatedly referred to God, the Holy Spirit not being mentioned in this context, and the imagery of body and breath (spirit) is not found. There is no attention to the problem of the more sensationalistic gifts of tongues, prophecy, and miracles, and Christian ministry is divided into the two main categories of word and deed (4:11). Thus 4:10-11 is not only Pauline, but already illustrates the combination of Pauline and Palestinian traditions found in 5:1-5 below. The plethora of *charismata* in Paul are now divided into ministry of the word of God and Christian service to others, as in Acts (6:1-7). The gifts are still directly from God, but are seen in terms of the community structured around presbyterial leadership.

The development of the discussion on spiritual gifts seems to have proceeded in three stages: (1) Paul's initial vigorous and somewhat polemical argument about "spiritual gifts" in 1 Cor 12; (2) the more reflective and toned-down discussion in Rom 12; (3) the development of the later version of this tradition in Rome after his arrival there, and after his death on the basis of Romans and 1 Corinthians (and Ephesians?); and (4) its appearance in 1 Peter and *1 Clement* (cf. *1 Clem.* 19:2; 23:2; 32:1; 35:1, 4; 44:3) in the next generation. In 1 Peter, there is no longer a detailed list of charismatic phenomena to be evaluated, but the essential understanding remains: it is God who speaks and acts in the church's speaking and acting. Thus those who speak (preachers, teachers, missionaries, any Christian who testifies to the truth of the Christian faith) are urged to consider their own speech the voice of God, and those who serve are to remember that the power at work in their ministry comes from God (4:11).

This theocentric affirmation modulates into a doxology, concluded by the usual responsory "amen." The question of whether the "to whom" of 4:11 means the doxology is directed to "God" or to "Jesus Christ" is misplaced, with either answer generating exegetical and conceptual difficulties. Word order seems to call for Christ as antecedent, but then "through Jesus Christ" in the same phrase is problematic. Without developing the insight conceptually, 1 Peter's theocentric Christology collapses the figures of "God" and "Christ" into each other; this is not the only text in which one should not attempt to distinguish them (cf., e.g., "Lord" in 1:3, 25; 2:3, 13; 3:12, 15, the equation of "Spirit of Christ" and "Spirit of God" in 1:11; "stone" used for God in the Old Testament text cited of Christ in 2:4; and the way in which love for Christ stands in place of love for God in 1:8; cf. on 1:17-21, 23-25; 2:21-25).

The doxology concludes a literary subsection of the letter, but does not signal the conclusion of a baptismal sermon or liturgy that has been incorporated into the larger epistolary framework of 1 Peter. This once-popular theory has been soundly refuted by detailed studies that present compelling evidence for the unity of 1 Peter). Such doxologies do not signal the end of a document or source. Doxologies such as 1 Pet 4:11 occur sixteen times in the New Testament, but only three times as the conclusion of a document (Jude 25; 2 Pet 3:18; Rom 16:27). They normally occur, as here, within the context of a letter when the subject matter brings before the author's mind a vision of the glory of God that calls forth a doxological response. Such doxologies can even occur near the beginning of a letter, as in the Rev 1:6, addressed to churches in Asia Minor about the same time as 1 Peter, using exactly the same wording. In the Pauline materials familiar to the Roman church, such internal doxologies occur in Rom 1:25; 9:5; 11:36 (which concludes a literary unit, as here); Gal 1:5 (cf. Eph 3:21). This feature of the literary tradition is continued not only in 1 Peter but in *1 Clement* (20:12; 32:4; 38:4; 43:6; 45:7; 50:6; 58:2; 61:3; 64:1).

The glorification of God with which the section closes also serves to bring the author's mind back to his previous reference to the glorification of God by Christian endurance of unjust suffering at the hands of their unbelieving neighbors (2:12), and thus serves as a transition to the next section, in which he resumes his main theme with a new intensity.

Suffering in Joy and Hope (4:12-19)

First Peter has no "theology of suffering" as such. Corresponding to its nature as a real letter addressed to a particular situation, 1 Peter does not deal, essay-like, with the problem of suffering in the abstract. There is no help here for the general human problem of physical evil, no theodicy, no explanation for the existence of evil in a world presumably ruled by a deity who is both almighty and loving. Nor is the question "why do Christians suffer for their faith" a theoretical problem, for the readers are already enduring social harassment, abuse, and occasional violence (see Introduction, pp. 33 and 44-45, and on 3:13-17 above). Their experience of suffering is the sharper because it is unjust, brought about not by accident or their own misbehavior, but by their membership in the Christian community and their adherence to the Christian faith. Suffering as such is not necessarily the adversary of faith and life; meaningless suffering is the enemy that must be overcome. Thus a theological response is called for. First Peter's theological perspective on the particular suffering experienced by the Christians of Asia Minor is intended not merely to comfort, but to equip (4:1). Thus 4:12-19 is not a "digression" from the theme of 4:7-11, which is then resumed in 5:1-5 (*contra* Michaels 1988, 257). The author wants to provide a realistic way of thinking that will place their experience in a meaningful framework and that will provide both rationale and motivation to endure unjust suffering as ingredient to the Christian life, so that the Christian mission may continue. While the letter as a whole is addressed to this issue (cf. especially on 1:6-7; 2:19-24; 3:13-18; 4:1-3), the concluding exhortation that begins in 4:12 provides something of a summary and "list," a series of overlapping and integrated perspectives within which to understand the meaning of their present experience of suffering.

It is also important to note what is not here. Despite the thoroughly eschatological outlook of the letter, the motivation for enduring unjust suffering is not merely the promise of future reward, nor is there any emphasis on the punishment of unbelievers and unfaithful Christians. There is no reflection on the positive value of suffering as such, as though suffering, correctly understood, is really a positive value that "develops character" or somehow makes its victims better. For 1 Peter, suffering as such is evil. However, unjust suffering is an evil that cannot only be endured but can be the setting for the joy of the Christian life. This parenesis is developed and supported in six affirmations.

◊ ◊ ◊ ◊

Suffering Belongs to the People of God as Inherent in Their Calling (4:12a): As Christians whose previous religious experience was mainly in the context of the tolerant hellenistic-Gentile world, the readers had little prior tradition of people being persecuted on religious grounds. The concept was likewise foreign to the mainstream of early Israelite and biblical thought. When Israel suffered at the hands of their Gentile neighbors, the prophets interpreted this in terms of Israel's unfaithfulness to their covenant with God (cf. Isaiah, Hosea, Amos, Micah). This perspective was schematized in the Deuteronomistic theology of history as found in Deuteronomy–2 Kings: when Israel is faithful to God, they flourish; when they are unfaithful, they are punished. This view is summarized in the blesses and curses of Deut 28. During the later periods of pre-Christian Jewish history, this theological scheme no longer worked, for it was precisely those who were faithful to God who were persecuted. Apocalyptic thought developed within this situation, as a means of affirming God's faithfulness when all empirical experience seemed to negate it. The Maccabean period, the setting for the book of Daniel, is paradigmatic. Not only did a new eschatology arise from these circumstances, a new understanding of the nature and mission of the people of God was also developed: to belong to Israel is to belong to the elect community called to witness to the world to God's ultimate rule and justice, though such witness will result in suffering at the hands of the powers of this world (Daniel; Qumran). Here as elsewhere, 1 Peter's understanding of suffering is a dimension of its apocalyptic understanding of the people of God.

Within such a perspective, it is indeed no surprise that suffering for the faith is inherent in membership in the elect community (4:12). The view that suffering is the "normal" state for the Christian thus has nothing to do with masochistic psychology or martyr complexes, nor is it an isolated view only to be related socially to the particulars of the Christian readership in late-first-century Asia Minor Christianity. That the Christian life as such includes suffering for the faith is a view not peculiar to 1 Peter but is the common perspective of earliest Christianity (cf., e.g., Mark 13:9-13 par.; John 16:1-2, 33; Acts 14:22; 1 Thess 3:4; 2 Thess 1:5; 2 Tim 3:12). The author shares this apocalyptic understanding of the people of God, and thus explains to his readers that their experience of suffering for wearing the name of Christ (see below) is a badge of their authentic membership in the continuing people of God (cf. the similar argument from the same Roman context in Heb 11–12, esp. 12:6). This does not mean, of course, that the author encourages people to seek out or provoke suffering in order to demonstrate that their membership in God's people is legitimate. The author begins with the reality that they are already suffering because they are Christians, and places their experience in the broader reality represented by his understanding of the role of the community of faith within the plan of God for the world (see pp. 156-57, 160 below and Appendix 1: The Narrative World of 1 Peter).

Suffering Is a Testing that Purifies and Refines Their Faith (4:12b): Taking up again a theme introduced initially in 1:6-7, the author presents no abstract doctrine on the "value of suffering," as though suffering as such were somehow good for character development. His more pronounced apocalyptic theology is to be distinguished from similar statements about suffering developed in the wisdom tradition (cf., e.g., Jas 1:2-4; Wis 3:1-9; Sir 2:1-6). The point in this context is that unjust suffering probes and refines, and strengthens the believer's own self-understanding as a Christian.

The author's metaphorical use of "fire" for the readers' trials thus has three overlapping connotations: (1) The primary reference is to the fire that tests and refines precious metal, burning away the dross, as in 1:6-7. (2) The apocalyptic framework also suggests the eschatological fire of judgment (as in the contemporary Rev 18:9, 18; cf. Matt 3:11*b*-12; *Did.* 16:5; see esp. Michaels 1988, 260). (3) Though like *1 Clement,* written with admirable restraint on this point, a letter from Rome written in the name of Peter that mentions "fire" could hardly fail to evoke pictures of the fiery ordeal endured by the Roman church under Nero in 64 in which Peter himself had perished.

Unjust Suffering for Christians Is Viewed from Within the Reality of the Believer's Life "in Christ" (4:13): The whole of Christian experience is interpreted as a segment within the Christ-centered narrative of salvation history (cf. Appendix 1: The Narrative World of 1 Peter). The believer's life is incorporated into Christ's; Christian existence is life "in Christ" (3:16; 5:10, 14). Without any "mystical" elaboration, and without developing it in explicit Pauline terms, 1 Peter has accepted this Pauline understanding and vocabulary, including the vocabulary of participating in Christ's sufferings by virtue of being "in Christ" (cf. Rom 8:17; 2 Cor 1:5; 4:10; Phil 3:10; cf. 2 Tim 2:11-13; Heb 11:26; 13:13). The specific terminology of this text reflects Paul: It was Paul who made the vocabulary of "participation" in Christ *(koinōneō, koinōnia)* Christian parlance (cf. 1 Cor 1:9; 10:16; 2 Cor 6:14; 13:13; Phil 2:1; 3:10); the phrase "sufferings of Christ" characteristic of 1 Peter (here; 1:11; 5:1) is found elsewhere only in Paul's letters (2 Cor 1:5; cf. Col 1:24); the pairing of present suffering and future glory is Pauline (Rom 5:2; 8:18; cf. 2 Cor 4:17). The statement that Christians share Christ's suffering is in the indicative. The readers are not exhorted to participate in Christ's sufferings. It is not the case that the Christian's suffering allows him or her to participate in the sufferings of Christ (contrast the REB translation). Rather, 1 Peter's meaning is that the Christian's life "in Christ" is prior to and the basis for seeing one's concrete sufferings as participation in the sufferings of Christ. The declaration here goes beyond a call to imitate Christ's suffering (cf. 2:20-25) and sees the Christian's story as embedded within the story of Christ, where God is revealed as the faithful creator (4:19). In the Christ-event, the character of God is revealed and the ultimate meaning of things is disclosed. The Christian's suffering, seen as suffering-for-others, is seen to be a participation in the suffering of Christ for others. The command to rejoice is thus not Stoic encouragement to keep a stiff upper lip despite external circumstances, but is the by-product of incorporation into Christ. As Christ once suffered and is now vindicated, so the Christian now suffers and will be vindicated. But the eschatological joy need not be postponed. Suffering Christians are called to celebrate now, not just in prospect. First Peter contains no suffer now/rejoice later theology. Not "suffer then rejoice," but "rejoice in sufferings" is the profoundly Pauline theology adopted by the author (cf. Rom 5:1-3; 8:17; 2 Cor 6:10; cf. Col 1:24).

In the Midst of Suffering, the Eschatological Glory Already Rests on the Community (4:14): The author pronounces a blessing on the suffering community reminiscent of the Matthean form of the Beatitudes (Matt 5:11), and sharing the same eschatological perspective. The saying of Jesus is not explicitly cited, however, nor is the declaration grounded in the teaching of Jesus. This is typical of 1 Peter, who never explicitly cites a saying of Jesus even in situations where Gospel texts known to us that would have supported his point come readily to mind (e.g., Mark 12:17 at 1 Pet 2:13). Rather, words from Isa 11:2 portraying the messianic deliverer, sometimes applied to Christ, are here applied to Christians (cf. Eph 1:17). For 1 Peter, the eschatological reality promised in Isaiah is already present, not only in Christ, but among Christians. When blessedness is pronounced upon the readers if they are insulted for the name of Christ, the conditional element is not whether or not they will be abused. Abuse is a given in their situation. The only question is whether or not their suffering is for the name of Christ, which is not to be a matter of shame but a badge of honor (4:14).

The readers of 1 Peter are understood to be suffering "for the name of Christ," mentioned twice in this context and identified with suffering "as a Christian" (4:14, 16). The once-popular view that 1 Peter is addressed to a situation in which Christians faced government persecution on the basis of their belonging to the Christian community has now properly been abandoned as anachronistic. Pliny's letter to Trajan (c. 112 CE) makes it clear that this was not yet the case, specifically in the area to which 1 Peter was addressed (cf. Introduction, pp. 44-45). The Christians' own self-understanding may sometimes have been that they were being persecuted for their Christian identity, that is, "for the name," when their non-Christian neighbors understood themselves simply as opposing a superstitious and unpatriotic new sect.

The name "Christian" was originally a derogatory term applied to the Jesus movement by its opponents (in the New Testament only here; Acts 11:26; 26:28). It is analogous to "Herodians" (= partisans of Herod; Matt 22:16; Mark 3:6; *Ant.* 14.450), or "Caesarians" (= partisans of Caesar; *Epic.* 1.19.19), but was probably first understood in a negative sense, "Christ-lackeys." Several religious movements have become known by the disdainful description with which their detractors had first labeled them (e.g., Methodists, Campbellites, [Ana-]Baptists, Dunkers, Moonies). These groups sometimes finally accepted such names as a badge of honor. Thus at least by the second century the followers of Jesus applied the name "Christians" to themselves in a positive sense. Ignatius is the first clear instance (cf. Ign. *Eph.* 11.2; Ign. *Mag.* 4; *Pol.* 7.3; Ign. *Rom.* 3.2; cf. also *Did.* 12:4; *Mart. Pol.* 3.2; 10.1; 12.1).

In 1 Peter's situation, to be called a "Christian" was a matter of social shame, no small matter in an honor/shame society. It is in this context that 4:15-16 is to be understood. The author wants his readers to grasp that, while there is a kind of suffering considered shameful by the society that is indeed disgraceful (suffering as a thief, murderer, or criminal), there is also a kind of suffering that brings no dishonor, even though the non-Christian social environment would consider it shameful—unjust suffering "as a Christian." Tacitus, who wrote in the same generation as the author of 1 Peter, stated matter-of-factly that Christians suffered for their crimes (*Ann.* 15.44). Thus the stereotyped vice list of shameful practices in 4:15 does not mean that Christians were likely to be guilty of such offenses (cf. on 2:1; 4:3), but is intended as a contrast to the kind of authentic Christian behavior considered shameful by the society, but actually a matter of honor. Though many speculative attempts have been made, there is still no satisfactory explanation for the rare word *allotriepiskopos* translated "mischief maker" (NRSV) or "meddler" (NIV). First Peter's admonitions are part of the general early Christian exhortation not to be ashamed of the gospel, the faith, the Cross, or Christ himself (cf. 2:6 above and Mark 8:38 par.; Rom 1:16; 9:33; 10:11; 2 Tim 1:8, 12, 16; 2:15; Heb 12:2). Suffering for the name of Christ is not a matter of shame; it not only brings honor to the believer but glorifies God (4:16).

In the Midst of Suffering, the Eschatological Judgment of God Already Rests on the Community (4:17-18): The temptation of a minority religious community suffering harassment and discrimination is to demonize its opponents and to assume a stance of (self-)righteous indignation that excludes itself from the judgment of God. First Peter resists that temptation, adopting the Old Testament view that election is not for privilege but for responsibility (Amos 3:2), that to belong to the elect and holy people of God does not mean exclusion from God's judgment, which begins at the "house of God." First Peter understands the biblical term to refer to the Christian community as both God's temple and the "household of faith" (see Appendix 2: Images of the Church in 1 Peter). The images tend to overlap and modulate into each other, since the church as the Christian household is identified as the temple community, a holy priesthood that offers spiritual sacrifice to God (2:5). Once again, instead of supporting his point with a saying of Jesus, the author cites an Old Testament text now understood from the perspective of Christian eschatology (Prov 11:31). Additional biblical language and imagery is employed to declare that judgment begins precisely at the "house of God" (Jer 25:29; Ezek 9:6; Mal 3:1-5), a view taken up elsewhere in the New Testament as well (e.g., Matt 13:24-30, 47-50). The reference to the worse fate for outsiders provides no emphasis or details on the punishment of unbelievers. The language of judgment is not descriptive language aimed at outsiders and their fate, but the confessional language addressed to insiders. Such exhortation functions within the relation that binds together God and the people of God, not as a threat to outsiders.

Suffering as a Christian Indicates the Believer's Place in the Eschatological Plan of God (4:17, 19): Though in the final position in the author's "list," the eschatological perspective permeates the whole. In the apocalyptic perspective shared by 1 Peter, just before the end the demonic powers are unleashed for a final assault on the faithful (cf. 5:8; 2 Thess 2:1-12; Rev 13:1-18 and *passim*). This view is here presupposed, but not developed and schematized. Thus the apocalyptic notion of the "messianic woes" that must precede the end is not brought into sharp focus, but hovers in the background. First Peter understands the troubles that must be endured by his readers within this general apocalyptic framework. In some streams of second-generation Christian theology influenced by Paul, the sufferings of the apostle are seen as of one piece with the sufferings of Christ (cf. Eph 3:13; Col 1:24). First Peter extends this view to the sufferings of Christians generally.

The author's point is not that the readers can identify specific enemies and problems in their context with predicted apocalyptic woes as the "signs of the times," but that nonetheless their experience is not meaningless since it is embedded within the framework of God's plan for history shortly to be brought to a worthy conclusion. This is the meaning of suffering "in accordance with God's will" (4:19). It is not the case that God wills these particular sufferings, but that God's plan is the framework for understanding their meaning. Thus "suffering in accordance with God's will" does not mean that particular afflictions are directly sent by God, but that the history in which their troubles are located is in the hands of God the faithful creator. Eschatology and protology, end and beginning, consummation and creation, are corollaries. Christian readers of 1 Peter may look toward the eschaton with joyful confidence not because they have worked out an apocalyptic scheme, but because all things finally reside in the hands of the Faithful Creator. The final word of this section on the Christian response to unjust suffering is not speculative theology but Christian ethics, not sullen resignation but active "doing good" (i.e., doing what is right; cf. on 2:14-15, 20; 3:6, 17).

Concluding Exhortation (5:1-11)

The concluding exhortation of 5:1-11 is composed of two subunits. Verses 1-5 form a coherent Petrine subunit, structured on the pattern of instructions to particular groups concluded by instruction to all, rounded off with a biblical citation (cf. the structure of 2:18–3:12). The second subunit begins at 5:6, with additional instruction to "all."

The text of verses 6-11 continues the admonition to all, calling for humility (vv. 6-11) and vigilance (vv. 8-9), promising eschatological vindication from the God who presently cares for them (v. 10), and concludes with a doxology (v. 11).

The structure is not crisply precise; some exegetes include verses 6-7 with the preceding unit, noting the change of tone and subject at 5:8 (e.g., Brox 1979, 225-26). The lack of structural precision is due in part to the fact that here, as elsewhere, the author is not composing freely, but reworking traditional parenetic material; compare the similarity in both form and content to Jas 4:6-10 and Acts 20:17-36.

◊ ◊ ◊ ◊

5:1-5 Church as Support Group Structured for Mission: This segment of the text may appear at first glance to be an abrupt introduction of a new subject—a discussion of the responsibility and attitudes of elders and their place in the church. Yet 5:1-5 is not a section of instruction on proper church order. A particular structure is assumed without explanation or defense. As is the case with real epistolary communication, the original readers were already familiar with the presupposed structure, and only we later readers must attempt to reconstruct it in order to understand the document.

Formal similarities between this section and the "household code" of 2:18–3:12 have suggested to some scholars (e.g., Kelly 1969, 204; Boismard 1961, 133-63) that this material in 1 Pet 5 was originally a part of the social code transferred here for the author-editor's own purposes. It is true enough that the general form used earlier by the author (instructions to particular groups, followed by instructions to "all," concluded with a quotation from Scripture) and even specific vocabulary (e.g., "Likewise, be subject" 3:1, 7/5:5) echoes his earlier language. It is appropriate that in addressing the issue of relations of church members within the structured community he takes up the same forms used earlier in the "household code," since throughout the letter he regards the church as the household of faith (cf. on 2:4-10 and Appendix 2: Images of the Church in 1 Peter). In the "household code" of 2:18–3:12 however, the concern was external, with how outsiders view the church. Here, the point is the solidarity of the congregation as a community structured for mission. While it is true that "effective pastoral leadership is indispensable if the community is to survive" (Achtemeier 1996, 322), the focus is not on survival as such but on the mission of the church. This mission requires not merely a collection of individual believers, but a cohesive community—and this means giving attention to relations of believers with one another within a structured congregation.

Thus the discussion of "elders," "younger," and "all" is not misplaced or randomly located, but plays its own role in this context. The particle *oun* (thus, therefore, so then), though absent from some manuscripts, should be considered original and given its full due, indicating a real connection with the preceding (cf. Michaels 1988, 276). The link with the preceding context is also seen in the motif that "judgment begins at the house of God" (see 4:17), related to the picture of Ezek 9:1-6, which "began with the elders." This is analogous to the related parenesis of Jas 3:1 directed to Christian teachers, who "will be judged with greater strictness." This section also stands in the developing tradition of early Christian letters according to which there is a section near the conclusion of the letter exhorting church leaders, with accompanying admonitions to followers (cf. 1 Cor 16:15-16; Col 4:17; 1 Thess 5:12-15; Heb 13:7, 17; Jas 5:14).

"Elders" and "Presbyters": For the first time since 1:1, where he identified himself as "apostle of Jesus Christ," the author refers to himself in the first person, this time as a "co-presbyter" addressing other presbyters. The term *presbyteros* (comparative of *prebys*) may be translated as "elder" (as in the NRSV) or transliterated as "presbyter." Since the whole context indicates that the presbyters of 1 Peter assume their role as a matter of choice and not merely by age (5:2), that being a presbyter involves authority subject to abuse and includes the potential for financial gain (5:3), the reference here is to a church office, a class of ministers. I will use the transliterated form "presbyter" rather than "elder" when referring to the Petrine meaning, though of course it was often the case that presbyters were chosen from among the older members of the congregation.

The basic meaning of *presbyteros* may be seen in Luke 15:25, where it is used in referring to the older brother of the "prodigal son." Thus the term may simply mean a person advanced in years (as LXX Gen 18:11 of Abraham and Sarah, precisely the same term as here). But very often in the hellenistic world, both Jewish and Gentile, "elder" was used to designate the holder of some official position unrelated to age, as in the case of our words "senior" and "senator." (We can speak of high school seniors, and in congress even of a "junior senator.") Elder/presbyter was generally a term of honor, without negative connotations, often associated with wisdom and leadership. Various guilds and associations were headed by boards of *presbyterioi*, and villages were governed by councils of elders (cf. Bornkamm 1968, 6:652-54). In some settings elders were religious functionaries. Not only were Jewish synagogues administered by elders, but in Egypt the priesthood of the god Socnopaios included elders with administrative responsibilities, listed with ages of forty-five, thirty-five, and thirty (Bornkamm 1968, 6:653). At Qumran there was not only a Mebaqqer corresponding to the later Christian bishop, but, subordinate to him and to the priests, a group of elders distinguished from the whole congregation (1QS 6.7-16).

The earliest Palestinian church adopted the eldership as a form of church leadership from the synagogue and general hellenistic practice (cf. Acts 11:30; 15:2, 4, 6, 22, 23; 16:4; 21:18). Acts also pictures Paul as having instituted the eldership in his Gentile mission churches (Acts 14:23; 20:17), although Paul's own letters never refer to elders. Although there was an identifiable leadership in Pauline churches (cf. for example, Rom 12:8; Phil 1:1; 1 Thess 5:12), Paul did not speak in terms of formal offices, but of the free sway of the Spirit that directed the life of the congregations through the gifts distributed to each member (cf., e.g., 1 Cor 12–14). Probably due to the large Jewish contingent of original Roman Christianity, the Roman church adopted the same model of presbyterial leadership developed in the Palestinian church, and continued to be directed by presbyters until the middle of the second century (cf. Brown and Meier 1983, 92-104). By the last decade of the first century, churches that had been founded on the Pauline model had adopted the presbyterial form of church government. The Corinthian church, for instance, that had no elders during Paul's time (otherwise their absence from 1–2 Corinthians is inexplicable) had both organized itself along presbyterial lines and had the authorized elders rejected by other factions in the church, a situation to which the Roman church responded by commissioning the letter of *1 Clement* to them.

The exhortation to elders in 1 Peter is a prime example of the blending of Pauline/Gentile and Petrine/Jewish tradition that had already happened in the Roman church (see Introduction, pp. 39-42). The author has already affirmed the charismatic ministry of the Spirit that functions through every believer, a perspective that is here combined seamlessly with Petrine "presbyters" (cf. Schweizer 1961, 110). Without surrendering the Pauline charismatic understanding of the Spirit that authorizes and empowers every member of the congregation for ministry (see on 4:10-12), he also affirms the role of elders as church leaders, a practice in continuity with the Jewish-Christian roots of the Petrine tradition. There is no hint of conflict between "charismatic" and "official" ministries.

Since Clement of Rome writes a pastoral letter from Rome to the church in Corinth that was experiencing internal conflicts at about the same time that the Petrine author writes to churches in Asia Minor plagued with external harassment, and since both authors presume that their understanding of church leadership is applicable to their respective addressees, what *1 Clement* says about presbyters may be used with critical caution to illumine the situation presupposed by 1 Peter. In both cases, elder/presbyter describes a church office, but continues the traditional etymological connotation of "older man." In both cases, "episcopal" terminology is used interchangeably with "presbyter" terminology, that is, elders are assumed to have a supervisory function. In *1 Clement*, the presbyters are the liturgical leaders who preside at the Eucharist, regarded as ordained "clergy" in distinction from the "laity." While 1 Peter uses "priesthood" in reference to the community as a whole rather than as a special class (see on 2:5, 9), it is still likely that the elders were congregational leaders who presided at worship. *First Clement* refers to deacons alongside presbyter/bishops. There is no reference to such "junior clergy" in 1 Peter, unless the "younger" of 5:5 are so understood (see below). In 1 Peter, the elders seem to be the sole leaders within the context of the general charismatic gifts given to every Christian.

"Peter" designates himself with the threefold description of (1) co-presbyter, (2) witness to the sufferings of Christ, and (3) participant in the glory to be revealed.

Peter as "Co-Presbyter" (5:1): While the name "Peter" is inseparably associated with apostolic authority (1:1), "co-presbyter" unites him with all the presbyters (and, more important, they with him), while the second and third designations unite him with all Christians. This manner of expression compactly combines a claim to leadership authority with democratic solidarity with the whole community. "Peter" addresses them both as their apostolic model and as one of them, at the same time (see on 5:5 below).

The author's referring to himself as a co-presbyter is thus not "a touch of modesty from an apostle" (Moffatt 1928, 161). Although the author is a sincere advocate of humility (5:5b-6), the self-description as presbyter is not a matter of humility. Just as "the Presbyter" of 2 John 1 and 3 John 1 is not the apostle John modestly referring to himself as an elder, but is *claiming* authority by virtue of this title, so also in 1 Peter it is not a matter of the apostle condescending to the level of the elders, but rather a claim that the presbyters represent apostolic authority. Presbyterial dignity, not apostolic humility, is the point. The situation is thus not parallel to bishop Ignatius speaking of the deacons as "fellow slaves" (contra Selwyn 1947, 228, followed by Kelly 1969 and others), since the bishop, humble though he was, never confused the authority of office and personal humility by speaking of himself as a "fellow deacon." The picture is rather analogous to a modern bishop's addressing the priests of his diocese as "my fellow priests." First Peter's manner of address is in continuity with the tradition initiated by Paul (*synergos;* "fellow worker"; see Rom 16:3, 9, 21; 2 Cor 8:23; Phlm 1:24; cf. *syndoulos;* "fellow servant"; Col 1:7; 4:7; Ign. *Eph.* 2.1; Ign. *Mag.* 2.1; Ign. *Phld.* 4.1; Ign. *Smyrn.* 12.2). Likewise, the idea of leadership by example is found in the New Testament only here and in the Pauline tradition, where it is common (1 Cor 4:16; Gal 4:12; Phil 3:17; 1 Thess 1:6; 2:14; 2 Thess 3:7, 9; 1 Tim 4:12; Titus 2:7).

The author wants to establish *continuity* between the apostolic office and the ministry of presbyters. This is done in a different way in the contemporary *1 Clement,* where the apostles ordain elders, but the intention is the same: to connect the presbytery of the second generation with the apostles of the first. Although 1 Peter has no doctrine of "apostolic succession" in any formal sense, he is interested in picturing elders as functioning by apostolic authority.

The author designates himself a witness "of" the sufferings of Christ (e.g., both NRSV and NIV) or witness "to" Christ's sufferings (e.g., REB; Beare 1958, 171; Kelly 1969, 195; Michaels 1988, 277). The noun *martys* ("witness"; later "martyr") is used two ways in the New Testament: (1) to designate an eyewitness who testifies to what he or she has seen (Matt 18:16; Acts 7:58) and (2) to identify a person who provides testimony on behalf of something, an advocate who is willing to speak up on behalf of a cause or person, even at great risk (Acts 22:15; Rev 2:13). Both senses can also apply to the same person, as in the case of Luke's understanding of the continuity between the first and later generations (Luke 24:48; Acts 1:8; 13:31). Thus in 1 Pet 5:1 "witness" could mean that (1) the writer is Simon Peter, who claims to be an eyewitness of Christ's Passion (so e.g., Selwyn 1947, 228), or (2) as part of the pseudepigraphical framework of the letter, that the fictive author claims to have been an eyewitness of Jesus' Passion, or (3) that the author bears witness to the sufferings of Christ, as do the other presbyters and the whole church. The first meaning is excluded not only by all the evidence that indicates Simon Peter is not the author (see Introduction, pp. 30-37), but by the unanimous tradition that the historical Simon Peter fled at the arrest, denied he knew Jesus during the trial, and was not present at the Crucifixion (Matt 26:75; Mark 14:50-72; Luke 22:54-71; John 18:13-27; 19:25-27). It would be ironical in the extreme if the Simon Peter who had slept through Gethsemane, denied, and abandoned Jesus during his time of suffering (Mark 14:32-42, 50; 15:66-72) should later, even if properly repentant, claim to be a witness of Jesus' suffering. Schelke's defense of 1 Pet 5:1 as a claim to eyewitness tradition is weak: "at least he [Peter] experienced the suffering and death of Jesus as present in Jerusalem when it happened, and was eyewitness of it at least in part" (Schelke 1988, 128). The same data must disqualify the second option: a pseudonymous author would be hesitant to represent Peter as courageously having been present at the Crucifixion. The clearly pseudonymous 2 Peter lets us see what such a claim to eyewitness experience would look like, and that Peter could be pictured as experiencing Christ's glorious revelation, but still not his humiliation (2 Pet 1:16-18).

The third option is then clearly the best: the meaning is that the co-presbyter author, along with the other presbyters and the church at large, is a witness to the sufferings of Christ, just as he along with them shares in the glory to come. Even authors who lean toward or explicitly affirm Petrine authorship agree that the meaning here is not a claim to eyewitness experience, but Christian testimony to the meaning of Jesus' suffering and death (Michaels 1988, 280; Davids 1990, 177). The situation is analogous to that pictured in Acts 20:17-35, which pictures Paul instructing *presbyteroi* successors as one of them, and using "witness" terminology of himself (*diamartyreomai*, cognate of the word used in 1 Pet 5:1), though he was certainly no eyewitness. The Acts passage is so close to this text in form and content that a common tradition must be presupposed. In both Acts 20 and 1 Pet 5, the intention is to show that the continuity between the founding apostolic generation and the continuing office of presbyters is in their testimony to the gospel. The *martys* terminology thus joins the author to the other presbyters, and does not distinguish him from them as though apostles were witnesses but presbyters were not.

This understanding is confirmed both by the grammar of the passage and by the author's use of "witness" terminology elsewhere. In 5:1, the single definite article binds together co-presbyter and witness, making "Peter" a co-presbyter and co-witness, just as the second occurrence of the article binds together witness and participation in the coming glory. Apart from this text, "witness" terminology occurs in 1 Peter only in 1:11 and 5:12. In the former passage, the Old Testament prophets are witnesses in advance to the sufferings that Christians would endure for Christ (cf. on 1:11). As the prophets bore witness in advance on the basis of the revelation given to them (not on the basis of eyewitness experience), so Christian leaders (and Christians generally) now bear witness on the basis of the Christian tradition and message they have received (not on the basis of personal eyewitness experience). The general affirmation of 4:13 that all Christians participate in the sufferings of Christ and will participate in the eschatological glory (see commentary there) is here concretized in the person of the apostle-presbyter "Peter," who models what all Christians are called to do and be (4:10-12). Thus the presbyters are exhorted to become such models themselves (*typoi,* 5:3). Congregation, presbyters, and apostle all participate in the ministry of Christ, which was suffering-for-others. So also in 5:12, "witness" is a verb corresponding to "exhorting," something that the author does in the letter, not something he did at the 30 CE crucifixion, and is no claim to eyewitness testimony.

The third element in the author's self-designation is that he is a participant in the glory to be revealed. This aspect of the author's self-description has sometimes been understood as a reference to Simon Peter's presence at the transfiguration (Matt 17:1-9; Mark 9:2-10; Luke 9:28-36; so e.g., Selwyn 1947, 228). A generation after 1 Peter, the historicizing 2 Pet 1:16-18 does indeed reinterpret this text as an explicit reference to Simon Peter's having seen Christ's glory "on the holy mount" (though even there it is not clear that the reference is to a pre-Easter transfiguration). In the present context, however, the reference must have the same meaning as the immediately preceding 4:14, where the eschatological glory is something in which the suffering church as a whole already participates. Rather than being a singular mark of the eyewitness author that separates him from the community, he is a paradigm of the life of the church as a whole, which both witnesses to the sufferings of Christ and already has a share in the eschatological glory to come. This is the significance of *co*-presbyter. The author exhorts his hearer-readers with apostolic authority, but as one of them who shares their common Christian experience.

The Exhortation (5:2-5): Following the same pattern established in 2:18–3:12, the author first addresses specific groups (the presbyters, the "younger") and then the whole community, concluding with a Scripture quotation. His most lengthy exhortation is to his fellow presbyters (vv. 2-4).

An admonition to presbyters was already diplomatically implied in the self-description of 5:1: the apostle is himself a model for how presbyters should function. The explicit exhortation is comprised of an exquisitely composed unit (5:2-3) beginning with the imperative *poimanate* ("shepherd") and concluding with the cognate noun *poimniou* ("flock"), which is then continued and grounded (5:4) in the cognate christological term *archipoimenos* ("chief shepherd"), thus embracing the pastoral ministry of presbyters in the pastoral ministry of the Risen Christ (cf. 2:25, which also makes the shepherd/overseer [*episkopos* = literally "overseer" = "bishop"] connection). The imperative with which verse 2 begins is elaborated in three balanced qualifying clauses. The whole is framed by the dual references to the glory to come (5:1, 4).

"Shepherding" was a common metaphor for the pastoral responsibilities of Christian ministers. At Qumran too, the Overseer cares for the community "as a shepherd his flock" (CD 13.9). God is the shepherd, and human leaders are considered to be stewards who will give account for their care of the flock (Ezek 34:31; John 10:16). Corresponding to the responsibilities of synagogue and community elders in Judaism and the more explicit references to elders in early Christian literature, the elders of 1 Peter were leaders charged with pastoral supervision that included the disciplinary and financial aspects of the community's life. For readers in the eastern Mediterranean, and for people who know the Bible whatever their cultural location, the image of shepherd and sheep is not warm, fuzzy, or idyllic, but connotes authority to guide and rule, the term often being used for kings. In Paul's charge to the Ephesian elders in Acts 20, they are made responsible for ensuring sound teaching (cf. 2–3 John), but orthodoxy is not at issue in 1 Peter.

In John 21:15-19 the Risen Jesus is pictured as commissioning Peter to be the shepherd for Christ's flock. The instructions here are similar enough that both the Johannine scene and the instructions in 1 Peter have been considered historical reminiscence, the latter written by Peter personally (e.g., Selwyn 1947, 229). But in Acts 20:28 "Paul" uses the same language, showing that it was general parenesis to Christian ministers of the late–first century. The Acts passage also combines the "episcopal" vocabulary with "presbyterial" terminology, as does 1 Peter. (Though some manuscripts omit *episkopountes,* "exercising the oversight" in v. 2, it was probably the original reading; cf. Goppelt 1993, 343-44 for full discussion of the text problem.)

The word *klēros,* literally "lot" as in Acts 1:26, translated "those in your charge" in the NRSV and "those entrusted to you" in the NIV, is ambiguous. In this context, it is parallel to the "flock" of 5:2. While not absolutely clear, the picture seems to be that each presbyter has pastoral responsibility for a particular "congregation," that is, a small house-church, which in their totality made up the one church in a given locality, which would have a plurality of presbyters (cf. Goppelt 1993, 347 and the literature he gives).

The author is not concerned to delineate what their function was; that was clear to them and their "parishioners" in their situation, though not so clear to us later readers. "Peter's" concern is with the *manner* in which they exercise their ministry, and their *motivation* for doing so. The exhortation to perform their presbyterial duty willingly, without compulsion from others (5:2) indicates that persons were sometimes reluctant to accept the office, due to the precarious position with the authorities in which it placed them.

The admonition against seeking the office for "shameful profit" shows that the office of presbyter presented opportunities for personal financial profit, whether from managing church funds (cf. 2 Cor 8:20) or because the eldership was already a salaried office in Asia Minor in the 90s (cf. 1 Cor 9:7-14; 1 Tim 3:8; 5:17-18; Pol. *Phil.* 11:1), or both. As the media commercialization of religion has illustrated in our own time, there has always been the temptation to assume ministerial functions because there is money to be made. The warning against lording it over their flock (5:3) reveals that the elders had authority that could be abused. As Christ the chief shepherd (5:4) exercises his authority by example to all Christians (2:21), so one aspect of the elders' participation in Christ's pastoral ministry is leading by *example* rather than command. The designation "chief shepherd" not only affirms continuity between the work of the elders and the work of Christ, but is also a clear but gentle reminder that they will give account to him of their pastoral work. The "crown of glory that never fades away" is not the author's ad hoc formulation but a stock image in apocalyptic thought, a traditional way of expressing the eschatological reward (cf. 2 Tim 4:8; Jas 1:12; Rev 2:10; *T. Benj.* 4.1; 1QS 4.7-8; *2 Apoc. Bar.* 15.8; cf. Schrage 1993, 118).

In comparison to the address to the elders, the instruction to "the younger" (5:5a) is brief to the point of abruptness, calling only for "subordination" to the elders. This is the same word as in the social code of 2:11–3:12 (see commentary there), and has the same sense, which does not mean servile obedience. Who are "the younger" so addressed? The five possibilities are (1) young people, in contrast to old people; (2) young people in contrast to presbyters; (3) newly baptized members of the community; (4) a subordinate class of "junior clergy" such as deacons; and (5) the remainder of the congregation (cf. Elliott 1970, who gives a succinct summary of each position and a detailed argument for #3).

While (1) seems at first to be the natural reading, it calls for understanding "elders" in a different sense than in 5:1-4, and there is no particular reason to introduce into this context a general admonition for young people to obey their elders. The second and third options leave the reader wondering why only (2) young people or (3) new converts should be instructed to be subordinate to church officials. There is no evidence for (4) a subordinate class of clergy in 1 Peter, where presbyters seem to be the only church officers. The "younger" thus seems to designate (5) the rest of the congregation, here called "younger" as counterparts to the "elders," in each case understood in terms of church structure rather than strictly a matter of age. This means that "elders" and "younger" comprise the whole congregation, which would correspond to the address to wives and husbands in 3:1-8 on which 5:1-5 is modeled. As wives and husbands form the totality of the unit addressed there, so here elders and younger comprise the whole congregation. Though "elder" is meant officially in both 5:1 and 5:5, the alternate meaning of "elder" suggests the use of "younger" as the corresponding group. Thus "all" of 5:5*b* does not mean "all the rest," as though there were three groups, with "elders" and "younger" having already been addressed but no longer so. (Goppelt 1993, 350, gives several texts in which elder/younger means the whole community.) It is rather the case that the author addresses the congregation as being composed of two groups, "elders" (presbyters) and "younger" (the rest of the congregation). This was facilitated by the fact that presbyters were mostly drawn from the older members of the community, and because "younger" can mean "novice" or "inexperienced" without regard to chronological age. (Compare Paul's use of "mature" and "infants" in 1 Cor 2:6–3:1, without regard to chronological age.) The pair "elder"/"younger" to designate the whole congregation seems strange to our modern ears, but *1 Clement,* from the same Roman location as 1 Peter about the same time has the same usage. In *1 Clement,* the "young" against the "elders" is parallel to "the church" against "the presbyters" (*1 Clem.* 3:3; 47:6).

The importance of the preceding discussion is that the concluding exhortation to "all" (5:5*b*) includes the presbyters. It is not the case that the author addresses three groups, "presbyters," "younger," and "all the rest," as though the final instructions were not addressed to "presbyters" and "younger." Rather, presbyters are first addressed, then the rest of the congregation as "younger." Then the address to "all" includes both presbyters and non-presbyters, and has the effect of placing them on the same level before God. While presbyters have authority in the structured church, which they must exercise in a Christlike manner as models to the flock, it is not the case simply that the congregation is to be subject to the presbyters, but that presbyters and non-presbyters are to be subject to each other, precisely as in the case of wives and husbands in 3:1-8 (where the "all" of v. 8 *includes* the wives and husbands of vv. 1-7). This calls for the attitude of *tapeinophrosynē*, "humility," which was considered servility in the hellenistic world, a self-understanding thought to be inappropriate for free persons. But 1 Peter's dialectic of free/slave (2:16) has set Christians free from this cultural pressure of concern with one's own self-image, so that *tapeinos* is a Christian virtue to be cultivated as the *sine qua non* of life together in the Christian *community*. As in the instructions given in the social code 2:18–3:12, the author seems to advocate a hierarchy without a hierarchical attitude, a nonauthoritarian concept of authority. There is a definite "chain of command" presupposed, though not explicitly articulated: God → Christ → Apostle → Presbyter → church. God is represented by Christ, the chief shepherd (cf. Heb 13:20, also of Roman provenance). Christ is represented by the apostle. The apostle is represented by the presbyter, who speaks as one of them and who instructs both presbyters and congregation in regard to the role of presbyters. The presbyters have portions of God's flock assigned to them for which they are responsible, and the members of the flock are to be subordinate to their authorized shepherds. But in every case this picture is saved from being a merely from-the-top-down authoritarian hierarchy. The figures of God and Christ are not kept distinct, but modulate into each other. So also the line between apostle and presbyter is not distinct, for the apostle is a co-presbyter, and the presbyters function by and with apostolic authority. Christ the chief shepherd shares the shepherding ministry directly with the presbyters, who are accountable to him. Just as the apostle is both "above" the presbyters and is a co-presbyter, so Christ is the chief shepherd and fellow pastor/bishop to the whole flock of God (2:25). It is thus important that the concluding "all" be heard as inclusive, not as "all-the-rest." The officers are included in the instructions to be subject. All, presbyters and non-presbyters, can afford to relate to one another in humility, because they have been freed from preoccupation with self-esteem (cf. on 2:4-10, 18-24).

As in 2:18–3:12, the exhortation is concluded with a citation from Scripture, now understood in a Christian sense. That it appears in a similar context in Jas 4:6 shows that it had become an element in stock Christian tradition. Once again, the modern reader notices that biblical texts play the role one would expect to be filled by sayings of Jesus, especially if the letter were actually written by Simon Peter. Appropriate Gospel texts come to mind (e.g., Mark 10:42-45). But the pseudonymous author has adopted the Pauline model of arguing from the Christ-event as such rather than citing the earthly Jesus as authority, so that neither here nor elsewhere does he introduce sayings of Jesus to support his point (see Introduction, pp. 22 and 34 and commentary on 3:8-12; 4:7-11, 14).

Concluding Exhortation to All (5:6-11): The concluding paragraph of the body of the letter does not trail off into random exhortations, but bears the marks of a thoughtful composition that both summarizes and intensifies the main themes of the letter as a whole, with several features that form an *inclusio* with the opening section. The opening imperative "Humble yourselves" is a Greek passive, "let yourselves be humbled," for in the author's understanding true humility is not a human achievement but the gift of God. Such humility has nothing to do with inferiority complexes, with a sense of self-worth or the lack of it, for it knows that it lives from the gracious judgment of God (Schweizer 1949, 102).

The "hand of God" is prominent especially in the Exodus narrative, and recalls the imagery identifying the Christian community as the continuing community of the Exodus with which the letter began (cf. on 1:3; 1:13-20). The image of the "mighty hand of God" can connote protection (e.g., Ezra 8:22; Ps 9:33), the power of God that gives one a strong and good heart (e.g., 2 Chr 30:12), or God's discipline of his own people (e.g., Job 30:21; Ps 31:4). But just as the hand of God can be perceived behind their adversities, they can also be summed up as encounter with the devil (5:8). In neither perspective are their troubles considered the direct work of either God or Satan. This means on the one hand that "suffering according to the will of God" does not mean that God causes the suffering (cf. on 4:19), and on the other hand that the human opponents and institutions under which they suffer are not demonized, but are themselves considered the victims of the "disobedient spirits" (cf. on 3:18-22). All is understood from the paradigm of the Cross in which both the devil and human evil are operative, but which ultimately is perceived as the grace of God.

The admonition for the readers to humble themselves so that God may exalt them is a common element in early Christian parenesis (cf. Matt 18:4; 23:12; Luke 14:11; 18:14; and especially Jas 4:10, where the exhortation is based on the same text as here, Prov 3:34). The "due time" when they will be exalted refers to the same eschatological *kairos* as 1:5 (cf. also the "day of visitation," 2:12 Gk). Here as elsewhere in 1 Peter, the idea is not a selfish strategy for being exalted, but a matter of living one's life as incorporated into God's plan for the world, when God's faithful people will be vindicated and participate in God's glory (cf. 1:7, 11; 2:12; 4:11, 13, 16; 5:1, 4, 10). A dimension of the humble trust that is here called for is to cast one's cares on God, since "it matters to him about you" (literal translation of 5:7, i.e., "what happens to you matters to God"). This is not the perfect but impassive god of Greek philosophy, but the God of the Hebrew Bible who cares for and actively intervenes for his people. While the thought is similar to that of the Sermon on the Mount (Matt 6:25-34), once again 1 Peter's teaching is not based on a saying of Jesus but on a biblical text: Ps 55:22 (LXX 54:23). The frequency with which this text is alluded to by Hermas (e.g., *Herm. Vis.* 3.11.3; 4.2.5) probably indicates its currency in the Roman church, also the setting for 1 Peter (see Introduction, p. 38).

With the command to be disciplined and alert (5:8), the substratum of apocalyptic that has undergirded the author's thought throughout becomes explicit, since "be alert" *(grēgoreō)* is a watchword of apocalyptic exhortation (cf. Matt 24:42, 43; 25:13; Mark 13:34, 37; Luke 12:37; 1 Cor 16:13; 1 Thess 5:6-10 [with "be disciplined," as here]; 1 Pet 1:13; 4:7; 5:8; Rev 3:2-3; 16:15; the parallels are more apparent in the literal translations given here).

So also, for the first and only time in 1 Peter, the devil appears as the eschatological opponent of the community of faith. In the apocalyptic tradition Satan is considered to be especially active just before his final eschatological defeat. Unlike the contemporary Apocalypse of John, 1 Peter does not develop and schematize this imagery. Yet the reference to the devil is not a casual reference, but is to be taken with theological seriousness. The point is that the distress in which the Christians of Asia Minor find themselves is not merely a matter of a conflict of lifestyles or different cultural understandings (Achtemeier 1996, 338). Rather, the readers are caught up in the eschatological conflict between God and the suprapersonal power of evil, a battle of which the outcome cannot be in doubt, since the decisive encounter has already occurred (cf. on 3:18-22). The readers are enabled to see their sufferings in a transcendent perspective that gives them ultimate meaning without trivializing the painful events that were very real to them. The devil *must* be resisted precisely because he is already defeated; to accommodate to him now is to switch at the last moment to the losing side. And the devil *can* be resisted because God is faithful (4:19) and supplies the strength by which Christians persevere (1:5). All this is said without demonizing the opponents by identifying them with Satan (they are to be respected along with all people, 2:17), without abdicating responsibility for one's own actions in a the-devil-made-me-do-that mentality, and without spinning out a speculative eschatological timetable.

Just as the introduction of the figure of the devil communicates the magnitude of the temporal context within which the readers are to see their struggles—they are part of the plan of God from creation to eschaton, a plan that is about to be brought to completion—so the reference to the sufferings of "your brothers and sisters in all the world" communicates the magnitude of the spatial context of the Asia Minor believers—they belong to a worldwide fellowship of Christians that suffers just as they do (5:9). Their social marginalization and minority status, in contrast to the proud hellenistic culture with its grand temples and religious institutions, pressured the readers into thinking that what they belonged to was something small. Each little house-church was hardly impressive in terms of size, numbers, and cultural significance; their members were tempted to think small when they thought of the church to which they belonged. They needed to know that they belonged to a community of faith that had endured through the ages and stretched around the world, and that this community shared its sufferings. The author reports this not on the basis of empirical data or because there was an empirewide persecution of Christians sponsored by the Roman government but as a theological judgment about the countercultural nature of the Christian life as such (cf. Introduction, pp. 43-44 and commentary on 4:12-19). Wherever there are Christians, they suffer, especially in the eschatological hour in which the devil roams about like a ravenous lion. As the devil does not operate regionally (Brox 1979, 239), wherever there are Christians they must encounter his last onslaught before the End. The Christians of Asia Minor do not belong to a congregational or regional church, but to the one people of God scattered throughout the world (another *inclusio,* cf. the Diaspora of 1:1).

The body of the letter ends not in the imperative but in the indicative mood, not with a command but with a promise (5:10). It is the "God of all grace" who meets the suffering community precisely in their troubles, not only beyond them (cf. 2:19-20; 5:12). With another *inclusio* recalling the letter's opening, God is portrayed as the one who took the initiative (1:1-2) and called (1:15; 2:9, 21; 3:9) the believers "in Christ" (Pauline language; cf. on 3:16). With a fourfold set of verbs, the author promises God's continuing care and eschatological vindication. The distinctions between the four verbs should not be pressed: that God will restore, support, strengthen, and provide the foundation for the believers' life all refer to God's activity in bringing the faithful community through the crisis into God's own eternal glory.

"After you have suffered for a little while" is to us a strange summary of the Christian life, yet that is precisely what we have here. The "little while" refers neither to the brevity of human life in general nor to the author's hope that the social situation will soon change and Christians can live a more trouble-free life, but to his conviction of the nearness of the eschatological consummation of

God's purpose (cf. on 4:7). "Suffering" (identified with "grace," 5:12) is the one-word definition of Christian existence as such, corresponding to the destiny of Christ into which Christians are incorporated (cf. on 4:12-19).

The concluding doxology (5:11) is not just a religious flourish with which to end. The power *(kratos)* attributed to God is cognate to the "mighty hand" *(krateia)* of 5:6 with which the unit began, the two terms forming an *inclusio* for the unit.

◊ ◊ ◊ ◊

The particular situation to which 1 Peter was addressed, and the author's understanding of Christian existence as essentially cruciform, provides a hermeneutical problem for later Christians who live more comfortable lives in less tension with their surroundings. On the one hand, modern readers must avoid a purely historical spectator stance, as though the changed social and political situation for many modern readers means that the text no longer speaks to us in our situation. The author understood himself to be portraying the nature of Christian life as suffering-for-others as integral to God's plan for history made known in Christ, in whatever social or cultural situation believers find themselves. The author of 1 Peter did not understand himself to be addressing an extraordinary situation of suffering, a temporary phase that would quickly pass and life would get back to normal; for him unjust suffering for others is the norm for Christian existence. For the author of 1 Peter, there would not be such a large gap between Christian life in first-century Asia Minor and twentieth- or twenty-first-century Christian life in North America, so far as what it essentially means to be a Christian is concerned: to live one's life as participation in Christ's sufferings. To be Christian is to suffer, to share Christ's sufferings for the sake of others. On the other hand, if this theology is affirmed today it must be done without either developing a superficial martyr understanding of ourselves or trivializing the real sufferings of the first readers of this document that were in fact very different from the experience of many modern readers.

CONCLUSION OF THE LETTER (5:12-14)

The letter concludes as it began, as the author's distinctive adaptation of the Pauline letter form (cf. on 1:1-2). The hellenistic letter typically closed with "farewell" (errōsthe, as Acts 15:29; 2 Macc 11:21, 33). Paul had modified the letter closing, as he transformed the letter opening, to be a vehicle of his distinctive theology. It is only our familiarity with the Pauline tradition that causes us to suppose 1 Peter follows the "typical" early Christian letter form. To the extent that it was typical, it was the influence of the Pauline letter corpus that made it so. The following points of contact with the Pauline epistolary tradition are adopted and adapted in the epistolary closing of 1 Peter:

1. Pauline vocabulary is concentrated in these closing words ("brother" as quasi-technical term for colleague in ministry [Rom 16:23; 1 Cor 1:1; 16:12; 2 Cor 1:1; 2:13; 8:18; 12:18; Phil 2:25; 1 Thess 3:2; Phlm 1]; "faithful" as the distinctive quality of a good minister [1 Cor 4:2, 17; 7:25; Col 1:7; 4:9; 1 Tim 1:12]; "son" or "child" for a younger ministerial colleague [1 Tim 1:18; 2 Tim 1:2] "consider"/"reckon" [logizomai] as the operative verb for evaluating ministry [1 Cor 4:1; 2 Cor 3:5; 10:2, 7, 11; 11:5; 12:6]; "in Christ" as the sphere of the Christian life [e.g., Rom 6:11; 8:1; cf. above on 3:16]).

2. Reference to the bearer of the letter that served as introduction and authorization (5:12; cf. Rom 16:1; 1 Cor 16:17-18; 2 Cor 8:16-19; Eph 6:21; Col 4:7, 9). The expression "through Silvanus" (5:12; tendentiously translated "with the help of Silvanus" in the NIV) could theoretically mean (a) that Peter dictated the letter to Silvanus as secretary; (b) that the letter was composed by Silvanus at Peter's behest; (c) that Silvanus delivered the letter to the churches of Asia Minor; or (d) that the name "Silvanus" is part of the fictive pseudepigraphical framework for the letter (see Introduction, pp. 30-37 for the spectrum of possibilities regarding authorship). For reasons presented in the introduction and throughout the commentary, the first two options must be ruled out. Silvanus is neither the secretary nor the drafter of the letter. The phrase to write

"through" someone (5:12) never refers to the letter's composer or drafter, but to its bearer (cf. Acts 15:22-23, of this same Silas/Silvanus; often in the church fathers). The time and distance involved make it difficult to imagine one person delivering this circular letter throughout the five provinces to which it is addressed. It is therefore better to see the reference to Silvanus as part of the pseudepigraphical framework of the letter, but this does not mean it is invented out of whole cloth. It is quite likely that the historical Silvanus had made his way to Rome where he was active in the continuing Petrine circle of teachers and missionaries. He was the ideal symbolic figure to associate with this letter, authorized by "Peter" himself, since he represented contacts with Peter and the primitive Palestinian church as a trusted and ecumenically minded leader who delivered apostolic messages (Acts 15:22-32) with Paul (Acts 15–18; 2 Cor 1:19; 1 Thess 1:1), and now in Rome where the Pauline and Petrine traditions were being amalgamated and sent forth into the hellenistic world. Thus when "Peter" says that he "[considers him] a faithful brother" (5:12), this is not an incidental expression of personal opinion, but the apostolic legitimization of the letter (cf. on 5:1, Peter as co-presbyter).

3. Greetings from congregation and coworkers that were more than merely personal, but expressed the unity and extent of the scattered church (5:13; cf. Rom 16:22-23; 1 Cor 16:19-20a; 2 Cor 13:12b; Phil 4:21b-22; Col 4:10-14; 2 Tim 2:41b; Titus 3:15; Phlm 23). The greeting from "my son Mark" (5:13) is analogous to the reference to Silvanus as "brother." "Son" does not refer to biological or adoptive parenthood (despite novelistic speculations about Peter's family history), but is used metaphorically, as Paul was pictured as calling his younger ministerial colleague Timothy his "child" (1 Tim 1:18; 2 Tim 1:2). The reference must be to John Mark, known from Acts as a representative of the early Jerusalem church acquainted with both Peter and Paul (Acts 12:12, 25; 15:37, 39) and in the Pauline letter tradition as a coworker in Paul's hellenistic mission (Col 4:10; 2 Tim 4:11; Phlm 24). If Philemon was written from the Roman prison, then this Mark certainly made his way to Rome, where later tradition located him in any case (Phlm 24). It is possible that he was part of the second-generation

"Petrine circle" in Rome from which 1 Peter emanated, or here too his name may simply represent part of the pseudepigraphical framework of the letter.

The greeting from "your sister [church] in Babylon, chosen together with you" (literally "co-elect lady in Babylon") refers to the Roman congregation (see Introduction, pp. 38-39). In addition to the actual greeting conveyed, the statement again makes the theological point of the unity of the one church scattered throughout the world (1:1; 5:9) and its solidarity in suffering and mission.

4. A pronouncement of grace (5:12; cf. 1 Cor 16:23; 2 Cor 13:13; Gal 6:18; Eph 6:24; Phil 4:23; Col 4:18; 1 Thess 5:28; 2 Thess 2:18; 1 Tim 5:21*b*; 2 Tim 4:22*b*; Titus 3:15*b*; Phlm 25). Whereas Paul had included "grace" as part of his closing benediction, the Petrine author composes a terse statement about God's grace as his own summary of the "exhortation" and "testimony" represented by the whole book. "This" of 5:12 refers to the readers' experience of unjust suffering as interpreted in the document as a whole. It is not a casual statement. First Peter takes the general (Pauline) understanding of God's grace made known in Christ and focuses it on their painful experience of marginalization, harassment, discrimination, and physical suffering. The point is not "although you suffer, God's grace is still available," but that the grace of God is present in and precise as their suffering (cf. 2:19-20). Unjust suffering is claimed to be grace not on the basis of philosophical explanation, but precisely because of the revelatory Christ-event and the readers' incorporation into it. The words are thus at the furthest pole from "cheap grace." Grace was costly for God and Christ (1:18-19). The suffering Christians of Asia Minor did not need to be reminded that it was costly for them as well, without grace ceasing to be grace. The statement is made as an indicative, but concludes with the final imperative of the letter: "stand fast in it," that is, in their experience of suffering that is also the grace of God. The Pauline combination of indicative and imperative appears once again in the concluding lines.

5. Paul's command to greet one another with a holy kiss becomes a "kiss of love" in 1 Pet 5:14. Kissing was a family greeting, early adopted by some streams of the Christian community as the

mark of mutual love and acceptance. In the second century it became a regular part of the liturgy. As in the letters of Paul, the command in 1 Peter indicates that the letter was intended not for individual private reading, but to be read aloud at the worship service of the community, and that the message of the letter was to be heard in the context of worship. Despite the author's orientation toward "holiness" as a mark of the community (1:15-16; 2:5-9), the author modifies Paul's "holy" kiss to the "kiss of love" *(agapē)* in accord with his theology of the church as family of God (1:3, 14, 23; 2:1, 17; 3:8; 4:8; 5:9).

The author has already elaborated the Pauline grace formula, and thus closes the letter with a pronouncement of "peace," resonant with the Hebrew *"shalom."* It is fitting that the last words of this letter speaking with the voice of Peter are the distinctively Pauline formula "in Christ," effectively combining the two traditions as testimony to the one holy catholic apostolic church.

APPENDIX 1:
THE NARRATIVE WORLD OF
1 PETER

The author wants to accomplish something, wants to achieve a change in the lives of his readers. The change he calls for is based on theological foundations, but it is not a matter of abstract theology, not second-level reflective theology, but first-level convictional theology. Hence he chooses the letter form, which had already been adopted and developed by Paul for this purpose. Fruitful studies of the narrative world of the Pauline letters have recently been made (Petersen 1985; Witherington 1994). To my knowledge, this helpful approach has not yet been applied to 1 Peter. From this perspective, the author is not attempting to teach or explain theology as such, but addresses the experienced concerns of the readers from within the narrative world presupposed by the letter. This world is projected by the letter itself as the real world, the world determined by God the creator who will bring it to a worthy conclusion at the near eschaton. This world is comprehensively defined by Christ as its source, goal, and revelatory midpoint.

"The world" is not just "there," is not simply an objective given that human beings observe. To be sure, there is a real world "out there," composed of a certain number of subatomic particles, energy, and whatever comprises "reality." But for human beings, the world is socially constructed (Berger and Luckmann 1966). The world we live in, our symbolic universe, is the result of our socialization, a construct expressed in language that selects and orders the subatomic particles into a habitable and meaningful world of space and time. We did not devise this world ourselves; it was communicated to us in the process of acquiring language and culture in a particular historical situation. Our world is comprised of the moving point on the horizontal line between our birth and our death, and the larger line in which we see it embedded, and all the realities and actions that impinge on that line. Whoever or whatever effects a change in our symbolic universe effects a change in us, in our sense of ultimate reality and who we are. We and our world are created by social imagination and communication expressed in language. "One becomes what one is addressed as" (Berger and Luckmann 1966, 165). Our world, its meaning and values, takes shape as we are spoken to by people who project upon us their vision of the world. Words are not decorative labels attached to reality, but, rather, constitute human reality. Language, embodied in stories and narratives, effects fundamental changes in us; it makes us who we are. "To speak a true word is to transform the world" (Freire 1970, 75-76).

The original readers of 1 Peter were suffering abuse for their faith, and needed to "know how things really are" (Elliott 1981, 19-20). The author places their experience within the framework of the real world constituted by God the creator who has acted in Christ, who is presently at work within them, and who takes responsibility to bring the world to a worthy conclusion. The author does this not by explaining metaphysics, history, or cosmology to them, but by addressing them from within this world, confirming the new world they received at their new birth, and by deepening and widening their perception of the new reality in which they live.

Letters are a narrative form (cf. Petersen 1985). They project a world as they presuppose the ongoing history in which both writer and readers are involved. For 1 Peter, this one world embraces the everyday lives of the readers within the story of God's mighty acts in history (see diagram on p. 185). Since, like letters in general, 1 Peter mostly refers incidentally and indirectly to this story, for readers such as ourselves who are not direct participants, it is helpful to reconstruct the narrative world presupposed and projected by the letter. The following reconstruction has been assembled by noting every word in 1 Peter that expresses or presupposes some action in the world regarded as real by the author. These are then arranged chronologically, and categorized according to the following types:

RS = Referential Series (events in the narrative world projected by 1 Peter, arranged in the order of real chronology)

PS = Plotted Series (events in the narrative world projected by 1 Peter, arranged in the order in which they are "plotted" in the text)

T = Type of action, in the following categories:

A = primary referential world (the immediate narrative world directly posited by the story), for example, the readers' faith tested, 1:6

B = secondary referential world (the narrative world that may be indirectly inferred from the text), for example, that the prophets of Israel unsuccessfully attempted to understand their own prophecies, 1:11

C = transcendent referential world
C^1 = acts in transcendent world by transcendent beings
C^2 = acts in this world by transcendent beings
C^3 = acts of this-worldly beings that transcend this-worldly reality

D = fictive referential world (as represented by the adoption of Peter's name)

( ) means the subject of the action is implied

[ ] means the action is implied

{ } means the chronological location is unclear

The narrative world projected by 1 Peter comprises 157 events. Each may be located on the line representing the author's narrative world, segmented according to the major divisions that determine his view of history:

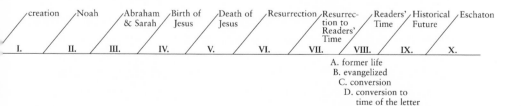

creation | Noah | Abraham & Sarah | Birth of Jesus | Death of Jesus | Resurrection | Resurrection to Readers' Time | Readers' Time | Historical Future | Eschaton

I. / II. / III. / IV. / V. / VI. / VII. / VIII. / IX. / X.

A. former life
B. evangelized
C. conversion
D. conversion to time of the letter
E. readers' present

We shall first arrange these 157 events of the story world of author and readers in the chronological order posited by this narrative world, which is structured by divisions into the following periods:

    I. (Before) Creation to Noah
    II. Noah to Abraham and Sarah
    III. Abraham and Sarah to Birth of Jesus
    IV. Life of Jesus
    V. Death of Jesus
    VI. Resurrection/Ascension/Session of Jesus
    VII. Resurrection of Jesus to Readers' Time
    VIII. Readers' Time
        A. Readers' Former Life
        B. Readers' Evangelized
        C. Readers' Conversion
        D. Readers' Conversion to Time of the Letter
        E. Readers' Present
    IX. The Readers' Historical Future: From the Readers' Time to the Final Revelation of Christ
    X. The Eschatological Revelation of Christ

On this basis we shall then present a series of observations and theses.

For details, see the commentary on the designated texts.

I. (Before) Creation to Noah

RS	PS	Action	T
1.	1:20	God foreknew/destined Christ before the foundation of the world.	C^1
2.	1:2	God foreknew the readers' election. It is not clear that God's electing activity chose Christians before creation. See commentary on 1:2.	C^1
3.	1:3	God was the Father of the Lord Jesus. Was there ever an event in which God "became" the Father of Jesus? This Nicean question is not yet posed in 1 Peter.	C^1

RS	PS	Action	T
4.	1:20	God founded the world.	C^2
5.	4:19	God is the faithful creator.	C^2

II. Noah to Abraham/Sarah

6.	3:19-20	Spirits are in prison in days of Noah.	C^1, C^2
7.	3:20	God's patience waited in the days of Noah.	C^2
8.	3:20	Ark was being prepared (by God? Noah?) in Noah's day.	B, C^2?
9.	3:20	God saved eight persons through water.	C^2

III. Abraham/Sarah to Birth of Jesus

10.	2:9	Israel chosen as the elect and holy people of God.	C^2
11.	3:5	Holy women who hoped in God were subject to their husbands.	B
12.	3:6	Sarah called Abraham "lord."	B
13.	1:10	Prophets prophesied of the grace that comes to Christians.	C^3
14.	1:11	The Spirit of Christ testified of *eis Christon* sufferings and following glories.	C^3
15.	1:11	Prophets tried to find out to (whom and) what time their prophecies referred.	B
16.	1:12	God revealed to the prophets that they were serving not themselves but the readers of 1 Peter (and other Christians).	C^2
17.	1:16	Scripture is written. "It is written" (perfect tense: it happened in the past and is still there).	C^{2-3}

RS	PS	Action	T
18.	2:6	"It stands in Scripture." [Sometimes Scripture is cited, explicitly calling attention to it; sometimes it is quoted without such notice; sometimes it is alluded to; all this refers to the after-Abraham-before-Jesus event. Several other references could be listed here.]	C$^{2\text{-}3}$
19.	1:12	{Angels longed *(epithymeō)* to peek into these things [God's saving plan that embraces suffering/glory of Christ and Christians] (from this time to eschaton?).}	C^1

IV. Life of Jesus

20.	1:20	Christ was manifest at the end of the times *(phaneroō)*.	C^2
21.	1:2	Christ was obedient (on one reading of 1:2); cf. 2:22 "committed no sin."	B
22.	3:18	Christ lived a righteous life.	B
23.	2:22	Jesus "committed no sin, and no deceit was found in his mouth." (Does this refer to the life of Jesus, or only to his death? "Sinlessness" as doctrine? [Isa 53])	B
24.	1:1	{[Peter became an apostle.]}	B

V. Suffering/Death of Jesus

25.	2:21	Christ suffered for you, giving you an example.	B
26.	4:1	Christ suffered in the flesh, made an end of sin.	C$^{2\text{-}3}$
27.	4:13	Christ suffered (in such a way that readers can share his sufferings).	B
28.	2:23	Christ did not threaten retaliation, but committed himself to the one who judges justly.	B
29.	2:22	Jesus "committed no sin, and no deceit was found	B

RS	PS	Action	T
		in his mouth." (Is this a general statement about the life of Jesus, or does it refer only to the manner of his suffering and death?)	
30.	1:2	The "blood of Jesus Christ" was shed (= Jesus' blood sealed the new covenant).	C^2
31.	3:18	Christ was put to death *sarki*, "in the flesh."	B
32.	2:24	Jesus himself bore our sins in his body on the wood.	C^{2-3}
33.	3:18	Christ suffered for sins once for all, righteous for unrighteous, to bring us to God.	C^{2-3}
34.	2:24	We are healed by his wound (singular).	C^{2-3}
35.	1:19	Redemption by blood of Christ. This event will be located differently on the narrative line depending on whether it is seen as referring to an "objective" event, before and apart from the believer's conversion ["ontological"] or as an aspect of it ["existential"] or both (see #69 and #77 below).	C^2
36.	2:4	Humans reject the stone chosen by God (perfect participle = continues in this rejected state; like "crucified" in the Pauline and Markan idiom).	B
37.	5:1	Peter the apostle was an eyewitness of Jesus' sufferings (?). (If the text is so understood— a reading rejected in this commentary—it is a dimension of the fictive pseudonymous literary world of the text.)	D
38.	4:6	{[Christ (was) preached to the dead. On one reading of this ambiguous text, Christ preached to the dead after his death but before his ascension.]}	C^1

VI. Resurrection/Ascension/Session of Jesus

39.	2:4, 6	God chose Christ as the elect stone (1 Peter is not concerned with designating the chronological	C^1

RS	PS	Action	T
		location of Christ's election, but to affirm God's election of Christ as the divine vindication of the one rejected by human beings)	
40.	3:18	God made Christ alive *pneumati,* "in the spirit."	C^1
41.	1:3	God raised Jesus.	C^2
42.	1:21	God raised Jesus from the dead and gave him glory (two stages or one?). God, not Jesus, is the active agent, "so that your faith and hope are set on God."	C^2
43.	3:19	Christ preached to the spirits in prison in/by the Spirit.	C^1
44.	3:22	Christ has gone to the right hand of God.	C^1
45.	3:22	Angels, authorities, and powers were made subject to him.	C^1
46.	1:20	{Christ was manifest at the end of the times *(phaneroō).* Is this Jesus' appearance in this world as such (as above, no. 20), or his manifestation at the Resurrection?}	C^2
47.	4:7	The end of all things has come near; the Resurrection as eschatological event.	C^2
48.	1:1	{[Peter made an apostle, an emissary of the risen Christ.]}	B
49.	2:4	Christ continues even after the Resurrection as the Rejected One, the stone rejected by humans but chosen by God (perfect participle = continues in this rejected state; like "crucified" in the Pauline and Markan idiom).	B

VII. Resurrection of Jesus to Readers' Time

RS	PS	Action	T
50.	1:3	God gave believers a living hope by raising Jesus from the dead.	C^2

RS	PS	Action	T
51.	2:4	{Jesus elected by God after the rejection by humans. (Order of rejection/election not clear.)}	C^2
52.	1:1	Peter ministers as an apostle. (Not connected to "stone" or "foundation.")	A
53.	2:6	God lays the chief cornerstone of the new spiritual house of God.	C^2
54.	2:8	Disbelievers stumble over this (as they were destined to do; 1 Peter does not speculate as to when this "predestination" took place).	A
55.	3:21	Baptism saves by Jesus' resurrection (note again combination of Jesus' time and the readers').	C^2
56.	5:1	"Peter" the co-presbyter witnesses to Christ's sufferings. (Cf. alternate understanding above.)	A
57.	3:22	Angels, authorities, and powers are subject to Christ.	C^1
58.	1:12	Angels long *(epithymeō)* to peek into these things.	C^1

VIII. Readers' Time
A. Readers' Former Life

RS	PS	Action	T
59.	1:14	Readers formerly lived by desires held in ignorance.	A
60.	1:18	Readers lived in futile ways inherited from ancestors.	A
61.	1:21	Readers did not believe in God before (became believers at conversion); but they were not previously atheists. Note "Peter's" evaluation of their previous religious life (cf. 4:3).	A
62.	2:9	Readers were previously in darkness.	A
63.	2:10	Readers had not received mercy, were not people (of God).	A

RS	PS	Action	T
64.	2:25	Readers once were straying sheep.	A
65.	4:3	Readers' former life was that of the Gentiles = licentiousness, passions, drunkenness, reveling, carousing, and lawless idolatry.	A

B. Readers' Evangelized

RS	PS	Action	T
66.	1:12	What the prophets prophesied and searched for was preached to the readers by evangelists empowered by Holy Spirit sent from heaven.	C^3
67.	1:25	Readers evangelized by the word of the living God, the good news that abides forever, referred to by Isa 40.	C^3
68.	4:6	{[Gospel preached to Christians who have since died. (On one understanding of this text.)]}	C^1

C. Readers' Conversion

RS	PS	Action	T
69.	1:2	Spirit sanctified readers (baptism reference?).	C^2
70.	1:1-2	{God elected the readers (1 Peter is not concerned with specifying the chronological location of God's election. Cf. commentary on 1:2).}	C^1
71.	5:13	{God elected the Christian community in "Babylon" as co-elect with the readers.}	C^1
72.	2:8	God destined unbelievers to stumble over the stone placed by God as the new spiritual house of God. (As the author of 1 Peter is not concerned with specifying the chronological location of God's election of believers, so he does not specify when the resulting destiny of unbelievers was determined. Cf. commentary on 1:2 and 2:8.)	C^1
73.	1:3	The readers are born again (God the actor) not of	C^2

RS	PS	Action	T
	1:23	corruptible seed but of the incorruptible living and abiding word of God.	
74.	2:2	The reborn readers are "newborn infants" at conversion. The metaphor refers to an event, not an idea.	C^2
75.	1:14	The readers live as obedient children of God. Since "new birth" precedes (1:3) and calling on God as Father follows (1:17), this refers to an event, not a static idea.	A
76.	1:2	God sprinkled readers with the blood of Jesus ([?] subject and action not clear). Cf. 1:19. (In Heb 10:22, "hearts sprinkled" apparently = at baptism.)	C^2
77.	1:19	God redeemed readers by the blood of Christ (event of both Jesus' time and readers' time?).	C^2
78.	1:3	God gave readers a living hope (by Jesus' resurrection; events of Jesus' time and the readers' time blend together).	C^2
79.	1:15 2:9 2:21 3:9 5:10	God **called** the readers ("effective call" 5x in 1 Pet + 3:6) —out of darkness into God's marvelous light. —to this (unjust suffering). —to return blessing for cursing. —into his eternal glory in Christ.	C^2
80.	1:21	Through Christ the readers became believers in God (resurrection is an act of God not Jesus, "so that your faith and hope are set on God").	A
81.	1:22	The readers purified their lives by obedience to the truth (cf. 1:2 "to be obedient"). Like Jesus' own obedience, on one reading of 1:2.	A
82.	2:3	You have tasted that the Lord is good (= "living . . . God," 1:23; Jesus Christ, 2:4). "Lord" modulates from God to Christ and back.	A

RS	PS	Action	T
83.	2:4	You come/came to Christ the living stone rejected by humans but elected by God.	A
84.	2:10	You had not received mercy (Greek perfect tense) but now receive mercy (Greek aorist tense).	C^2
85.	2:11	{Readers are beloved (if "of God," refers to an event, not characteristic); vs. NIV's "dear friends").}	C^2
86.	2:16	Something happened (God's act) that made them free/servants of God. They had all been slaves, now all are freed. But as freed persons, they are God's slaves (neither of these a "natural" state, but refers to an event). They are liberated/enslaved.	C^2
87.	2:25	Straying sheep have returned to their shepherd and overseer.	A
88.	3:6	Readers have become Sarah's daughters (= heirs of the promise, now part of people of God; corresponds to Pauline "sons of Abraham").	C^2
89.	3:21	Baptism as antitype now saves you, not as removal of dirt from the body, but as an appeal to God for a good conscience, through the resurrection of Jesus Christ (note again the combination of the time of Jesus and the readers' own time again).	C^2
90.	4:10	Each Christian has received a charisma (God has given it) to be used for one another, as good stewards of God's varied grace.	C^2

D. Readers' Conversion to Time of the Letter

91.	4:6	{Some Christians who were judged by their non-Christian contemporaries according to human standards have since died (but they will be vindicated at the Last Judgment). (According to one reading of this difficult text; cf. Commentary.)}	C^2

RS	PS	Action	T

E. Readers' Present

RS	PS	Action	T
92.	1:1	Peter's apostolic authority continues to be expressed through the letter.	A, D
93.	1:4-5	Salvation is "ready" in heaven. The inheritance kept in heaven for you/us (cf. 1:13 "the grace that Jesus Christ will bring you").	C^1
94.	1:1	Readers live as elect resident aliens of the Dispersion (cf. 2:11 sojourners and resident aliens).	A
95.	2:11	Readers live as sojourners and resident aliens.	A
96.	1:2	Grace and peace pronounced.	A
97.	1:3	God is declared to be blessed (= thanked, praised).	A
98.	1:17	Readers call on God as Father (cf. 1:3).	A
99.	3:7 4:7	The community prays (the letter contains nothing directly about a eucharistic community or other liturgical or missionary acts).	A
100.	1:5	Believers are kept (by God) through faith.	C^2
101.	1:6 4:12 5:10	Faith is being tested by fire.	A
102.	1:6	Readers rejoice in God (or "in the preceding").	A
103.	1:6	Suffer various trials for a little while.	A
104.	2:12	Gentile neighbors malign them as evildoers.	A
105.	3:16 4:14, 16	The readers' good life in Christ is reviled. Readers are reviled for the name of Christ, and suffer as Christians.	A
106.	5:8	The devil prowls about like a roaring lion seeking someone to devour.	C^2

RS	PS	Action	T
107.	5:9	The family of God throughout the world is enduring the same suffering.	A
108.	5:10	"After you have suffered for a little while" (the only picture of the historical future). Cf. 1:6.	A
109.	4:13	Readers participate in Christ's sufferings.	A
110.	1:8	Readers have not seen Christ, but love him.	A
111.	1:8	Readers believe and rejoice with inexpressible and glorified joy.	A
112.	1:9	Readers are receiving the goal/culmination of your faith, salvation (present participle; future or present meaning?).	C^2
113.	1:17	God judges without partiality (present? or only eschatological future?). Cf. 4:17.	C^2
114.	2:2	Readers are "growing in" salvation (see NIV) or "into salvation" (NRSV).	A
115.	2:5	Readers are being built (by God) into a spiritual house of God, to be a holy priesthood, offering spiritual sacrifices acceptable to God through Jesus Christ.	C^2
116.	2:9-10	Readers are a chosen race, a royal priesthood, a holy nation, God's own people, the people of God, who have received mercy.	C^2
117.	2:9	Readers proclaim God's mighty acts.	A
118.	2:11	Desires of the flesh war against the self.	A
119.	2:13	Human institutions have rightful authority (the letter does not say they are established by God).	A
120.	2:16	The readers live as free/as slaves of God.	A
121.	2:18	Slaves have non-Christian masters.	A

RS	PS	Action	T
122.	3:1-6	Women have non-Christian husbands.	A
123.	3:7	Husbands have Christian wives.	A
124.	3:15	Outsiders ask believers to give a reason for their hope.	A
125.	4:1	Readers (like Christ) suffer in the flesh, make an end of sin.	A
126.	4:4	Readers no longer live in their former Gentile vices, and are reviled for it.	A
127.	4:11	Readers graced by God speak, serve, and are empowered by God.	C^2
128.	4:14	The Spirit of glory and of God rests upon them.	C^2
129.	4:17	The time has come for judgment to begin with the house of God = "us."	C^2
130.	5:2-3	Presbyters tend the flock, exercise oversight.	A
131.	5:5	Presbyters have authority to which ("younger") members are to be subject.	A
132.	5:7	God cares about the community of believers.	C^2
133.	5:12	The present (resulting from the past acts of God), including its unjust suffering, is here described as the "true grace of God." Their only task is to stand fast, to live in and out of the grace of God represented by the new symbolic universe, the narrative world projected by the letter.	C^2
134.	5:13	The readers belong to the same community as the (co-elect) sister church in "Babylon."	A
135.	1:1; 5:12	"Peter" writes to them through "Silvanus."	D
136.	5:13	"Mark" sends greetings.	D

RS	PS	Action	T
137.	5:13	Christians from Rome greet them.	A
138.	5:14	They greet each other with an *agape* kiss.	A
139.	5:14	Present Christian existence is "in Christ."	A

IX. The Readers' Historical Future: From the Readers' Time to the Final Revelation of Christ

140.	5:10	"After you have suffered for a little while" (the only picture of the historical future) is God's restoring them, making them strong, firm, and steadfast, the historical or eschatological future?	A

X. The Eschatological Revelation of Christ

141.	1:7, 13	The revelation of Jesus Christ (same phrase as Rev 1:1) will occur; this is the eschaton. Believers do not meet someone at the End different from the one they have already met in history; who Jesus Christ is is presently concealed, but will be eschatologically revealed. (Objective genitive. Something happens to Jesus at eschaton.)	C^2
142.	1:13	Grace comes to readers at the eschatological revelation of Jesus Christ (something happens to readers at eschaton).	C^2
143.	2:2	The eschaton will be the fulfillment of "salvation." The present life of believers is "growing into salvation" (see NRSV; NIV = "in" salvation).	C^2
144.	1:9	Believers will receive the goal/culmination of their faith, salvation (present participle; future or present meaning?).	C^2
145.	1:5	Salvation that is now "ready" will be "revealed."	C^2
146.	4:13	Christ's glory will be revealed as the counterpart to his sufferings.	C^2

RS	PS	Action	T
147.	5:1	Glory is to be revealed.	C^2
148.	5:4	The Chief Shepherd will be manifested *(phaneroō)*.	C^2
149.	1:7	Believers' faith will result in the praise and glory and honor (by God).	C^2
150.	1:17	God will judge impartially according to everyone's works.	C^2
151.	2:12	The day of God's visitation is coming ("when he comes to judge" NRSV).	C^2
152.	2:23	{God is the one who judges justly (at the eschaton?), to whom Jesus committed himself.}	C^2
153.	4:5	Gentile sinners shall give account to the one who will judge the living and the dead (does this phrase connote a universal judgment at the end of time, that interrupts human history and brings it to an end, or merely an otherworldly judgment scene?). Cf. 4:17.	C^2
154.	4:6	{Those dead to whom the gospel was preached will be judged in the flesh as everyone is judged (on one reading of this difficult text; cf. Commentary).}	C^2
155.	2:12	(Some?) Gentile neighbors will glorify God on that day.	B
156.	5:4	Faithful presbyters will receive the unfading crown of glory.	C^2
157.	5:6	God exalts those who have humbled themselves.	C^2

Observations and Theses

1. The orientation of the author, and the shape of the projected narrative world delineated by his letter, is horizontal, not vertical.

The axis of the story is the moving line of history, not the vertical line to the heavenly world.

2. The narrative extends from creation to eschaton. There is nothing plotted after the eschaton, and only one reference to action before the creation. Like the Bible in general, it is historical human life under the dome of heaven, not mythical pictures of before creation, after the eschaton, or of the present transcendent world, that forms the exclusive focus of the author's world.

3. The story of the world is: creation/judgment and salvation in Noah's time/covenant with Israel, the prophets speak/the Christ-event/the time of the readers/the eschatological consummation.

4. This creation-to-eschaton history is the "mighty acts of [God]" the church is called to proclaim (2:9). It is a divinely determined history.

5. The God who is the principal actor in this history is defined by Christ, who is active in each stage: elected before the foundation of the world, spoken through the prophets, appeared as Jesus, suffered, died, and was exalted, is the sphere of the believer's present existence, and will be revealed in glory at the eschaton. "God or Christ" is a false alternative; the two terms modulate into each other for 1 Peter.

6. The linear mode of representation of saving history given above should not be construed only as uninterrupted, straight-line evolutionary development. Alongside continuity is discontinuity (e.g., "once you were not a people, but now you are God's people" [2:10]; "the stone that the builders rejected has become the very head of the corner" [2:7]). It is not the case that each segment evolves from the preceding, but is determined by God's active incursion into history. The series of the "mighty acts of [God]" (2:9) should perhaps be thought of as a drama in which there is coherence and continuity, but also differing "acts" in which the curtain that opens and closes both separates and binds together the different segments of the story.

7. Two major items of God's saving acts are not plotted, that is, are not located at a specific point in the line of saving history. (1) It is presupposed throughout that God chose Israel as the elect and holy people of God (continued in the Christian community),

but this is never specified, the term "Israel" or its synonyms never appears, and the actual acts of the election of Israel are not plotted. There is no specific Moses-Sinai-wilderness-conquest-kingship tradition. (2) It is presupposed throughout that at some point God chose Jesus and constituted him as the Christ, but this is never located at a particular chronological point.

8. Scenes from the life of Jesus play a minimal role in this story. It is important to the author that Jesus lived, that his life was righteous, and that he suffered unjustly for the sake of others without threatening retaliation. Otherwise, there are no details from the "life and teaching of Jesus." This has obvious implications for authorship, as does the shape of this story world as a whole. As in the Pauline tradition, the saving act of God in Jesus is concentrated in his suffering, death and resurrection, not in his life.

9. More events from the *experience of the readers* are plotted than all the other segments of the narrative combined.

10. Although the narrative world is nonmythological and this-worldly, the mundane world is penetrated by the transcendent world (note the number of C^2 and C^3 events).

11. The fictive world of "Peter" is barely represented. While the pseudonymous framework is adopted, the narrated content is from the real lives and times of the real author and readers, not the fictive world postulated by the adoption of Peter's name.

APPENDIX 2:
IMAGES OF THE CHURCH IN
1 PETER

The word *church* does not occur in 1 Peter, yet this letter (along with Ephesians) is one of the most ecclesiologically oriented documents in the New Testament. Ecclesiology is central to the imagery and metaphor system of the author. If one reads carefully through 1 Peter looking for explicit vocabulary or imagery referring to the community, and for phrases that address the readers in terms that infer an ecclesiological identity they are assumed to have or should have, the result is a list of at least forty-five terms and images for the church. Twenty of these have already been introduced by the end of chapter 1. The corporate identity of the readers is also indicated by the use of pronouns: there are fifty-four second-person plural pronouns, but not a single instance of the second-person singular. Even imperatives in the singular and expressions about what "each" should do are minimal ("each" only 1:17; 4:10; imperatives in the third singular only 3:3, 10, 11; 4:15-16, in all cases generalizing). The document is oriented not to "individual responsibility" but to the Christian community, its identity and nurture as a communal fellowship of believers, the continuing people of God through history.

The following list of terms and images is arranged in the order in which they occur in 1 Peter. They could easily be arranged according to some systematic structure (e.g., one, holy, catholic, apostolic), but this would give the impression that 1 Peter presents a systematic "doctrine of the church," which is not the case. The author does not present his profound ecclesiological understanding by means of a systematic statement, but, corresponding to the letter form, as a linear parade of images that have their own effect on the reader. For elaboration, see the Commentary on the passages cited.

1:1	"Elect": The Chosen Community
1:1	"Sojourners": The Community of Resident Aliens
1:2	"Foreknowledge" "Destined" (NRSV): The Community Embraced by God's Foreknowledge
1:2	"Sanctified": The Community Sanctified by the Spirit
1:2	"Sprinkled with His Blood"; "Obedience": The Covenant Community
1:3	"Blessed Be God": The Community of Praise to God
1:3	"New Birth": The Community of the Reborn
1:4	The Community with a Heavenly Inheritance
1:5	The Community Kept by God's Power
1:5	The Believing Community
1:6	The Rejoicing, Overjoyed, Exulting Community
1:6	The Distressed Community
1:7, 13	The Community of Hope
1:8	The Loving Community
1:10-12	The Community of Fulfillment
1:14	The Community of Obedient Children
1:15	The Community of the Called
1:19	The Redeemed Community
2:2	The Community in Need of Nourishment and Growth
2:5	The Temple Community
2:5	The Community of Priests
2:9	An Elect Nation
2:9	A Royal Priesthood
2:9	A Holy Nation
2:9	A People That Is God's Own Possession
2:9	A Community That Witnesses to the Mighty Acts of God
2:10	The People of God
2:10	The Community That Has Received Mercy
2:10	The (Be-)Loved Community
2:14-15	The Community of "Zealots for Good" (Cf. 3:13)
2:16	The Community of the Free
2:16	The Servant Community

2:17	The Family of Believers
2:21	The Community That Follows in the Steps of Christ
2:25	The Flock of God
3:7	The Community That Celebrates the Goodness of the Gift of Life
3:12	The Community of the Righteous
3:14	The Blessed (by God) Community
3:16	The Community "in Christ"
3:20	The Saved Community (in the "Ark of God" ?)
3:21	Community of the Baptized
4:10-11	The Graced Community
5:3	The Structured Community
5:9	The Ecumenical Community
5:12	The Community of Grace

Missing Terms

In view of the comprehensive ecclesiological range of the letter's imagery and terminology, it is striking that a number of terms do not appear:

Church (Ekklēsia)

The absence of the word *church* in so ecclesiological a document (except in some manuscripts at 5:13 supplementing "co-elect") is especially startling, since it is written in the name of Simon Peter (cf. Matt 16:16-18). The same is true of the striking absence of the "rock" terminology of that passage. Both items are further confirmation that neither Matt 16 nor 1 Peter is directly related to the historical Simon Peter.

Israel

The author never mentions Israel, empirical or otherwise, nor does he reflect on the relation of the Christian community to the Israel of past history or to the Jewish community of his own present. As in 1:10-12 the prophets only function "for you," so also the Scripture citations in 2:4-10 are relevant for the present alone. The Petrine author sees a seamless continuity and identity between the

Old Testament history of Israel and his present, thus reading the Old Testament christologically.

Covenant (Diathēkē)

While from the first line onward 1 Peter utilizes the covenant language of the Old Testament (cf. on 1:2) and regards the church as the continuing covenant people of God (e.g., 2:4-10), in contrast to Paul and the Gospels the covenant terminology itself is not explicitly found. Thus one notes the absence both of central terms from the Pauline tradition and key terms and imagery one would expect if Simon Peter, the companion of Jesus, were the author. While 1 Peter is influenced both by Pauline tradition and Palestinian Christian tradition, in ecclesiology, as elsewhere, the author formulates his own distinctive understanding of the tradition.

Apostolic

Though the church is not called "apostolic," *apostolos* of 1:1 is not merely a claim to personal authority on the part of the author, literal or pseudepigraphical, but shows that apostolicity is an essential dimension of the author's ecclesiology.

Along with "apostolic" one must place "one" and "catholic." Though neither word occurs in 1 Peter, the letter assumes that its readers in the five provinces belong to the one church scattered throughout the whole earth, and are undergoing the same troubles (5:9). An apostle belongs to the whole church, and the letter, especially if pseudepigraphical, partakes of this apostolic and universal nature of apostleship to the one church.

Holy Ones, Saints (Hagioi)

The church is considered the holy community (see above), but the term "holy" (8x in 1 Peter) is used as a qualifying adjective, not as a substantive or term for the church. Paul often refers to the Christian community as "holy ones" ("saints," *hagioi*), but again a key ecclesiological term for Paul is absent from 1 Peter (45x in the Pauline and Deutero-Pauline letters, especially in the greeting formula and in direct address to his readers).

Disciples (Mathētai)

It is also striking that "disciples" is missing, in contrast to the prominence of "disciples" as a term identifying Jesus' followers in the Gospels and Acts, especially in contexts in which Peter is active. In this regard 1 Peter is like the Pauline tradition, where the word is never found, in contrast to the Gospels and Acts, where it occurs 261 times.

Body of Christ (Sōma Christou)

The author has much contact with and sympathy for Pauline tradition, but the absence of a key metaphor in Paul's own understanding of the church (cf. Rom 12:4-8; 1 Cor 10:17; 11:29; 12:12-30; Eph 1:23; 2:16; 4:4, 12, 16; 5:23; Col 1:18, 22, 24; 2:19; 3:15) is another indication that he is no mere "Paulinist."

Rock (Petra)

The imagery of the church being founded on the *petra* (rock) is entirely missing from 1 Peter. This is striking in view of the dual phenomena that (1) the word *petra* is indeed used, but not in an ecclesiological sense, and only negatively (2:8). This corresponds to Paul's usage reflecting the LXX (Rom 9:33/Isa 8:14), not to the key role played by the word in Matt 16:18. (2) "Rock" terminology is used of the church, but in different terminology than *petra,* and in a different frame of reference than in Matt 16 (cf. on 2:4-5 above).

SELECT BIBLIOGRAPHY

WORKS CITED IN THE TEXT

Balch, David L. 1981. "Let Wives Be Submissive . . .": *The Domestic Code in 1 Peter.* SBLMS 26. Chico, CA: Scholars Press.

Bartchy, S. Scott. 1973. *ΜΑΛΛΟΝ ΧΡΕΣΑΙ: First Century Slavery and 1 Corinthians 7:21.* SBLDS 11. Missoula, MT: Society of Biblical Literature.

Barth, Karl. 1957. *The Word of God and the Word of Man.* New York: Harper.

―――. 1963. *Evangelical Theology: An Introduction.* New York: Holt, Reinhart and Winston.

Barth, Karl, and Johannes Hamel. 1959. *How to Serve God in a Marxist Land.* Introduction by Robert McAfee Brown. New York: Association Press.

Bauer, Walter. 1979. *A Greek-English Lexicon of the New Testament and Other Early Christian Literature.* Translated by William F. Arndt and F. Wilbur Gingrich. Second Edition revised and augmented by F. Wilbur Gingrich and Frederick W. Danker from Walter Bauer's 5th edition, 1958. Chicago: University of Chicago Press.

Beker, J. C. 1962. "Peter, Second Letter of." *IDB* 3:767-71. Nashville: Abingdon.

Berger, Peter L., and Thomas Luckmann. 1966. *The Social Construction of Reality: A Treatise in the Sociology of Knowledge.* Garden City, NY: Doubleday.

Best, Ernest. 1969. "I Peter and the Gospel Tradition." *NTS* 16:95-113.

Boismard, M. E. 1957, 1961. "Une liturgie baptismale dans la Prima Petri. II.—Son influence sur L'Epitre de Jacques," *RB* 64:161-83. Elaborated in *Quatre Hymnes Baptismales dans la Première Épître de Pierre.* Lectio Divina 30. Paris, 1961, 133-63.

Boring, M. Eugene. 1984. *Truly Human/Truly Divine: Christological Language and the Gospel Form.* St. Louis: Christian Board of Publication.

———. 1993. "Interpreting 1 Peter as a Letter [not] Written to Us." *Quarterly Review.* 13:89-111.

Boring, M. Eugene, Klaus Berger, and Carsten Colpe. 1995. *Hellenistic Commentary to the New Testament.* Nashville: Abingdon.

Bornemann, W. 1919/20. "Der erste Petrusbrief—eine Taufrede des Silvanus." *ZNW* 19:143-65.

Bornkamm, Günther. 1968. "πρέσβυς, κτλ." *TDNT* 6:651-83. Grand Rapids, MI: Eerdmans.

Brown, Raymond E. 1976. "Peter." *IDBSup.* Nashville: Abingdon.

———. 1984. *The Churches the Apostles Left Behind.* New York: Paulist.

———. 1997. *An Introduction to the New Testament.* New York: Doubleday.

Brown, Raymond E., Karl P. Donfried, and John Reumann, eds. 1973. *Peter in the New Testament: A Collaborative Assessment by Protestant and Roman Catholic Scholars.* Minneapolis: Augsburg; New York: Paulist.

Brown, Raymond E., and John P. Meier. 1983. *Antioch and Rome: New Testament Cradles of Catholic Christianity.* New York: Paulist.

Brunner, Emil. 1947. *The Divine Imperative.* Philadelphia: Westminster.

Bultmann, Rudolf. 1924. "Die liberale Theologie und die jüngste theologische Bewegung." Translated by Louise Pettibone Smith in *Faith and Understanding,* edited by Robert W. Funk, 28-52. Philadelphia: Fortress, 1987.

———. 1951. *Theology of the New Testament.* 2 vols. New York: Scribner's.

Childs, Brevard S. 1984. *The New Testament As Canon: An Introduction.* Philadelphia: Fortress.

Cothonet, Edouard. 1988. "La Premièr Epître de Pierre: bilan de 35 ans de recherches." *ANRW* II 25,5: 3685-712. Berlin: De Gruyter.

Crouch, James E. 1972. *The Origin and Intention of the Colossian Haustafel.* Göttingen: Vandenhoeck & Ruprecht.

Cullmann, Oscar. 1953. *Peter: Disciple, Apostle, Martyr: A Historical and Theological Essay.* Translated by Floyd V. Filson. Philadelphia: Westminster.

Dalton, William J. 1965. *Christ's Proclamation to the Spirits: A Study of 1 Peter 3:18–4:6.* AnBib 23. Rome: Pontifical Biblical Institute.

Dillenberger, John, ed. 1961. *Martin Luther: Selections from His Writings.* New York: Doubleday.

Dinkler, Erik. 1959, 1961, 1965-66. "Die Petrus-Rom Frage." *TRu* 25:189-230; 289-335; 27:33-64; 31:232-53.

Dockx, Stanislas, O. P. 1987. "Chronologie zum Leben des heiligen

Perkins, Pheme. 1994. *Peter: Apostle for the Whole Church.* Columbia: University of South Carolina Press.

Petersen, Norman R. 1985. *Rediscovering Paul: Philemon and the Sociology of Paul's Narrative World.* Philadelphia: Fortress.

Preuss, Horst Dietrich. 1995. *Old Testament Theology* 2 Vols. Louisville: Westminster/John Knox.

Ranke-Heinemann, Uta. 1994. "Petrus in Rom?" In *Petrus, der Fels des Anstosses,* edited by Raul Niemann, 62-75. Stuttgart: Kreuz Verlag.

Reicke, Bo. 1946. *The Disobedient Spirits and Christian Baptism: A Study of 1 Pet. III.19 and Its Context.* ASNU 13. Copenhagen: E. Munksgaard.

Rowley, H. H. 1950. *The Biblical Doctrine of Election.* London: Lutterworth.

Schneemelcher, Wilhelm. 1991. *New Testament Apocrypha I: Gospels and Related Writings.* English version edited and translated by R. McL. Wilson. Louisville: Westminster/John Knox.

Schrage, Wolfgang. 1993. "Der erste Petrusbrief." In *Die Briefe des Jakobus, Petrus, Johannes, und Judas,* edited by H. Balz and W. Schrage, 60-121. NTD 10. Göttingen: Vandenhoeck & Ruprecht.

Schrenk, Gottlob. 1967. "eklektos." *TDNT* 4:181-92. Grand Rapids, MI: Eerdmans.

Schweizer, Eduard. 1961. *Church Order in the New Testament.* SBT 32. London: SCM.

Setzer, Claudia. 1997. "Excellent Women: Female Witnesses to the Resurrection." *JBL* 116:259-72.

Simmel, Georg. 1950. *The Sociology of Georg Simmel.* Translated and edited by Kurt H. Wolff. Glencoe, IL: Free Press.

Snodgrass, Kent R. 1977. "I Peter ii:1-10: Its Formation and Literary Affinities." *NTS* 24:97-106.

Soards, Marion L. 1988. "1 Peter, 2 Peter, and Jude as Evidence for a Petrine School." *ANRW* II. 25,5:3828-49. Berlin: De Gruyter.

Talbert, Charles, ed. 1986. *Perspectives on First Peter.* NABPR Special Studies Series Number 9. Macon, GA: Mercer University Press.

Thiede, Carsten Peter, ed. 1987. *Das Petrusbild in der neueren Forschung.* Wuppertal: Brockhaus Verlag.

Thrall, Margaret. 1980. "Super-Apostles, Servants of Christ, and Servants of Satan." *JSNT* 6:42-57.

Thurén, Lauri. 1995. *Argument and Theology in 1 Peter: The Origins of Christian Parenesis.* JSNTSup 114. Sheffield: Sheffield Academic Press.

van Unnik, W. C. 1962. "Peter, First Letter of." *IDB* 3:758-66. Nashville: Abingdon.

Witherington, Ben. 1994. *Paul's Narrative Thought World: The Tapestry of Tragedy and Triumph.* Louisville: Westminster/John Knox.

Wuellner, Wilhelm H. 1962. *The Meaning of "Fishers of Men."* Philadelphia: Westminster.

COMMENTARIES (BOTH CITED AND NOT CITED)*

Achtemeier, Paul J. 1996. *1 Peter: A Commentary on First Peter.* Hermeneia. Minneapolis: Fortress. — Detailed and thorough historical-critical study with theological perspectives. Argues for pseudonymous authorship by a writer dependent on a tradition shared by Paul, but not dependent on the Pauline letters.

Beare, Francis Wright. 1958. *The First Epistle of Peter: The Greek Text with Introduction and Notes.* 2nd rev. ed. Oxford: Blackwell. — An original baptismal liturgy has been encased in a later epistolary framework. Pseudonymous author directly dependent on Paul's letters.

Best, Ernest. 1971. *1 Peter.* NCB. Grand Rapids, MI: Eerdmans. — A midrange critical commentary with an extensive and thorough discussion of introductory issues.

Bigg, Charles. 1901. *A Critical and Exegetical Commentary on the Epistles of St. Peter and St. Jude.* ICC. Edinburgh: T & T Clark. — Classic older commentary defending Petrine authorship.

Brox, Norbert. 1979. *Der erste Petrusbrief.* EKKNT 21. Neukirchen: Neukirchener Verlag. — Strong case for pseudonymous authorship. Argues the author had no thought-out structure, but assembles his materials somewhat randomly.

Craddock, Fred B. 1995. *First and Second Peter and Jude.* Westminster Bible Companion. Louisville: Westminster John Knox. — Readable recent commentary directly relating insights from 1 Peter to contemporary Christian life.

Davids, Peter H. 1990. *The First Epistle of Peter.* NICNT. Grand Rapids: Eerdmans. — Conservative critical commentary with good discussion of theological issues, especially 1 Peter's "theology of suffering." Defends "Petrine" authorship in the sense that Silvanus composed the document (in *Paul's* style) at Peter's commission, though Peter himself may never have seen it.

---

*Unless otherwise noted, all authors argue for or assume pseudonymous authorship.

Elliott, John H. 1982. "I Peter." In *James, I–II Peter/Jude,* by R. A. Martin and John H. Elliott. Augsburg Commentary on the New Testament. Minneapolis: Augsburg. — Concise critical commentary presenting the views of a leading contemporary interpreter of 1 Peter, whose interpretation will be elaborated in the forthcoming Anchor Bible commentary.

Frankemölle, Hubert. 1990. *1 Petrusbrief, 2 Petrusbrief, Judasbrief.* Die Neue Echter Bibel. 2nd ed. Würzburg: Echter Verlag. — A historical commentary with a theological and pastoral orientation that sees many parallels between the situation of the community addressed in 1 Peter and that of the contemporary church in a secular world.

Goppelt, Leonhard. 1993. *A Commentary on 1 Peter.* Edited by Ferdinand Hahn, translated and augmented by John E. Alsup. Grand Rapids, MI: Eerdmans. — A translation from the 1978 standard work in the classic series *Kritisch-exegetischer Kommentar über das Neue Testament* (Meyer), slightly revised and brought up-to-date. Combines rigorous historical scholarship with theological and pastoral orientation. Pseudonymous author not directly dependent on Paul's letters, but on tradition shared with the Pauline churches.

Grudem, Wayne. 1988. *1 Peter.* Tyndale New Testament Commentaries. Grand Rapids, MI: Eerdmans. — Evangelical commentary arguing the apostle Peter, who was fluent in the language and thought of the hellenistic world, composed the letter in the 60s.

Krodel, Gerhard. 1977. "The First Letter of Peter." In *Hebrews, James, 1 and 2 Peter, Jude, Revelation,* edited by Gerhard Krodel. Proclamation Commentaries. 2nd ed. 1995. Fortress: Philadelphia. — One of the few recent commentaries maintaining the older critical view that 1 Peter is not a literary unit but incorporates an extensive earlier document, 1:3–4:11, a homily to newly baptized Christians.

Marshall, I. Howard. 1990. *1 Peter.* IVP New Testament Commentary. Downers Grove, IL: InterVarsity. — The work of a careful evangelical scholar. Argues (not assumes) for Petrine authorship, but directs the main thrust of his exposition to the question "What has 1 Peter to say to us today?"

Michaels, J. Ramsey. 1988. *1 Peter.* WBC 49. Waco, TX: Word. — The most scholarly and detailed of recent evangelical commentaries. Based on the Greek text with extensive bibliographies for each section. Argues the letter was written from Rome c. 80, and not by Peter personally, but maintains "Petrine" authorship by arguing Peter lived into the 80s, when his "ideas" were then written up by a disciple and approved by Peter before being circulated.

Moffatt, James. 1928. *The General Epistles: James, Peter, and Judas.*

MNTC. New York: Harper & Row. — Classic older commentary based on his own (occasionally idiosyncratic) translation, but still containing perceptive insights. One of the last critical commentaries to argue the letter was "a pastoral letter sent by Peter [though dictated to Silvanus who shaped its language] from Rome during the seventh decade of the first century."

Perkins, Pheme. 1995. *First and Second Peter, James, and Jude*. IBC. Louisville: Westminster/John Knox. — Not a verse-by-verse treatment, but, in accord with the series to which it belongs, provides a good exposition of the general message of 1 Peter in its original setting, with insights for contemporary application.

Reicke, Bo. 1964. *The Epistles of James, Peter, and Jude*. AB 37. New York: Doubleday. — Brief, relatively uncritical commentary utilizing the author's own translation. To be replaced by the much more extensive critically up-to-date commentary by John H. Elliott. Assumes Petrine authorship in the 60s, but the language and thought were shaped by Silvanus, the disciple of Paul.

Schelke, Karl Hermann. 1988. *Die Petrusbriefe, Der Judasbrief* HTKNT 13/2. 6th ed. Freiburg: Herder. — Detailed critical commentary by a contemporary Roman Catholic who thinks it possible that Silvanus wrote after Peter's death but expressed Peter's views. Argues for heavy dependence on Pauline tradition without denying that independent Petrine tradition is also present.

Schweizer, Eduard. 1949. *Der Erste Petrusbrief*. Zürcher Bibelkommentare. 2nd. ed. Zürich: Theologischer Verlag. — A brief commentary oriented to biblical study in the church by laypeople in the European situation after World War II in which the readers found many points of contact between their context and that of the original readers of 1 Peter.

Selwyn, E. G. 1947. *The First Epistle of St. Peter: The Greek Text with Introduction, Notes, and Essays*. 2nd. ed. New York: Macmillan. — Classic, thorough commentary on the Greek text with several extensive excurses on key issues in 1 Peter. Argues for Petrine authorship ("through Silvanus") on the basis of a stream of firmly fixed tradition widespread in early Christianity.

Windisch, Hans, and Herbert Preisker. 1930. "Der erste Petrusbrief." In *Die Katholischen Briefe*. HNT 15. Tübingen: Mohr-Siebeck. — Brief commentary especially oriented to history-of-religion issues. Contributed to the popularization of the older critical view that 1 Peter contained an older baptismal liturgy or homily.

INDEX